I
DIDN'T
SURVIVE

— A True Story —

Emerging Whole After Deception, Persecution, and Hidden Abuse

I DIDN'T SURVIVE

— *A True Story* —

NAGHMEH ABEDINI PANAHI
with EUGENE BACH

WHITAKER
HOUSE

Front and back cover photos by Daniella Maile.

I Didn't Survive:
Emerging Whole After Deception, Persecution, and Hidden Abuse

Naghmeh Panahi
IDidntSurvive.media@gmail.com

ISBN: 979-8-88769-053-7
eBook ISBN: 979-8-88769-054-4
Printed in the United States of America
© 2023 by Naghmeh Abedini Panahi

Whitaker House
1030 Hunt Valley Circle
New Kensington, PA 15068
www.whitakerhouse.com

Library of Congress Control Number: 2023943509

1 2 3 4 5 6 7 8 9 10 11 ᵁᴶ 30 29 28 27 26 25 24 23

NOTE TO THE READER

This book includes depictions of emotional and physical abuse against the author that may be disturbing. Please use your discretion in reading certain passages, particularly if you have suffered a form of abuse in the past.

Events in this book are described to the best of the author's recollection. Various names and events have been changed to protect the privacy of certain individuals mentioned in the book.

—The Publisher

THIS BOOK IS DEDICATED TO...

Maman, who has shown me, as a woman, what love, sacrifice, and strength look like.

My children, Rebekka and Jacob, who are God's beautiful gifts in my life and whom God has used to motivate me to continue speaking out for truth and justice.

Baba, who passed away from Covid-19 in 2020. You always encouraged me, as a woman in the Middle East, to be strong and courageous. You would have been so happy to see me publish my book.

Pastor Robert Needham and Mrs. Barbara Needham, who spent countless hours directing me to the Word of God and the ministry of the Holy Spirit, where I found my identity in Christ and healing.

Sarah Pulliam Bailey of the *Washington Post*, who asked the question "Whatever happened to Pastor Saeed's wife?" and came looking for me after Saeed's release and after the news of the abuse came out. Thank you for your genuine care and for being a voice for the oppressed and the voiceless.

Eugene Bach, who helped me tell my story and, in the process, spent countless hours praying and seeking the Holy Spirit.

Christine Whitaker and Whitaker House, for wanting to publish my story; and Lois Puglisi, for the countless hours of working with me in editing my book.

God, for His glory and for the benefit of His church.

CONTENTS

Prologue.. 9

1. Child of Revolution and War.. 11

2. A Long, Bitter Winter.. 17

3. "We Can't Stay Here Any Longer" 22

4. Respite from War..27

5. "God Loves You"...30

6. The Opportunity to Dream 35

7. Escaping Jesus 38

8. Life in Idaho..44

9. "Show Them Who You Are".......................................48

10. Discovering My Calling 52

11. Back to Iran...58

12. God's Persistent Call...64

13. Meeting Saeed...70

14. Falling in Love...75

15. The Heartbeat of Change 80

16. A Proposal? 84

17. Pushing the Boundaries..91

18. Revival in the House Church.....................................95

19. Planting Churches and Evangelizing 98

20. Arrested and Tested...105

21. The Wedding 111

22. Honeymoon from Hell 115

23. Begging for Love 119

24. Falling Apart 125

25. The Beating 129

26. Church Split 2.0 135

27. A Baby Born in Chaos 151

28. An Alternate Universe...158

29. Attempted Escape 166

30. Trapped in Iran...171

31. The Phone Call 177

32. A Different Kind of Arrest 182

33. Keeping Saeed Alive..188

34. Tortured for Christ 194

35. The Campaign...200

36. A New Friend 207

37. Confronting the Iranian Presidential Delegation 210

38. Hospital Revelation..215

39. A New Prison 218

40. Downward Spiral...224

41. President Obama..229

42. God's Daughter...233

43. Confession 238

44. The Emails...243

45. Released from Prison...247

46. An Unwanted Divorce 256

47. In the Wilderness 263

48. A New Kind of Ministry...267

49. Processing the Past...273

50. A Renewed Vision 277

Epilogue...284

About the Author...286

PROLOGUE

I am not sharing my experiences to spin a tale of how I was able to make it through tough times in my marriage, but rather to tell you *who I became* because of those tough times.

I can't tell you how I was able to make it through, because "I" didn't. *I didn't survive.* The old me died in the process, burned in the fires of trials. I am not the same person today that I was before. People who have a hard time getting out of an abusive relationship are often those who attempt to drag their old selves, their old ways of thinking, through it. I couldn't. I didn't. Like the phoenix rising from the ashes, a new me arose from the catastrophe of my marriage.

This book is about how I learned and grew along the way, despite my mistakes, false perspectives, confusion, and battered self-image. As my understanding grew, I also grew. As my challenges grew, so did my faith, and, with this faith, my ability to endure pain. The pain didn't become easier—it never does. But I became stronger.

In order to survive, I had to change—and that is my story. I didn't want to change, but the obstacle of Saeed's imprisonment finally forced me to. The obstacle led to the solution. What had stood in the way ironically became the way. If Saeed had not gone to prison in Iran, it is highly likely that I would still be sitting in my own prison. I would still be living in the chains of an abusive marriage. But his imprisonment eventually set me free from mine. I believe God wanted Saeed to be delivered from the Iranian prison, yet He did not want me to remain in my own captivity.

When I realized I needed to change, I didn't yet know what that change would look like, but I was certain the solution to the problem started at the genesis of my failure, and confronting that failure would give birth to thinking differently and redefining who I was according to the Word of God.

Obstacles have a unique way of breaking the chains of how we define ourselves. The fake me had to die. It began to disintegrate when it collided with the immovable wall of reality, which presented problems I couldn't solve by my old ways of thinking and old methods of survival.

I know some people reading this book may think that I gave up on my marriage. I never quit on my marriage. I fought to keep my marriage—but I had to learn to let it go. I had to learn that quitting and letting go are not the same thing.

I could have been the wife of a Christian hero, but I gave that up. Christian leaders even told me to hide the abuse in my life in order to keep up appearances, in order to maintain the advocacy. That life of lies offered a guaranteed income, favored status, and a comfortable lifestyle, but I decided to give it up for truth. I could have continued to mold a public image that people looked up to, and I might even have convinced myself that I was doing it for God, but I gave it all up.

When I realized I was an abused wife, I was holding a handful of broken dreams but not a broken future. My false self was crumbling away, but healing and wholeness were entering into me through my wounds like light breaking through the cracks in the walls of an abandoned building.

The Light shining through was teaching me that many of my dreams had been shattered only because they were not really my dreams. I had long held the dreams of someone else, and I had been caged in by the expectations of others. I had also been trapped for years in memories of fear and loss that reached all the way back to my childhood in war-torn Iran. This is my story of how I was able to break free.

1

CHILD OF REVOLUTION
AND WAR

I was too young to remember what peace tasted like. From my earliest memories, I was intimately familiar with all the flavors of war.

My twin brother, Nima, and I were born in Tehran, the capital of Iran, in 1977—only two years before the Iranian Revolution and three years before the beginning of the long conflict between Iran and Iraq. Our little sister, Nazanin, was born five years later.

My birth had been a surprise. My mother didn't realize she was carrying twins during her pregnancy. Because I was so small as I shared the space in her womb with my brother, the doctor completely missed my presence during all of my mother's prenatal checkups. After I was born, the doctor warned my parents that, most likely, I would not survive infanthood.

I was a sickly child, needing extra nourishment in order to grow. Even years later, my sister could wear my clothes when she was only a toddler. I also had eye problems and had to wear an eye patch and special glasses in order to see straight. In addition, I experienced bladder problems, having constant infections that required medication to control.

Anyone looking at pictures of my parents in Tehran in 1977 would not be able to tell if they lived in the Middle East or Europe. Universities in the capital city flourished, with both men and women flooding the academic halls. Shopping centers were full of young men in bell-bottomed jeans and women in form-fitting shirts with vivid, pastel colors. Many families like ours had their own car, house, shag carpet, television, and record player.

The eruption of the Iranian Revolution, one of the most defining moments in the history of Iran, completely changed our society. Religious leaders overthrew the secular government, led by Mohammad Reza Shah Pahlavi, and turned the nation into an Islamic theocracy. The young people protesting in the streets in favor of the Revolution did not recognize the freedoms and the other good aspects of life they experienced in Iran. Instead, they saw what they didn't have. The people didn't have the luxurious life of the Shah or his many wealthy, frivolous friends. They didn't have hundreds of millions of dollars flowing in from Iran's oil reserves. There were millions of poor people in Iran's more conservative Islamic villages who couldn't even afford proper health care for their children, while the Shah was throwing lavish parties for his friends that would cost half a billion dollars today.

My parents were split down the middle in their reaction to the Revolution: my father promoted the uprisings, and my mother actively worked against them. Their different opinions led to never-ending discussions at home between them. Our family was a microcosm of two of the clashing ideologies that were igniting the national conflict.

My father, whom I affectionately called "Baba," was from a wealthier, more educated sector of society. Looking around and seeing the financial inequality, he believed that Islam, wrapped in the elements of equality being championed by the Communists of that time, was the way forward. So, he joined in the protests, marching in the streets against the Shah. Baba embraced the same Islamic utopian ideology as the other protestors, and this put him in direct support of the revolution's leader, Ayatollah Ruhollah Khomeini. Khomeini didn't just lead the revolution; he *was* the revolution.

My mother, whom I lovingly called "Maman," came from a very poor family, but she didn't feel that the way forward for Iran was a more centralized, radical path. As a female officer in the army, she had sworn an oath to protect the Shah, and she viewed the Islamic Revolution with great skepticism. She was not a devoutly religious Muslim woman. She did not pray three times a day or attend mosque, and she had no desire to give up her miniskirt. While Baba was out demanding that Iran bring about an Islamic revolution, my mother was defending the Shah's push to make Iran more secular.

In the end, Khomeini's Islamic Revolution triumphed, and suddenly Iran's culture was transformed—and left in tatters. We all hoped for better days with the transition to the Islamic government: equal distribution of wealth and equal access to education and healthcare. But that day never came.

Baba was still convinced that Ayatollah Khomeini was going to be a great leader. My mother was not as hopeful. Whenever Maman would worry, Baba would try to calm her down by reminding her, "We are the direct descendants of the prophet Muhammad." Our family name is *Sayyid*, or *Hashem*, meaning that we are in the royal bloodline of Muhammad, the founder of Islam. Ayatollah Khomeini would have to respect our connection to the Prophet, Baba said, because he benefited in the same way, since he himself was directly descended from Muhammad.

An emphasis on leadership by those related to the prophet Muhammad is what separates Iran from all the other Muslim nations in the world. In the seventh century, after Muhammad died, the Sunni and Shia branches of Islam fought over who would assume power. Iran is a Shia nation, believing that the leader of Islam after Muhammad must be in the royal bloodline of the Prophet. Sunnis, representing all the other Muslim nations in the world, take a more democratic approach and believe that someone who is not related to the Prophet should be appointed as leader. The Sunnis and Shia are still in conflict over this.

One could say that our family took more pride in our name than in our religion, because we received favor due to it. We never had to tell people that we were related to the Prophet—they automatically understood this. On certain days of the year, strangers would even give us money as a religious duty, just to honor our name, similar to what occurs with the caste system in India. In Iran during the Revolution, being related to the prophet Muhammad meant everything. And within my earliest memories linger echoes of my father's voice, whispering to me the same words he would say to my mother, even before the days when I could understand them: "We are the direct descendants of the prophet Muhammad."

My father was a fairly rotund man with a jet-black goatee that was so thick and broad, it almost passed for a full beard. With the Revolution, he had developed a deep passion for following Allah and living by the teachings of Muhammad. We would watch him pray, and although he didn't push Islam on us, he taught us how to be good Muslims, and my brother eagerly followed in his footsteps.

The end of the Islamic Revolution was quickly followed by the war with Iraq. The Sunnis in Iraq were extremely nervous that Khomeini would export Shia Islam into their nation, so they launched an attack to preempt it. My memories of the war start when I was about five, after my sister was born. I remember the howling sounds of sirens, people burning tires in the streets, and the chaos and panic as everyone desperately attempted to dive for shelter before the Iraqi planes screamed overhead. During that time, most evenings, Iranians went without using electricity to illuminate their homes, in order to prohibit the Iraqi fighter pilots from having the aid of any residential lights to use as targets.

I remember that when we heard the air-raid sirens, my mother would hurry downstairs with our baby sister; my father would follow, carrying my brother and me. He could go from a seated position, eating bread and reading a newspaper at the table, to a full sprint, swooping us into his arms and hurling himself down the stairwell to the basement. He would do it so fast and so effortlessly that I would mostly be unaware that I was even being held until we were almost on the final flight of stairs. My body naturally molded to my father's arms and shoulders with his makeshift fireman's carry, and I was as comfortable there as I was playing with my toys on the floor.

During the raids, each of us in our family had our usual spots in the basement of our apartment building where we would lie in the darkness and wait for the bombing to end. Although I couldn't see anything in front of me, in my mind, I had a picture-perfect image of everything around me. The floor was littered with dusty pillows and stale blankets where my father would entertain us for hours with guessing games and intricately woven stories about our Islamic heritage—some true, some maybe not so true. In the far corner were water jugs and shovels for emergency use in case we became trapped by the building falling in on us and had to dig our way out.

Night after night, we listened to sounds from outside and tried to guess what was making each one. "Can you hear that?" Baba would ask. A moment of silence would follow as my brother and I tried to guess what the sound was.

"What is it, Baba?"

"That!" he would exclaim in a soft voice, just as a thunderous clap cracked through the night air, echoing off the mountains surrounding Tehran. "That is an Iraqi plane coming in and…now, wait for it…." He would pause, and my brother and I would hold our breath, not wanting to miss what was coming next. "Wait for it…."

"*There!*" he would whisper, just as we heard an explosion. His timing was impeccable. His anticipation of the explosions and his exclamations were so closely knit together that it was hard to tell if he was commenting on the war outside or orchestrating it. "We got 'em," my father would proclaim in victory, hearing the sound of what he assumed was the antiair defense system shooting down an Iraqi plane.

As my father whispered these narrations to us, we would listen carefully, as if our lives depended on it. We tried to keep our eyes open as much as possible because we were afraid of falling asleep and then waking up to the terrifying reality of a bombed-out apartment building and finding ourselves orphans. As children, our identity was connected to our parents, to whom we belonged. We felt that being orphans would mean we did not belong to anyone any longer, and that would mean we had no identity. Eventually, we would slowly drift to sleep listening to the sounds of falling bombs, streaking missiles, and antiair defenses.

As we lived under the constant threat of bombs, I developed a terror of losing my mother. Every morning, for years afterward—all the way through high school—I would go to sleep worrying about losing her, and I would wake up in a state of anxiety, call out my mother's name, and run to look for her to make sure she was still alive. When I became an adult, my mother confided in me something her father had told her: children are not really orphaned by the loss of their father, but they are truly orphaned by the loss of their mother. There was something about the thought of losing my mother that made me feel completely alone in this world.

My first thoughts about God were formed during those dark nights listening to bombs and missiles being dropped on our city. Even though I was a child, the war had shaken me out of my childish bubble of daydreams and brought me into the harsh reality of death and the frailty of life. "Where are you, God?" I would pray. "Why are you allowing all this to happen? Who are you?" These questions plagued my mind and were often the topic of conversations with my twin brother. I remember our first conversation about it, which went something like this:

"Hear that sound?" Nima asked me.

"The screeching sound, you mean?"

"Yeah. They say when it is the screeching sound, it is a missile. A bomb would make more of a 'boom' sound. And I have heard that when a missile hits a neighborhood, it destroys the entire neighborhood."

"Do you think God is at the houses that get bombed and with the children that die? You know God judges every sin, and every time we do something bad, the angel on the left hand records all of the wrongs, and the angel on the right hand records all of the good that we do. We haven't done very many good things recently. I have been so bad. I keep peeing on myself. I don't know what's wrong with me. Sometimes I just get so scared."

"I did learn at school today that God is angry and that we are all going to hell—that is, unless I die in a holy war. I want to sign up. I want to go to heaven."

"Do you think God is mad at me?" I whispered. "I have said a few lies to Baba and Maman about my grades. Do you think our house might get hit next? They say God is vengeful."

"Who is this God, anyway?" Nima replied. "How can we please him? Should we be praying every day like Baba? Should we try to fast during Ramadan?"

I didn't know how to get God to answer our questions.

2

A LONG, BITTER WINTER

Looking back on the early days of my childhood, I remember feeling moments of terror fueled by the imagination of a small child. Yet, at the same time, I had a raw confidence from the knowledge of my holy bloodline to the Prophet, the comfort of Baba's stories, and the women in my life who had blazed paths as cultural warriors.

Not only was I born Naghmeh Shariat Panahi, meaning "Naghmeh, protector of Islamic Law," but I was born into a line of strong women who knew how to fight in a society dominated by men. The Iraqi army didn't scare them, and it was going to take more than the enemy's bombs to stop them.

My grandmother was a fierce woman who taught the Koran and was one of the first female pharmacists in Iran. In the early 1920s, when she was a young single lady, not only was it almost unheard of for a woman in the Middle East to be a pharmacist, but one would have been hard put to find a female pharmacist at that time even in Europe or America. My grandmother shattered the glass ceiling of her day and danced atop its shards.

My mother was just as tough. She had fought her way into Persian history by being one of the first female officers to be accepted into the Shah's army. After her officer candidate school graduation, she went on to become an officer of the guards and was in charge of running various duties for security throughout Iran, eventually making her way up to the rank of major.

My mother earned her black belt in martial arts and was the top shooter in her unit. It felt very natural for me to see my mother posing in our early family photos wearing a miniskirt and carrying a sidearm. As the stories go, she could often be seen pushing my stroller with one hand and carrying a pistol in the other. Her military discipline taught her to always be armed and ready for action.

Although it was strange in our culture in the 1970s for a woman to have such a manly job, Baba didn't mind my mother's vocation. In fact, he openly declared that this was part of his fascination with her. He loved that she was an officer in the military and had a career she felt fulfilled in.

Even more than that, he was infatuated with my mother. He had met her when he was only a young teenager at a family reunion and had often tried to court her, but she paid him no attention. Even when he attended Oregon State University in America to earn his master's degree in electrical engineering, he never forgot her. Eventually, he returned to Iran and was able to win her approval for marriage—and he never stopped courting her. His face would beam when she walked into a room where he was.

After their marriage, my mother never grew into a "happy homemaker," and while Baba loved her for that, he did daydream from time to time about what it would be like to have a wife who cooks. "Just one time," I remember hearing him say to her, "I would like to taste your cooking."

"Tough!" she had instinctively rebuffed, without even looking up at him. He had laughed out loud and simply shook his head. That day was clearly never going to come. He had expected nothing different from her.

We had a full-time nanny who lived with us to take care of the day-to-day household chores. The very earliest memory I can summon is of my nanny, Naneh, rolling a ball to my brother and me. She had begun working for our family long before I was born, after she lost her husband in a tragic accident and had four young girls to support.

My grandfather on my mother's side had taken Naneh in, along with her children, and provided her with a job caring for my grandmother. My mother was the only daughter in her family, and, before my grandmother passed away, Naneh promised to go with my mother's family and look after her in the manner that she had so lovingly looked after Grandmother. She kept her promise.

Naneh was a short, stout woman with a sturdy center of gravity. As a devout Muslim, she made sure that she always wore her headscarf. She wore sandals, but never without socks because that would be scandalous. Although she was a stern woman, she adored my brother, having a soft spot for him.

Naneh would often lift her sleeve to show off her wealth of gold bracelets. Pointing to one of the many ornaments, she would say, "This bracelet is for you, Naghmeh, when you get married." Then she would move her finger from her wrist to her elbow, indicating the remaining bracelets as she looked at my brother and said, "And all of these bracelets are for you, Nima, when you get married. If I am lucky enough to see that day," she would add as tears rolled down her face.

When Naneh prepared meals for my brother and me, she made sure to give him a larger portion. She would always make my brother's bed, but I was expected to make my own. When we played, she would concentrate on him. If I got into trouble, my father would rap my hands with a stick while Naneh busied herself in another room with cleaning and cooking. But if my brother got into trouble, all of a sudden, she would become alert, throw herself in front of my father, and beg him, "No, please, punish me instead."

I wasn't jealous of my brother as much as I was annoyed by Naneh's behavior.

I was also observant. Naneh came from a culture that valued boys more than girls, but her devotion to my brother was more than that. Perhaps it was because she had four daughters and no sons of her own, or maybe she just naturally connected with my brother more than she did with me. Whatever the reason, despite the accomplishments of my strong-minded mother and grandmother, I was being conditioned by the idea that I had less value as a person because I was a girl. This was a mindset I would have to fight against over and over in my life.

Baba's caring nature brought some balance to my conception of myself. I knew that I always had a special place on his knee and a formidable ally when I needed to win an argument with my brother. "You know, you are a lot like me," he would often tell me. Any inadequacies I felt were largely overcome by the love I received from Baba. But, as I would come to discover, not even his influence in my life could change the subjugation of women that came with the Iranian Revolution.

Our daily life in Tehran was carved out around the war. When there weren't bombing raids, we made attempts to live a normal life. We had an apartment in a high-rise on Amirabad Street, a middle-class neighborhood in the least-destroyed section of the city. Our wide, rectangular building was flanked by slender, crooked walkways, extending north and south. The seven-story structure was not oversized for our neighborhood, being squeezed between equally impressive neighboring buildings on the same street. The upper floors were often not fully visible from the outside, being partially obscured by a thin curtain of smog and particle dust that seemed to constantly hover over the city.

My grandmother owned the entire apartment building, and she only rented to family members, never strangers. Several of my father's siblings lived in their own apartments on their own floors. My grandmother lived on the bottom floor, with easy access to the fruit-tree-laden garden in the back; my aunt lived on the top floor, and all the other families were sandwiched on the floors in between.

My immediate family lived in the middle of the building on the third floor. Our apartment had four bedrooms, a living room, a formal dining room, an informal dining room, a kitchen, and two bathrooms. Nima and I were never lonely or bored. During the day, our building buzzed with all the energy of a Persian bazaar, with people running up and down the stairs, going from apartment to apartment, visiting together, playing backgammon, and feeding off the "drama" dragged in from the city by my aunts, uncles, and cousins.

One day, I fell and gashed my forehead while playing. My father took me to a nearby hospital, but because the doctors were busy tending to patients with war casualties, we waited for hours to receive help, with blood gushing from my forehead. Finally, Baba stopped a hospital worker and asked them to stitch me up. There was no anesthetic available, so I felt every thrust of the needle as it went in and out. Because I was not stitched up by an expert, I developed a scar right in the middle of my forehead—in the form of a check mark—that remains to this day.

When my brother and I were not chasing each other between the floors of our building, we played games with our best friends, Shokoofeh and her sister. My brother was the only boy among us, but he didn't seem to mind. We had a few toys that Baba had given us, but, most of the time, we played games, including endless hours of tag in our back garden. The garden served as my family's own personal orchard, having fig trees, apple trees, tangerine trees, and persimmon trees. My favorite tree in the courtyard didn't have any fruit on it. It was a red maple, and, in the late spring, the tree would bloom with thousands of helicopter-shaped seeds that fell to the ground with a spinning movement and rode on the slightest breeze across our yard. Those seeds provided endless entertainment and competitions for my friends and me.

In the middle of the garden was a spot marked with black charcoal from the burned logs we used every year to build a fire during the Iranian New Year celebration, known as Nowruz. Nowruz is the biggest holiday of the year, occurring at the spring equinox. The fire was for *Charshanba Suri*, an ancient Persian tradition that dates back long before Islam, where we would say, "I give my illness to you, and I receive your life for me," and then jump over the fire to receive life from it.

Day after day, for hours, my grandmother would sit motionless in our garden, like a sad memorial statue, unmoved by the world around her. Her reverie was interrupted only by our running in and out of the garden with our friends. When I ran around her, I sometimes called out her name, but she wouldn't respond. I knew what she was thinking about. The whole family did. Her glassy eyes held painful memories as she sat in motionless silence.

On several occasions, I thought about sitting with her to keep her company, but she always had the air of someone who was content to be alone, her sad mahogany eyes gazing beyond me, beyond the walls of our garden, reaching out to see a faraway place she couldn't go to but desperately wanted to. She was mourning her youngest son, who was only in his teens. He languished in notorious Evin Prison for the political crime of being a part of the Mujahedin, a group of Muslims that opposed the rule of Ayatollah Khomeini.

My grandmother had experienced the Iranian Revolution and its aftermath as a long, bitter winter: one son, my father, had supported the Ayatollah, while his wife had been oath-bound to the Shah; another son had been sucked into the Mujahedin at an age when he was too young to know better. The Ayatollah, the Shah, and the Mujahedin were not merely three political parties with opposing views running against each other in an election. They were three sworn enemies playing for keeps and fighting to the death.

My grandmother spent her days thinking of her young, innocent, beardless, skinny boy, fading from existence in a dark prison. She knew that few people made it out of Evin Prison alive, but she was hoping against hope.

3

"WE CAN'T STAY HERE
ANY LONGER"

Death to America! Death to Israel! Death to America! Death to Israel!" I yelled in unison with my classmates as we were lined up for morning formation, throwing my fist into the air as our teacher had taught us to do.

"Death to America! Death to Israel!" my teacher shouted again, turning and glaring down at us with her furrowed brow and stern, demanding eyes, silently charging us to repeat her words.

"Death to America! Death to Israel!" we all repeated—but I shouted the loudest, with as much enthusiasm as I could muster, with the hopes of catching the teacher's attention. I knew that my devotion would impress her and she'd think I was an exceptional student.

I didn't know what the chant of this holy jihad against the "Great Satan," America and Israel, meant, but it felt exciting. I had never heard the word *Israel* before, but the electric charge of the chant seemed to surge through the entire student body like an extra alarm bell for those who hadn't fully woken up. It was invigorating, although we didn't really know anything about America or Israel. Our incantations didn't have any practical meaning for us.

After our morning formation, we proudly marched into the school. I followed my column into our classroom, took a seat at my dented black wooden desk, and, together with the rest of the class, waited for our teacher. I stretched my feet under the desk, pointing my toes toward the chalkboard. My legs were too short to reach the ground as I sat in my chair, and I swung them back and forth in a rocking motion that kept quick-paced time.

The teacher looked up at the clock as she closed the door behind her. Then she immediately took out her Koran to instruct us. The Koran was our primary focus and was woven into every academic subject of our day. "Today, we are going to talk about one of the most fundamental pillars of Islam: fasting."

It was not difficult for me to understand the written Koran because it was in Arabic, which I had been learning to read. But it was hard for me to say the words because I was not fluent in speaking Arabic. Our family normally spoke Farsi, or Persian. But after the Revolution, it was mandatory for students to learn the Arabic language, study the Koran, and adopt Sharia law. I didn't know all of the details about Sharia law, but I could see its effects.

Under Sharia law, women were no longer allowed to wear Western clothing or walk freely in the city. Now they had to be covered from head to toe. The men grew beards and prayed toward Mecca three times a day on special rugs they carried with them everywhere. Homosexuals and adulterers were executed. Those caught participating in *haram*, or forbidden, sinful acts denounced by Islam—such as dancing, listening to music, watching pornography, making alcohol, or dealing drugs—were punished by being whipped or hit with a cane, or were executed by decapitation, hanging, or firing squad. It felt like our entire nation, not just the students in our class, was relearning the meaning of *haram*.

Besides the "Great Satan," my classmates and I understood there was another enemy that Allah had called us to fight in "jihad," and it was closer to home—Iraq. Fighting Iraq was not theoretical for us; it was part of our daily lives. Thousands of Shia fighters were dying in an effort to repel the attacks of the Sunni aggressor, and more troops were needed.

The number of men of fighting age was quickly dwindling, and the Ayatollah looked to young boys—as young as six or seven years old—to join the battle. Iraq was planting explosive land mines along the front lines of the battlefield, and young, "expendable" boys were being recruited to walk through the maze of explosives to find or "make" a safe path for the rest of the soldiers to follow.

It was a suicide mission, but schoolteachers were trumpeting it as an act of holy jihad. Young boys were told that they would be guaranteed a place in paradise, with virgins to entertain them for eternity. They themselves were virgins and didn't fully understand the meaning of the word, but that didn't stop the teachers from pumping their minds full of stories of heroic deeds that awaited them on the battlefield.

One by one, my brother's classmates signed up to serve and were promptly shipped out to the front lines. If any parents objected, they were labeled as being anti-revolutionaries and enemies of Allah—the two worst labels anyone could have in postrevolutionary Iran.

"It's time for me to go!" Nima announced one day after school, giddy with excitement.

"Time to go where?" my mother asked.

"Jihad! To fight against the evil Iraqis," he answered, clearly perplexed that she had to ask. "My friends are signing up. If I die, it's jihad, and I will go to heaven."

As soon as she heard my brother's words, my mother froze in place. Not even her eyes moved. Because she was in the army, she knew what he meant and was cognizant of exactly how he'd be used. Since the beginning of the war, she had been seeing reports of all the carnage taking place on the front lines. She knew that the young boys being sent out would not be returning home. They would walk in the minefields and not stop until the explosive was triggered. That was their job.

When the Ayatollah assumed power in Iran, my mother was stripped of all her power because she was a woman. She was forced to wear a headscarf that covered both her head and her rank. The new Islamic army of Iran didn't want to see a female showing any rank that was higher than that of a male. Eventually, she was forced to remove her rank insignia altogether to avoid confusion. She had to turn in her guns and would no longer be allowed to carry a weapon.

She hadn't complained. But to recruit her son was going too far—Iran was asking her to send her baby boy to be slaughtered.

When Baba arrived home and heard the news, he was shaken to his foundation. Both my parents knew there was nothing they could do to protect Nima from going to war in the near future. Without warning, the true weight of the Revolution and its implications had come crashing down on them.

Like my mother, my father had seen the carnage of the war firsthand. After the Revolution, the government had offered him a high-profile position with the new regime for his role in the riots and the overthrow of the Shah. He was offered the position of Minister of Communication, which included overseeing agricultural satellites. He didn't jump at the opportunity because he, like my mother, knew that powerful positions could be more of a curse than a blessing. It was often the people in the most visible positions who were executed when things went wrong. My father had seen too many people hastily executed by angry mobs that needed no more evidence of a person's guilt than a flimsy accusation.

Instead, Baba decided to help the war effort by supporting the medical needs of Iran. When the conflict with Iraq began, most medical companies left the country. Medical devices were continually breaking down and needing repair, and my father was skilled at fixing them. His clients were so impressed with him that they told him that if he would import medical supplies, they would purchase them from him. Since the economic sanctions against Iran by the United States did not include medical equipment, my father started a highly successful medical supplies distribution company. He provided supplies to hospitals and also repaired their equipment, frequently traveling outside the country to conduct his business.

Because of his contacts with these hospitals, my father saw up close the horrible carnage of the war, especially when Iraq launched chemical warfare against Iran. He would often stumble shell-shocked through the door of our home after a long day at work, flop down at the kitchen table, and recount the horrors he had seen at the hospital: maimed men with missing limbs blown off at minefields; helpless infants suffering from chemical attacks that had left them plagued with festering, oozing blisters that covered the places where their eyes, noses, and lips used to be.

I imagine that now, as he thought about my brother going to war, all those vivid, gruesome images filled his mind.

"Why is Allah allowing this to happen?" Baba grieved aloud while sitting at the table. He pulled his strong, veiny olive fingers down his face as if trying to draw the answer from the top of his head. "Why is Allah allowing this to happen?" he asked again. He wasn't waiting for anyone in the room to answer him because, deep down, he knew what we all knew—no one had an answer to all the pain and suffering, not even Allah.

The despair of that moment left our family sitting in awkward silence, no one wanting to speak. My brother's decision to volunteer to be a minesweeper for the Iranian army had changed everything we thought we knew. Suddenly, our newfound Islamic devotion had taken on entirely new significance. Many of our fellow countrymen had cried out for the Revolution, my father had supported the Ayatollah, my mother had given up her rank and job, and my grandmother had given her youngest son—but it wasn't enough. The

Revolution wanted more, and its angel of death was now at the threshold of our home, demanding a tax that could only be paid in blood.

Although Nima had declared he would sign up for jihad, there were only a few recruiting times during the year. After my brother's startling announcement, my father privately told my mother, "We can't stay here any longer. We have to find a way to get our family to America."

4

RESPITE FROM WAR

Through a maze of concrete lanes and not-so-carefully planned knolls of grass and friendly trees, my brother and I made our way back home from school. We had just said goodbye to our classmates for the last time and did not know what the future held for us.

The fresh, bracing air swooping down from the Alborz mountain range clashed with the dust that hung like a tattered curtain over our path, choking out the sunshine before some rays eventually broke through. Floating particles scratched the back of my throat whenever I took a deep breath. The smell of sulfur, burning rubber, and shattered cinderblock from the previous day's bombings wafted back and forth in the afternoon breeze.

Stray dogs foaming white froth from the corners of their mouths darted from rubble pile to rubble pile, desperately looking for dead carcasses or decomposing animals to devour. I kept my head down, trying not to look at these dogs. Every day that we were able to attend school was a day that we heard the story of yet another classmate who had gone missing. In some ways, I shuttered at the thought that the wild dogs might have found one of those missing students, and I refused to look at the scavengers for fear that they might be feasting on one of my classmates. There was little chance this was the case, but I didn't like the probability, so I kept my gaze fixed on my feet as I hastily shuffled through the debris.

Tehran was quickly growing into a city of orphans with an alarming number of waifs roaming the streets looking for food and shelter. The city had once had an ample supply of devotion to her citizens, but the needs had simply grown too substantial and the supplies had run out. Every citizen felt overwhelmed by their own tragic stories. Children walked the city streets like zombies with blank stares and void faces, hoping someone might notice them and take them in. No one did. They cried until their eyes were dry and empty. Tears take energy that can't be fed with empty stomachs, reminding us that war is no place for parentless children. They see things that their virgin eyes should never see, and they lose something they will never regain.

My parents were concerned that my brother and I might suddenly go missing or be killed as they made arrangements to leave Iran. So, several months before we said our final goodbyes to our classmates, during our summer vacation, my parents had driven us and my grandmother to the coast of the Caspian Sea in northern Iran to keep us safe. We stayed with my grandmother at a magnificent vacation retreat owned by my grandmother's brother, while my parents returned to Tehran to work.

It was the first time in my life that I experienced what it was like to be a carefree child. Our respite in the north was blissful, with no sounds of bombs or missiles competing with the splashing waves of the sea—even though I was also anxious at times about what might be happening to my parents. The days of innocence on the Caspian Sea seemed endless and washed us clean of the terrors of the war in Tehran. The escape was temporary, but the therapy was eternal. I spent every day on the beach, playing make-believe and gathering a wide assortment of shells, frogs, snails, worms, and bugs. The long days at the shore were a million miles away from my days of walking the zigzag, war-torn paths between home and school.

The villa where we were staying was three stories tall. It was covered with vines, and it was surrounded by jasmine bushes. To this day, whenever I smell jasmine, memories of that wonderful period of my life come drifting back to me. I even choose perfumes with jasmine in them to recall those pleasant days. Whenever I went out exploring and got lost, I could easily find my way back by looking up and spotting the large, vine-blanketed villa, and heading in that direction. Those vines were beautiful, but they could also be dangerous—they housed many beehives, a fact I didn't realize until one day when I ran past the villa and was chased by angry bees, getting stung six times!

The people in northern Iran are more relaxed than those in the capital city of Tehran and were far more flexible about the Islamic religious laws. My grandmother walked around without her head covered, and no one seemed to care. My brother and I didn't have regular mealtimes or a set bedtime; we ate when food was prepared and slept wherever we collapsed after a day of playing hard. My grandmother's ideas about raising children were different from my parents': she felt that children grew best when they were allowed to independently explore the world around them.

Looking back, it seems strange how fast my brother and I forgot about the war; but, in truth, it was never far away. Although my grandmother tried to be strong for us, in many ways, she was a shell of her younger self. She still waited endlessly for her youngest son to be released from prison, and she endured many sleepless nights imagining what they were doing to him. She had prayed to Allah again and again every time we heard cracking gunshots while visiting relatives who lived near Evin Prison, as political prisoners were systematically executed by firing squad. Once, my grandmother was able to visit my uncle in prison, and she took my brother and me with her. It was a temporary step back into reality for me. I remember the narrow halls, the stark waiting room, and the glass window that separated us from my very thin and scared uncle. When my uncle was first incarcerated, he had not yet hit puberty and had no facial hair. Now, after several years, he had grown into a young man with a long beard. It was extremely painful for my grandmother to see him in his changed state, looking at us with desperation and great fear, staring off in a daze as he talked about the carefree times he had spent as a little boy, running in the backyard of our apartment building, as if it were more of a dream than a memory.

One day, my grandmother received the phone call she had been waiting for. "He is free; you can come get your son," a prison guard said over the phone.

"He's free!" she told everyone when she got the call. With great excitement, she rushed to the prison—only to find that their idea of freedom was different from hers. Evin Prison had simply waited for my uncle to turn eighteen, and, on his eighteenth birthday, they executed him.

It was a sadistic joke. While my grandmother stood wailing at the grate, crying over the death of her youngest child, the guards gleefully gave his clothes to her and promptly told her to get out. It seemed like the cruelty of the Iraqi military attacks on Iran were never as torturous as what the Ayatollah's henchmen were capable of inflicting on their own people.

5

"GOD LOVES YOU"

Six months after my brother and I arrived home from the north, my parents told us to get ready for our "going-away" party. Baba allowed us to invite all our friends to come and celebrate our birthday on February 3 before we would fly to America. They told us we were moving to an exciting land where my father had lived and attended graduate school before my parents were married. It would be an adventure and relieve us of all the troubles connected with the war.

My brother and I got caught up in Baba and Maman's enthusiasm. Nima's growing anticipation about going to America distracted him, overpowering his desire to sign up to serve in the army—which is just what my parents had hoped for.

Since Baba still had a green card from the time he had lived in the United States, he was able to secure green cards for the rest of the family too. My father had two brothers in California, one who was just out of college and another who worked as an engineer for a company called Lockheed Corporation. One of my mother's brothers also lived in California.

My uncle who worked for Lockheed would help us get settled once we arrived. Baba told us this uncle had also become a famous radio personality, and he used our radio to try to locate the station that broadcast his brother's program, but he wasn't able to.

"Aargh...I can't find it. Never mind," Baba said, tossing his hands at the radio.

Even though Baba had been unsuccessful in finding my uncle's program, Nima and I were not disappointed in the program he had landed on, which we could understand because it was in Farsi. A man was speaking, and it sounded like a fun program, so, when my father left the room, we kept listening. We were excited to hear something that was not about the war.

Suddenly, without warning, the man began saying something I had never heard before: "God loves you. All you need to do is speak to Him from your heart. He can hear your prayers. If you would like to know Him more, you can ask Him to reveal Himself to you." His words echoed in our room and fascinated us.

The God that this strange, invisible man was talking about seemed to be different from the one we had been learning about in school. This God apparently loved us and wanted to know us on a personal level.

"God loves you," the man said again in a tender voice. His words lingered through the airwaves and dangled in my thoughts. I had never heard that phrase before. I looked over at Nima, and he looked back at me with his big, round almond eyes bulging in surprise. He was as bewildered at the thought as I was.

"Is this man saying that God loves us, or is he talking about a different *Khuda?*" I asked myself, using the word for "God" in the Persian language.

"God created you," the man on the radio continued. "He knows your name. He loves you so much that He gave His life for you, and He will reveal Himself to you if you will only ask."

Again, Nima and I looked at each other incredulously. The idea was crazy. The concept that God loved us and wanted us to know Him was unheard of.

"Repeat after me," the invisible man said in a very caring voice. "God, I want to know who You are." He paused for us to follow along.

Nima and I paused, too, before we eventually repeated, "God, I want to know who You are."

"Please show me who You are," the man prayed.

"Please show me who You are," we said in unison.

I had never prayed directly to God before. In school, we prayed to Allah, but nothing about those prayers was personal. The prayer we said with the invisible man on the radio was intimate in a way that I had never experienced before.

That moment altered the course of our lives. Soon after my brother and I uttered that prayer, our prayer began to be answered. At the time, we didn't know that our move to America was being orchestrated by God not only for our physical safety but also for our spiritual well-being. In the meantime, we were unprepared for some cultural surprises about the country we would be moving to.

Nima and I didn't know anything about America, except that it was the great enemy we had been taught in school to hate. I wanted to hate America, but it was hard to do that when Baba said so many good things about it.

On his many work trips, he would often purchase things for us from other countries to teach us about America. One day, he burst through the door with his suitcase bouncing behind him. Hearing that Baba was home, we all rushed to greet him.

"Hey everyone, come! You have to see this!" he said excitedly as he dropped to his knees and unzipped the case in the middle of the floor in front of us. Lying neatly on top of his folded clothes was a brown paper bag with big yellow markings on it. He reached inside the bag and pulled out a fist-sized package wrapped in yellow waxed paper. Then he slowly unwrapped it as if it were a treasure.

"What is it? What is it?" I asked, bouncing up and down. "Baba, what did you bring us?"

"This is called a cheeseburger," he said as he gingerly broke it into small portions and offered each of us an equal-sized portion.

I ripped the piece from his hand, shoved it into my mouth, and swallowed it. The savory flavors were all completely new to me and lingered on my tongue, even though the exposure time had been short. We all stared at each other with our eyes bulging.

"Wow!" I said. My brother looked toward me and then back at Baba.

"More, Baba!" my brother demanded. "We want more of whatever that was."

"Sorry, I only brought one, but they have those everywhere in America."

On another occasion, Baba went on a work trip to Japan. His meetings with the company there were not close to his hotel, so his hosts gave him money for bus fare. Instead of taking the bus, Baba walked to each meeting and used the money to buy me an American Barbie doll. When he brought the doll home to me in Iran, I immediately fell in love with it. I had never seen anything like that doll, and I was instantly crazy for anything with the Barbie logo. I spent hours escaping the woes of war playing with my new toy. I would lose myself in it, pretending to be living in Barbie's blonde, carefree world.

Before the Islamic Revolution, Tehran had been painted with advertise-ments of famous singers and performers. After the Revolution, it was illegal to even listen to popular music in the privacy of your own home. Our family broke these laws. We had a VHS tape player that we had secretly kept after the Revolution, and certain family members helped to smuggle special videos for us. My brother and I spent hours watching Tom and Jerry cartoons and several dubbed Disney movies with singing and dancing.

The tapes I enjoyed the most were those featuring famous female Persian singers who had escaped Iran after the Revolution and now performed abroad. They sang songs about life and romance instead of Islam and war. While watching them, I would hold my Barbie doll and dance to the music. I was fascinated by the ornate gowns and lavish hairstyles of the singers.

For my final birthday party in Iran, my mother bought me a yellow dress with blue frilly stripes and white ruffles, similar to one worn by my favorite Persian pop star, Neli. I had a special white doily that wrapped around the top of my dress, highlighting my slender Persian neck. The entire ensemble was shiny and silky, just as I imagined Barbie wearing. I also cut my hair short like Neli in a way that was edgy and independent from Ayatollah control. I twirled around in the whole ensemble feeling like a princess.

Our home was decorated with festive streamers stretching from one corner of the living-room ceiling to the other, with balloons dangling from the ceiling as well. The formal dining room, with its pastel-colored walls and white lace curtains—which we were usually banned from using—was now in full function. On the top of our dining table, which was surrounded by brown chairs with white-and-brown-patterned cushions, sat a massive cake decorated in the shape of a book, with my name on one side and my brother's name on the other.

After the guests arrived, the white tablecloth on the kitchen table, where the cake was moved, did not stay white for long, with people flinging chunks of crème and icing from the cake knife as they hurriedly cut slices for them-selves to enjoy. Whenever the knife was misplaced in the commotion of the moment by some rushed guest, my mother would grab a spatula or whatever else was easily accessible so the cake could continue to be served. Snacks were lined up on the table beside the cake, but additional food items were arranged on the stainless-steel countertops.

A line formed at the far left-hand side of the stove, where Naneh kept the bronze copper pot to warm the tea throughout the day. Tea in Iran is not just a beverage—it is the dry-leaf and cardamom liquid bond that holds the society together. Every home in Iran—whether the country is at war or not—keeps a pot of tea on the stove throughout the day. If the leaders of the Iraqi army had known how to drink Persian tea, the disputes of the war might have been settled in an afternoon.

The number-one rule of tea in Iran is that you never let the teapot go empty or cold; you keep the pot full and warm the entire day. It was imperative that Naneh stayed on her toes to ensure that no guest was ever without tea.

After they had eaten cake and snacked on the other foods, everyone stood around drinking tea and speculating what life would be like for us in America. In between sentences, my family members and their guests would briefly pause to place a hard white sugar cube in between their teeth before drinking more tea, as is customary in Iran. This custom enables people to take a breath, slow the pace of the conversation, and carefully select the words they wish to share with others, while at the same time heightening the flavor of the tea with sweetness, without permitting the sugar to fully dissolve into the tea.

An Iranian without tea can be dangerous, allowing thoughts to be expressed that should never be shared publicly. The Persian way of drinking tea allows for a very clever, socially acceptable constraint that imposes time restrictions on how much can be shared in a conversation.

Our going-away party felt like the perfect day. Only a few weeks later, in mid-March, during the Iranian New Year holidays, our family was packed up in our car and headed to the international airport. As we pulled away from the house, Naneh was crying and throwing water behind us. In Iran, throwing water behind someone is a blessing for their trip to give them good fortune.

I wish we could have turned around and thrown water behind Naneh. She would need the blessing staying in Iran more than we would need it by going to America.

6

THE OPPORTUNITY TO DREAM

I didn't know I had a phobia of airplanes until the moment we arrived at the airport in the late evening. I had never been on an airplane before, and, up until that point, I had always associated planes with bombing raids.

Baba could see I was growing more concerned by the minute. "It's going to be okay, Naghmeh. These are the kind of planes that I fly in all the time," he said after taking the tickets from the ticket agent. "These are the kind of planes that carry businessmen like me to and from their meetings. Families with little children like you take airplanes like this one every day to go on vacations to fun places around the world."

I held his strong hand and carried my Barbie close to me, under my arm, tightly squeezing both of these sources of comfort.

When we boarded the plane, the stale air was cold and pinched my cheeks. I saw the big English letters KLM. As we looked for our seats, I heard a language over the intercom system I didn't understand.

"What are they saying, Baba?" I asked.

"They are saying that we need to quickly find our seats to allow other passengers to board in a timely manner," he answered while dragging me down the aisle by my arm. Not long after we sat down, a sweet flight attendant came by and gave me a small toy. I couldn't understand what she was saying, so she talked to me through her smile. Her kindness immediately put me at ease, and, in only a few minutes, I was asleep, nestled into Baba's arm.

Later, we stopped for a quick transfer to another flight, and then we arrived in San Jose, where my uncle greeted us at the airport. We didn't have much luggage because we'd had to leave most of what we owned back in Tehran.

I had departed Iran in the middle of the night and arrived in America in the middle of the day, which, thinking back to that time, was a metaphor for my experience, because the difference between Iran and America seemed like night and day to me. In Iran, I had often had nightmares about being bombed or getting in trouble from the authorities for not being covered up. In America, I didn't have to worry about either. I saw no piles of rubble from bombs, and none of the women were covered up. During the first week, I constantly felt panicked when I realized I had not covered my head, and I would have to remind myself that it was not a problem in America. My mother also no longer wore a head covering, and we both felt a feeling of freedom.

My uncle and his family lived in a townhouse in a subdivision outside San Jose. My uncle had arranged for our family to have a room upstairs. Baba and Maman slept on the only bed in the room, while my brother, our baby sister, and I slept on the floor. There were two more rooms for my uncle and his children.

"See that out there?" my father asked, pointing to a swimming pool in the middle of the courtyard.

"Yes," I said shaking my head in excitement.

"You can swim in that pool anytime you want!"

"Wow!" I screamed as I ran to take a closer look.

Soon after we arrived, my uncle took us to a place called Safeway to buy food. It was the largest grocery store I had ever seen in my life. I had never imagined anything like it, with aisles and aisles of food that seemed to go on forever. All the shelves were so perfectly aligned and neatly arranged. There were no venders calling out to you, trying to sell you things you didn't want or haggling with you on the price.

In Iran, if you want bread, you go to the baker. If you want meat, you go to the butcher. If you want vegetables, you find a vegetable stand. Here, everything was in one single, convenient place. There were so many things to see and explore in that store that my brain was quickly overwhelmed, and I was no longer able to process any additional sights or sounds.

When we had first driven to my uncle's house from the airport, I had peered out the window and been fascinated by all the modern-looking buildings and massive freeways. Lines of fast-moving cars seemed to go on for miles. In Iran, traffic crept along smaller roads, and the flow seemed less efficient. As we went along, I spotted a large yellow "M," just like the one I had seen on the package Baba had brought home from his travels.

"Baba—look!" I said, pointing to the sign.

"Yes, that's McDonald's. That is where I bought the cheeseburger I gave you that one time."

I smiled back at him as if I had just discovered something new. "I want to eat there every day, Baba."

"That is the amazing thing about America," he replied. "If you want to eat at McDonald's every day, that is your choice. In America, it is all about what you make it. America is a country where you can do what you want and be whatever you want to be, if you are willing to work hard." He paused and looked at my mother. "It is the land of opportunity," he said, squeezing her hand.

"I came to university here with no scholarships and no money in my pocket, but I studied hard, worked odd jobs to pay for my education, and earned my degree. In America, we have a great future."

It was odd hearing Baba speaking so optimistically. It was as if something had awakened in him. In Iran, I had never heard him dream about the future. Even when he shared with me about Islam and the Revolution, it wasn't in an optimistic way; it was about changing things to avoid destruction. Now he was talking about changes that would bring hope and promise.

As Baba spoke, dreams of growing up filled my mind for the first time. I had not been able to dream in that way in Iran. With death all around me, I had never considered what it meant to have a future. The minds of my family members were constantly on survival, not knowing if we would be alive the next day.

What did I want to be when I grew up? It was strange thinking about having the opportunity to grow up in America. It was strange to think that I had just been chanting "Death to America" at school a few days earlier, and now I was in a car with my uncle and his family in the United States, with the possibility of never leaving it.

7

ESCAPING JESUS

As I adjusted to life in America, the heartfelt prayer I had said with my brother while listening to the man on the radio was long forgotten—until one day when I was standing in a hallway of the townhouse getting ready to put on my bathing suit. It was a warm spring day and the pool was open. We had not yet started school because Baba wanted us to wait for the fall semester to begin.

Nima came barreling toward me. I could tell something tragic had happened because he was crying. Nima *never* cried.

"Naghmeh!" he yelled with tears streaming down his face. "I found the God that we have been looking for, and He loves us!"

"What?" I was confused.

"I said," he repeated, trying to fight through the tears, "I found the God that we have been looking for, and He said He loves us!"

If it had been anyone else, I might have laughed. But Nima did not get emotional about anything. Between the two of us twins, I had received all of the "emotions" genes, while he had received none of them.

"I saw Him, Naghmeh. I saw God. He came to me," he said with his bottom lip trembling up and down. "I found the God we have been looking for. His name is Jesus."

I didn't know what to do or how to comfort him. Our parents were not at home. Baba was traveling and our mother was out shopping.

"What do you mean? You mean Isa? He is God?" I asked. "Isa" is the name for Jesus in the Persian language.

Nima gulped and then explained, "I was just sitting in the room, and Jesus appeared. He came into the room with me, and I wasn't scared. All I felt was complete love."

With our parents away and no other family member available to talk to about this experience, we grabbed hands and rushed outside looking for someone who could tell us who Jesus was. We ran around the housing area and asked random people, "Can you tell us who Jesus is?" But because we were not speaking English, no one understood what we were saying.

Suddenly, as we were running out of people to ask, my uncle returned home. We pivoted on our heels and rushed right up to him as he was getting out of his car.

"Who is Jesus?" we shouted in unison, standing toe-to-toe with my uncle. He jerked back at first, and then a large smile came across his face. His eyes glanced over to the townhouse as he put his fingers up to his lips and motioned for us to be quiet. "Shhh," he said and then winked at us as if to say he would tell us the secret. I followed his gaze to the side yard of the townhouse and noticed that our mother was there. I instantly understood that something about the conversation was a secret and that my mother was not in on that secret.

My uncle's wife took my mother on a walk so he could spend some time with us alone.

"Now, tell me what happened," my uncle said to Nima.

Nima told him everything about his vision of Jesus. I sat and watched in amazement as my brother grew more animated as the story unfolded, and he retold every little detail. My uncle joined in with his excitement. I was surprised that he was taking Nima seriously. I thought that he would have laughed at my brother's silly, fairytale-sounding story, but the opposite was happening. My uncle was sharing in the joy of my brother's story.

"Did you know, Nima, that God created us to be in a loving relationship with Him?" he said in the same kind of manner as the faceless man on the radio. "That is why God created Adam and Eve. But Adam and Eve disobeyed God, and their sin of disobedience created a separation between God and themselves. This is when sin and death entered the world. Man's disobedience didn't end the love that God had for man, and He had a plan to bring man back into a relationship with Him. Without God's plan, all would be lost, because man could not come back to God on his own. Sin had created too great a debt for man to ever pay on his own. God came in human form to pay the penalty of sin by dying on the cross for the sin of all humanity so that everyone on earth could have the opportunity to have a relationship with Him. That is who Jesus is—God in the flesh. And whoever believes in Jesus has their sin forgiven and is reconciled to God. You become a child of God."

After my uncle shared that simple explanation, he followed it up with, "Would you like to believe in Jesus?"

"I already believe," my brother responded. I was shocked at his boldness. "I already believe in Jesus. I saw Him. What do I need to do to follow Him?"

My uncle rephrased his question: "Would you want to be a follower of Jesus?"

We both nodded our heads up and down with a rapid motion. Then, like the invisible man on the radio that day in Iran, my uncle told us to repeat after him as he prayed with us to receive Jesus and become His followers.

"What do we do now?" Nima asked.

"Now you should be baptized," he said.

"What does that mean?" I questioned.

"I'll show you. Follow me." He motioned with one hand while walking toward the pool. We followed him, and he baptized us in the water. When we returned to the house to change into dry clothes, my uncle handed us a little dark-green book with Farsi letters on the front cover.

"This is a special book," he said. "It is called a Bible. Read it every day, and it will tell you who Jesus is and what to do in life." My uncle signed the Bible with both of our names and the date of the baptism and then handed it to Nima.

My brother took it, held it up to his face, and stared at it like it was a piece of valuable treasure. I pulled it from him to take a look inside. One of the first pages I turned to was in a section labeled "Psalms." I saw a large number 2 in the corner of the page and then the number 7, and I read that portion out loud:

> 7I will proclaim the LORD's decree:
>   He said to me, "You are my son;
>   today I have become your father.
> 8Ask me,
>   and I will make the nations your inheritance,

the ends of the earth your possession.[1]

I dropped the Bible to my waist as I recited the verse in my head. "Ask me, and I will make the nations your inheritance."

Just then, our mother arrived, and we immediately ran up to her to share the good news.

"Maman! Maman! Guess what? We are Christians! We accepted Jesus!"

"What?" my mother shouted back, clutching her chest with both hands. Nima repeated what we had said, but with much less enthusiasm. Each word progressively faded in volume. It was clear from the growing anger in her face that this was not good news to her. We quickly learned that this was her worst nightmare.

She saw the Bible I was holding in my hand and snatched it away. Then she grabbed Nima and me by our hands and rushed us up the stairs to our room. Once we were there, she pointed her finger at us and yelled, "You are not going to talk to your uncle again. Do you understand me?"

We were confused. We didn't know what had happened, but we realized that it wasn't good. "Your father will be back soon from his trip, and until that time, you are going to stay in this room. You are not going to leave it. Do you understand me?"

I nodded that I understood her instructions, but I didn't understand why.

For the next couple of days, our mother guarded our room like she was back in the military standing post. On Wednesday evenings, our uncle had friends come over to read the Bible together in his home and sing worship songs together. To keep us from hearing what they were saying and singing, my mother turned on the radio in our room, with the volume loud enough to drown out all the other sounds in the house.

When Baba finally returned and heard what had happened, he exploded. "Pack up everything! We are moving out," he told us. Then he turned and shouted at my uncle, "We are leaving and never coming back."

We packed up, and Baba found another place for us to live. As we drove away from my uncle's house, Baba started shouting with anger-laced rants, half talking to us and half talking to himself. "The worst thing that could have happened to you happened," he said to my brother and me. "You lost your religion," he said, slamming his hand down against the dashboard and bringing

---

1. Psalm 2:7–8 (NIV).

it back up again, "You lost your culture." Again, he banged his hand down on the dashboard. "You lost everything. We lost everything.

"Nima, I thought losing you in the war would be the worst thing that could ever happen, but I was wrong. This? This here, with you losing your religion, losing your culture, is even worse than your dying in a war."

My brother cried, but he wasn't backing down. Not even our father's harsh words could turn him away from what he had seen in that vision. "I don't want to go back to Iran," he blubbered, making his words barely understandable. "I don't want to die in holy jihad. I don't believe in jihad anymore."

I covered my mouth. We didn't talk back to Baba. We never disagreed with him.

"I don't want to do all this Islamic stuff anymore. I don't believe in it anymore," Nima said, referring to the chants that he had to say at school in Iran.

I turned and looked at my brother. I didn't know who he was any longer. In only a couple of days, he had completely transformed. It was as if he were a new person with his own mind, and making his own decisions. I was only a witness to it.

"Too bad," Baba shouted back. "You are a Muslim. End of story!"

Baba found us a small two-bedroom apartment on the other side of town in an immigrant community where the rent was cheaper. However, the community didn't feel as safe. We hadn't been living with my uncle for long, but I had already developed a circle of friends there, and I missed them. My first real friend in America was a white girl named Kimberly. She was my age and lived a few doors down from my uncle. I had never had a white friend before. I didn't understand English, but we communicated through smiles, laughs, and hand gestures.

When we walked into our new apartment, it was completely empty with sandy-beige walls and triple-tone brown matted wall-to-wall carpet. We slept on the floor for the first couple of weeks but slowly began to add donated furniture. Kimberly's parents kindly gave my parents some things that we needed.

I had clothes that Kimberly had given to me with the permission of her parents. In Iran, I hadn't had more than three sets of clothes—one set for playing, one set for school, and a special set for festivals and family gatherings. Americans like Kimberly had closets full of clothes and could wear a different outfit every day of the month.

There weren't any immigrants in our new complex who spoke Farsi because most of the Persians who had escaped from Iran were professionals like my father and chose to live in other communities. I tried to make friends, but most of our neighbors spoke their own languages from Africa or South America. Many of them were suspicious of outsiders and dealt harshly with each other.

One day, while riding bikes with my brother in the parking lot, I was hit by a car. Fortunately, I wasn't hurt, but the driver got out and started yelling at me, clearly upset that her car had been scratched by my bike when she hit me. She threatened my mother that she would take me to the police if we didn't pay her five hundred dollars. My mother didn't want any trouble, so she paid the woman and told me to stay away from the parking lot with my bike.

Although my father no longer wanted anything to do with my uncle, and they were not on speaking terms, his other brother who had just graduated from college had obtained a new job in another part of America called Boise, Idaho. Our younger uncle proposed that we move there with him and help him set up a new life in the middle of the country. He urged my father to give Idaho a try instead of returning to war-torn Iran.

"If you move your family to Idaho, you will not have to worry about Christians there," he said. "It is a small rural area where there aren't many Christians. Naghmeh and Nima are so young. They will soon forget about this Jesus."

My father grew excited about the prospect, so, at the end of the next school year, in the summer of 1987, we loaded up our car and moved our lives to Idaho to escape the Christians in California and their Jesus.

8

LIFE IN IDAHO

Outside our home, I didn't see any other Iranians besides our family. But, inside our home, it was as if we had never left Iran—the aromas alone transported us right back to our house in Tehran. McDonald's and Burger King were just down the road, but their offerings were not on Maman's menu. Instead, a "fast-food" meal in our family consisted of cucumbers, tomatoes, and onions lightly covered with olive oil, lemon, and salt. You could not get this meal for takeout, however. You had to sit and eat it with everyone else.

Both breakfast and lunch were considered to be quick affairs. Lunch was usually little more than feta cheese and bread or perhaps an egg sandwich if you were really hungry.

Dinner was the real meal.

Unlike the Americans in Boise who often consumed their dinners between five and six o'clock in the evening, we didn't begin our dinner until nine or ten o'clock at the earliest. Although my mother was not fond of the American meal schedule or the wide selection of processed foods for sale, my father would often find flavors and concepts in the local cuisine that he enjoyed and then make them at home—passing them off as his own ideas.

From time to time, when our family prepared a salad, we would add lettuce to it, like the Americans did. Baba would mix mayonnaise, ketchup, salt, pepper, and lime as a dressing to put on top. It wasn't until later that we discovered this was basically his interpretation of Thousand Island salad dressing! He did the same with French toast—he just didn't call it that. He would take bread, dip it in egg, fry it, and then serve it with melted butter and fresh honey and tell us he had invented the recipe.

Idaho has a way of growing on you. Although there weren't very many foreigners there, unlike at the apartment complex in California, and we felt out of place in many settings, the people were all very friendly. Boise's small size made it more digestible for newcomers like me.

When my brother and I first attended middle school, I was intimidated. I was the only dark-haired girl in my class, and everyone automatically assumed I was Mexican. I did perceive some prejudice and racism toward me, but there were certain students who were curious about my dark complexion and my Middle Eastern background and wanted to get to know me better. Nima had a similar experience. In some ways, our distinctiveness made us exotic and special to them.

Some of my classmates were intrigued when I told them my family was from Iran. Not many of them knew where Iran was located, but they thought it sounded "cool." Before long, most of my fellow students grew to accept me, and I made a lot of friends, which helped me to learn English more quickly.

During our time in California, my little sister Nazanin had spoken English the best in our family. Although she was only four years old at that time, she was speaking English like an American after only two months and had become our de facto translator. But, in Boise, Nima and I soon became fluent.

There were many things I liked better about living in Idaho than in California. Boise didn't have the kind of graffiti and ghetto areas that we were used to seeing in and around San Jose. The people in our new neighborhood were welcoming and engaging instead of suspicious and combative, like the residents at our old apartment complex had been.

But there were two things Boise didn't have that I dearly missed: my friend Kimberly in California and my best friend Shokoofeh in Tehran. I attempted to stay in touch with both of them by frequently writing them letters, and we wrote back and forth; but, over time, our letters grew fewer and fewer.

Boise is as un-Iranian as any city can possibly be, but there was something about both the weather and the mountains surrounding the city that reminded Baba of Tehran and inspired him. "This is where you can work and actually get somewhere," he commented to my uncle shortly after we arrived. Baba was able to run his medical supplies company from the United States, and, in the years to come, he would travel often as he oversaw the company, which continued to be very successful. He made regular trips to Iran, where our family still owned an apartment and other property. Baba also started a business with my uncle in Idaho.

To Nima and me, he gave a similar message as he wagged his finger and lowered his head so we could see his face more clearly: "You two need to focus on going to school, getting good grades, and making something of yourself. There is no ceiling here. If you put your minds to it, you can make good money; you can become doctors, lawyers, professors, or engineers. It doesn't matter if you are a woman or a foreigner. Do you understand me?"

I didn't answer because no answer was needed. Baba was not looking for an indulgent reply or nod of the head; he was imparting his advice with the assumption that it would be blindly followed.

We did not discuss Christianity or what had happened in California. My parents hoped that Nima and I would soon forget about Jesus and instead set our minds on the American dream. Their goal was to get us through school in the best possible manner and into a good university.

For both Nima and me, American schools were easier than Iranian schools and, in some ways, more enjoyable. Because math and science are not as heavily reliant on language, we both excelled at those subjects. In fact, in the first year, Nima skyrocketed to the top of our class academically.

Shortly after we arrived in Boise, my grandmother moved to America to be near us, having applied for and received her visa. She found a house close to where we lived, and Baba would pick her up twice a week and bring her to our home. We would visit with her, playing cards and other games, until it was time for her to return to her house.

Within a couple of years, my whole family became American citizens. My parents raised their right hands and swore allegiance to the Constitution of the United States of America. That day was an especially happy one for Baba.

I felt more American and less Iranian with every passing year. I also felt more Christian. Even though my parents had instituted rules to keep Nima and me from becoming overly exposed to Christianity, they were never able to fully prevent our contact with Christians. They forbid my brother and me to secretly pray together. We were only allowed to go straight to school and then straight home again. They didn't want to risk any Christian friends inviting us over to their houses. We were not even allowed to have friends who were Christians, and we were not permitted to hang out with friends without our mother being with us. Once in a while, my parents would allow us to spend time with our Mormon friends from school. Yet, in spite of all the problems my Christian faith brought me, I never turned my back on Jesus. My life had been forever transformed when I was baptized in the pool as a young girl.

When people at school asked me about my religion, I said that I was a Christian. It felt foreign to say this at first because I was not sure about everything that went along with that title, but I grew more and more accustomed to it.

I didn't realize it then, but each time I told someone that I was a Christian, I was solidifying my relationship with Jesus Christ. Following Jesus was a personal choice I had made apart from my relationship with my family. I really started to understand that my faith was a personal journey, not one that could be dictated to me by friends, family members, or national leaders. I, as an individual, had made a choice that was outside the control of my parents, outside the control of our mosque in Tehran, and outside the control of Iran. My mother and father were Muslims, I came from a Muslim nation, and I was born and raised a Muslim, but that didn't dictate who I was now. I had made a personal decision to follow Jesus Christ, and I now belonged to Him.

> But now, this is what the LORD says, He who is your Creator, Jacob,
> And He who formed you, Israel:
> "Do not fear, for I have redeemed you;
> I have called you by name; you are Mine!"[2]

---

2. Isaiah 43:1.

9

"SHOW THEM WHO YOU ARE"

During my early years in Iran, except for those brief months on the coast of the Caspian Sea, I had not been able to have a real childhood as my family and I sheltered from bombing raids, and as Nima and I faced the hazards of war even when walking to and from school. But now that my family had been safely living in America for several years, and I was entering my teens, I had the opportunity, for the most part, to live the typical teenage life that most of my schoolmates experienced.

However, the transition to living in America had been difficult for my mother. She had once been a respected officer in the Iranian military, in charge of large units and conducting operations in the interest of national security. Now, in rural America, she was a housewife on what seemed the frontier to nowhere, and she couldn't even leave the house without being accompanied by someone who could help interpret the language and customs for her. She wasn't confident speaking a new language and was embarrassed anytime she needed to express herself in English.

When Baba was traveling, Maman was on her own, feeling purposeless. In her mind, she was completely helpless. She also felt that our family was losing its culture and traditions, becoming rootless in America, and she mourned our former way of life.

For three years, she became extremely depressed. Her illness shook my world, and, once more, I was left without a sense of security and stability in my life. And my nightmares about losing my mother, which had begun years earlier in Tehran, were still plaguing me.

Most days, after school, I would come home to a dark and depressing house, with every curtain drawn. My mother had not only completely closed the curtains, but she had even blocked, with thick, dark cloth, every crack around the curtains that might allow any sunlight into the house. It was not uncommon for me to come home and find Maman curled in a fetal position in the corner of a room, crying. I didn't know what to do, what was really wrong, or how to help.

Whenever I saw my mother in this state, I would secretly pray for her. Again, I found myself praying the same prayer that I had heard the invisible man pray on the radio: "God, I want my mother to know who You are. Please show her who You are."

It was at school that I found comfort and hope. When I entered high school, I learned about a group called the Fellowship of Christian Athletes that met during the lunch break on certain days of the week. Nima became a part of this fellowship, and even though I was not an athlete, like he was, I was allowed to join the group. This gave my brother and me an opportunity to study the Bible, talk about our faith, and pray together without my parents being aware of what we were doing; they couldn't object to something they didn't know about. I grew to understand so much about the Bible during that time.

On numerous occasions, I found myself repeating the same prayer I had prayed years before as a little girl when I first read the Bible after my baptism: "God, You say in Your Word that I am Your daughter now, that I belong to You. I ask that You would give me the nations as my inheritance, as You promise in Psalm 2. I don't desire money or fame but to see nations hear the gospel. God, I want my family to know who You are. I want my nation to know who You are. Please show them who You are."

When I was thirteen, my mother was hospitalized for clinical depression. Although she received treatment, depression and anxiety continued to be part of her life. My uncle with whom we had moved to Idaho had kept his own Christian faith a secret until my mother's illness, but he began to share with her about Jesus and tell her he knew someone who could pray with her. "I know that you have tried everything, but I have an idea," he said. "There is place here in Boise called Calvary Chapel where I would like to take you."

My mother smiled at the idea but held out very little hope that her life could change. She was almost at the end of her rope but agreed to go to Calvary Chapel. One of the leaders there, named Pastor Bob, prayed for her, and, from that day, she began to feel better. She wondered if the Jesus we had believed in might be real, and, as I would later learn, she began secretly reading the Bible she had confiscated from Nima and me years earlier. She had never thrown it away because even though Muslims do not believe in the Bible, they still regard it as a holy book that should be treated with respect.

The clinics had not been able to help Maman out of her depression, so now she was giving Jesus a try. As she continued to battle depression, she found herself turning to the hope through Jesus described in the Bible; through His healing power, her depression left, and she got better. Nima and I were not aware until later that when my father saw this change and asked her about it, he began to seek faith in Jesus too.

As Christmas season approached, life felt more and more festive. The weather grew colder, and the celebration of Jesus's birth made everything seem more jubilant. I was participating in a Christmas concert at school, and I knew that I would be singing songs about the birth of Jesus, so I invited my parents to come. I was excited when they agreed. It felt like there were more open doors with them than ever before. They were no longer militantly against the idea of Jesus, which was huge progress for our family.

Things really changed during the year I turned seventeen, when our family had a reunion in California. The uncle who had baptized me had reestablished a connection with my parents, and, slowly, they were starting to communicate again. This uncle hosted a special family gathering in Lake Tahoe.

As soon as we arrived for the reunion, my uncle began asking Nima and me about our faith. He was curious to see if we still considered ourselves Christians. It had been the better part of a decade since he had baptized us. He seemed very impressed that we had been able to weather the storm of our parents' objection to our newfound faith and maintain our belief. And he was astonished to hear that not only had we hung on to our faith, but we had also found ways to secretly grow in Christ by attending Bible studies and joining fellowships at school.

My uncle had openly asked Nima and me about our faith in front of our parents, and I noticed that they did not seem concerned or threatened by this. I half expected them to react with anger toward his questions and our answers, but they didn't. They were listening closely and nodding their heads. I thought that Baba would be shocked to hear that I had been attending fellowships without his knowledge, but it turns out that he was the one about to deliver a shock: he explained that he and my mother had been secretly reading the Bible they had taken from me when I was a little girl, and now they wanted to become Christians and give their lives to follow Jesus!

Everyone was stunned. Although I had never seen this coming, I felt it was a direct answer to the simple prayer I had learned from the invisible man on the radio: "Please show them who You are."

We also had another joyful surprise: when my sister, Nazanin, heard my parents tell my uncle that they believed in Jesus, she acknowledged that she, too, had also been a believer in Jesus for years but had been afraid to say anything about it because she had seen what had happened to my brother and me when we confessed our faith in Jesus.

I felt a stirring in my spirit, and I told my uncle that I wanted to be baptized again. Although I believe my first baptism was sufficient, I really wanted to be rebaptized to make a public declaration of the inward transformation that had taken place within me. My uncle agreed, and Nima, Nazanin, and I were all baptized. My parents were baptized at a later time when they fully understood what it meant to make a commitment to Jesus Christ.

I felt great peace as I was raised from the water.

Our whole family was now following Christ.

10

DISCOVERING MY CALLING

The year I turned eighteen, I didn't have a clear direction about which university to attend, so I let my brother do the research, and I followed him to the University of Puget Sound in Washington State. Nima studied physics and mathematics and eventually earned his doctorate in quantum physics at the University of Chicago.

I decided to study microbiology, a subject that I thought would be helpful for getting into medical school. I was not aware that the University of Puget Sound was one of the most politically and religiously liberal universities in the US until I arrived on campus, but, during my time there, I learned much more about my own faith and steadily grew as a Christian.

I loved the university's reddish-brown English Tudor Gothic brick buildings, which contrasted with the vibrant emerald-green quads. In many ways, the campus had an atmosphere that I imagined felt similar to what it would be like to attend a New England Ivy League school.

Not long after I arrived on campus, I met other Christians and joined a group called InterVarsity Christian Fellowship. The student body at Puget Sound was quite small, and Christian students comprised only a fraction of that number, so it was easy to get to know everyone. I started going to church on campus on a regular basis, hosted Bible studies in my dorm, attended prayer meetings every Friday night, and established a deep connection with my Christian friends. My time at the university is when I really got an opportunity to be an independent believer in Christ and see Him move in my life.

In my sophomore year, I co-led a Bible study for "seekers," or those who wanted to learn more about Christianity and Jesus. Because I still felt like a new Christian myself, I felt a strong desire to engage unbelievers in the Bible and discussions about faith. Our campus fellowship had traditionally focused on Christian students and had never really held a Bible study for seekers. For Bible-believing Christians on a campus like Puget Sound, where the classrooms could quickly turn into verbal battlegrounds over the existence of God and Christian beliefs, it felt like a victory just to survive the criticism and hostility of some of the teachers and other students. However, I had a desire to connect with people who were seeking God, even if they didn't realize it.

Thankfully, the leadership of our fellowship group agreed with my plan and helped me to launch a Bible study for people were not yet Christians but were curious about God and open to learn more about Him. With my Muslim background, I was excited to share with others about my Christian faith and give my testimony of what God had done in my life.

My Iranian background was a huge asset at the university, just as it had been when I first started school in Idaho. There weren't a lot of minorities on campus, so people thought I was interesting, and foreign students found me approachable. This provided me with many open doors to share the gospel. It wasn't long before we had atheists among those attending our Bible study.

By my senior year, I felt that God was moving me on a clear path toward medical school, and I had a desire to be a doctor on the mission field. I was inspired by Noble Peace Prize-winner Dr. Albert Schweitzer, who transformed nations for God's kingdom through his work in medical missions. I envisioned myself in Africa, helping the sick, serving the poor, and preaching the gospel message.

Before graduation, our Christian fellowship group held a retreat in the mountain forests of western Washington. The annual trip, featuring cabin life with other believers my age, was something I always looked forward to. This year, the fellowship had invited a special guest speaker to share with and inspire our small group of believers.

"I know that everyone has plans for how they would like to spend this weekend," the speaker started off, "but I want to do something a little different this year. I know that you have plans for what you are going to do after university. Some of you are going into your careers, and a few of you plan to go straight into grad school. Some of you plan to be loafers and will move back in with your mom and dad!"

We all laughed and nodded our heads at this accurate statement, knowing that almost all of us would move back in with our parents if we could.

"But, during this time, I want to ask you to fast. I want you to fast from food, from talking, and from each other. I want you to cast away all of your future plans and go into the forest, find a secluded space, and just get away from everyone else. This forest is big enough for you to find a place to get alone, and when you are by yourself, ask God what *His* plans are for your life. Do not say what you want God's plans to be; be silent and listen to what He really wants for your life."

The speaker dismissed us and sent us into the forest. I wandered in a direction away from everyone else and found a little spot where I could be alone.

At first, I just sat and listened to the sounds of the forest. One might think that the forest is quiet when there is no one around to disturb it, but I found it to be a noisy place to a silent audience. An orchestra of leaves clapped against each other, water in a nearby stream perpetually slapped against banks and echoing rocks, and large tree branches cracked and popped under the strain of unexpected gusts. There was so much noise in the forest that it seemed as if the birds were forced to sing more loudly just to have their melody heard by other birds, adding even more decibel levels to the forest's symphony.

After a few moments of sitting in silence in the clamorous forest, I began to pray something like this: "I am here, Lord. I want to hear from You. Show me what You want me to do with my life. You know that I want to serve You. I have plans to be a doctor. I want to be a missionary doctor for Your kingdom in the way that Dr. Albert Schweitzer was. I know that this is what You have for my life, so I follow after You."

I was certain that God wanted me to be a doctor because Baba wanted me to be a doctor. In my mind, if I made my earthly father happy, then I was making my heavenly Father happy.

As I prayed, I saw something piercing through the forest. I was surprised to see that it seemed to be an image of a multitude of women gathered together. When I looked more closely, I could see that the women had their heads covered; it looked like they were wearing the hijab that many Muslim women wear. The women were all facing a stage, listening intently. As the vision came into even clearer focus, I could see that I was there as well. Although I was on the stage, I wasn't preaching like an evangelist or a charismatic pastor would; instead, as I stood in front of everyone, I looked broken and unable to speak. I was straining to say something, but my grief was so thick that I couldn't force the words to come out. As I struggled to speak through my pain, these Muslim women—an ocean of them—were kneeling and accepting Christ.

I shook my head and tried to move away from this vision, but I could still see it. I had never had a vision before—it was like watching a movie screen.

I looked around at all the Muslim women who were kneeling and praying, and I was confused. Why were all these women coming to Christ from my broken message of pain? Where was this happening, and why was I there? I didn't have a dream to preach to Muslim women. My family had *fled* the Muslim world to find freedom in America. I didn't ever want to go back!

"God, I know that You have called me to the mission field. I am ready to be a doctor and go to the furthest reaches of Africa to minister to the poor, but my chapter with Islam is over," I prayed.

Suddenly, God revealed to me my own heart. Deep inside, I was willing to serve God in any place in the world as long as it was not where I didn't want to be. I argued that I didn't need to be in the Middle East to serve God. During my college years, I had tutored low-income children, and I had a heart and a passion for the poor. Wasn't that good enough? I could go to Asia or Africa. I could go to the poorest areas of America or South America—but I did *not* want to return to the Middle East.

It was not long before I realized that the one thing I didn't want to give to God was the one thing He was asking of me. My red line, the one I would not cross, was going back to the Middle East. It turned out that my red line was God's starting point.

The vision disappeared, but its impact remained. I stood with bated breath, both unwilling and unable to move. The vision was speaking to me in a clear way, and I interpreted it in the only way it could be interpreted: God was telling me to return to Iran.

After the retreat, I went back to my dorm room and continued to debate the vision. Had I truly seen it? Was it real? What did it mean? With all these questions running through my head, I was unable to sleep. "No, this can't be right," I rationalized to myself. "My parents risked everything to bring our family to America. They wanted to keep us safe from the violence in Iran. I would be throwing away everything they sacrificed if I went back to Iran."

I found a thousand excuses for why I shouldn't go back. I argued with God and listed all of the reasons why it didn't make sense and why it would be better for me to go anywhere else. I laid out the argument of travel bans for

American citizens, how it wasn't fair considering what my parents had sacrificed, and how ineffective I would be as a woman in a male-dominated society like Iran. If I were to go back there, I would be doing so as a Christian. I would be an apostate of Islam, and Christian converts in Iran were being killed on a regular basis.

I left my dorm room to go to the store. I would regularly lend my car to other students in my dorm, and someone had just brought the vehicle back. I was grateful it was available. As soon as I turned the ignition switch to the on position, a Christian song came on the radio. That had never before happened after someone had borrowed my car, because so many people from my dorm who used it were not Christian. They often left the radio on a local secular station. But, this time, Christian music was playing, with a song I had never heard before and have never heard since. The lyrics were about needing to go and share God's light to a world lost in darkness.

The song took me completely by surprise, and I broke down, giving myself fully to God to do His will. "Okay, God!" I cried. "I give up. I surrender to You." I heard myself quoting the words of the prophet Isaiah: "Lord, 'here am I, send me!'"[3]

In that moment, I had a glimmer of hope. I had one more request of God before I would believe that He wanted to send me to Iran. I made a deal in the same way that Gideon from the Bible did when he asked God to show that He was with him—I used a "fleece":

> *Then Gideon said to God, "If You are going to save Israel through me, as You have spoken, behold, I am putting a fleece of wool on the threshing floor. If there is dew on the fleece only, and it is dry on all the ground, then I will know that You will save Israel through me, as You have spoken." And it was so. When he got up early the next morning and wrung out the fleece, he wrung the dew from the fleece, a bowl full of water. Then Gideon said to God, "Do not let Your anger burn against me, so that I may speak only one more time; please let me put You to the test only one more time with the fleece: let it now be dry only on the fleece, and let there be dew on all the ground." And God did so that night; for it was dry only on the fleece, and dew was on all the ground.[4]*

---

3. Isaiah 6:8.
4. Judges 6:36–40.

With my own fleece in mind, I prayed, "If it is Your will for me to go to Iran, God, I need to know that my parents are okay with it. If my parents do not agree for me to return to Iran, then I will know that this is not Your will."

My request was very simple. I knew that God had better things to do than to reassure unwilling servants like me, but in the footsteps of Gideon, I laid out my fleece.

Still sitting in my car, I regained my composure, then made my way back to my dorm room. As soon as I walked through the door to my room, I heard the phone ring. It was Baba. He eagerly asked me what my plans were for after graduation.

"I plan to take a year off to study for the exam to get into medical school," I replied, most likely sounding a bit confused. It was not common for my father to sound so urgent, and I was curious to know what the phone call was all about.

"Naghmeh," he said in an excited voice, "I was just talking to your mother, and our company has had an opportunity come up for you to go to Iran and help with some of the business there."

I almost dropped the phone as the realization hit me: I was going to Iran.

11

BACK TO IRAN

In the summer of 1999, right after my graduation, my father and I were planning a trip together to Iran. My father's medical supply company was growing rapidly, with offices in the US, the Middle East, and Europe, and he needed an international representative. He had several candidates in Tehran who could possibly fill the role, but they would need to be trained by someone who understood the mindset of the international client, and Baba thought that I might be the perfect person to do that training. This would also allow me to enter Iran as a businessperson without raising the suspicions of the Iranian government.

The plan was for us to fly from Boise to Chicago, and then to Germany, where we would take a train to France. There, we would meet with a French company that sold medical equipment and reach a deal to be their distributor for Iran. I would watch how my father conducted his presentation and learn from him how to engage potential clients in the future. It would be a crash course in international relations.

The flight to Chicago went smoothly, but just as we were about to board our plane for Germany, Baba was stopped at the gate. "Sorry, sir, you cannot board this flight," the flight attendant said to him. "Your passport has expired. Do you have one that is not expired?"

We were both traveling with two passports—one American and the other Iranian. Baba's Iranian passport was not valid for traveling to Europe, and his American passport was apparently no longer active.

With my eyes, I begged my father to say he had another passport that was not expired.

"No, sorry, this is my only one," he sadly admitted.

"Sorry, sir," the attendant said again, "we cannot allow you on this flight."

"What do we do?" I asked.

"You go on the flight. No problem. I will fix this and be right behind you," he said, as if everything was completely fine.

"Baba, I can't go without you," I protested.

"No, really, it is fine. I will get an emergency passport and be on the next flight to Germany. I'll meet you there," he said optimistically. Baba was always the optimist. He always believed things would work out.

I was terrified. I had never traveled internationally on my own before, and I didn't know anyone in Germany; but, by the time I arrived, Baba had worked everything out for me. He had arranged for one of his relatives to pick me up and take me to the train station. At the station, another family member would put me on the correct train. Our family had its own Iranian diaspora network, with relatives all over the world.

The same is true for many Iranians today. In 1979, when the Ayatollah took over Iran, many people had to flee, and they spread out to the four corners of the world. With the continued persecution of Christians and political opponents in Iran, the diaspora continues. Most Iranian families do not end up in one country. Instead, they end up dispersed throughout America, Canada, Turkey, and various European nations.

I cried during the entire trip. I wept on the flight to Germany, and I wept on the train to France. Although I had relatives to point me in the right direction when I needed to make connections, I was frightened to be traveling alone. I didn't know what I was doing, and I didn't know what I would do when I arrived in France. This was supposed to be my time to observe how my father engaged his customers, and now I would have to face them alone.

When I arrived in France, I was picked up by my business hosts and driven to the headquarters of their large multinational company. They escorted me to a boardroom full of executives who expected to hear me give a thorough presentation of our company. I was also expected by my father to negotiate a deal, design a future plan, and sign an agreement.

I was trembling as I walked into that boardroom. I looked around at the faces of all the executives and realized that they assumed I would take charge of the meeting and start the presentation. The president of the company and the director of the marketing team had their notepads out, ready to take notes.

I made a very simple presentation based on the information that Baba had given me, and the longer I spoke, the more comfortable I felt. Before the meeting was over, I felt as if I were friends with everyone in the room.

The company signed the agreement, and I felt a huge sense of accomplishment and worth. I had just made my very first international corporate deal.

I called Baba to give him the good news. He was very proud and excited, but he also told me regretfully that his passport renewal was taking longer than expected, so I had to stay in Europe for a little bit longer than originally planned.

During my short time there, I connected with a Dutch company in Holland and secured another contract. It felt like the longer I was in Europe, the more deals I was able to make.

A few days later, Baba arrived in Germany, and we flew together to Iran. As soon as we touched down, I felt a bustle in the air. Although the immigration officers weren't heeding the call to prayer, the airport was full of reminders that Islam was ever present.

The green, white, and red flag of Iran had meant little to me when I had fled with my parents as a young child, but seeing it again brought back feelings of dark nostalgia. The green band at the top symbolizes Islam, and the red band at the bottom represents martyrdom. On the white band in the middle is the national emblem in red, which includes the word *Allah*. Along the inner edges of the green and red bands is written, "*Allah hu Akbar*" or "God is Great!"

Though the flag rustled up old memories, my home city of Tehran was no longer the war zone I had known as a child. Instead, it had seemingly changed into a modern, progressive, and inclusive city. But hiding in plain sight was the dark side of Iran that had compelled my parents to flee. Hovering over the urban center was an inescapable heavy cloud of oppression and hopelessness that seemed to seep into your lungs like the smog that used to cover the city. The faces of the Islamic Revolution—Supreme Leaders Ruhollah Khomeini (who passed away in 1989) and his successor, Sayyid Ali Khamenei—were ever present, displayed on colossal, centrally placed posters.

However, the faces I was eager to see were the familiar faces of my family members who had never left Iran. They were used to seeing Baba because he often visited Tehran during his numerous business trips, but this was the first time I had seen many of my relatives since I was a young girl. I had gone back to Iran to visit a couple of times, first with my parents when I was seventeen and again with my father right after college, but I hadn't had an opportunity to visit with all of my family members. During the first visit, Naneh had been there, waiting for me with a big hug. Seeing her was like seeing my own mother again after a long absence, and it was a joyous reunion. Unfortunately, soon after that visit, she had a heart attack and passed away. Now, being back with my extended family in Iran, my memories of Naneh from that earlier visit prompted a deep sadness and loneliness within me at her absence. At times, I would imagine her coming down the hallway or calling my name, but I had to wake up to the harsh reality that Naneh—the woman who had raised me during the first nine years of my life—was gone.

The family celebrations over our arrival awakened something within me that surprised me—a longing for some familiar foods that I hadn't even known I had missed until I tasted them again. The Iranian pomegranates that we couldn't get in the United States were so deliciously plump and sour. The ice cream with saffron and pistachio was a tasty combination that is distinctively Iranian. And *faloodeh*—oh! Faloodeh is a dish of frozen white noodles made with sugary syrup and rose water, served with lemon and crushed pistachios on top.

My family fed me well, and I gave everyone gifts from America that I had brought with me, including American chocolate bars. For my cousins, in particular, I brought CDs of the Christian group DC Talk. My cousins were all Muslim, so it was fun watching them walking around the house singing the song "Jesus Freak." They didn't know what the words meant; they were just ecstatic to have American music to listen to.

After I was settled in at my uncle's house, where I would be staying, Baba left, and I was alone with my Iranian family. I began to purposefully share the gospel with each of my family members, but my Farsi language skills were not very good. Those skills had basically stopped developing the day I left for America. I couldn't pronounce certain syllables correctly, and many of my relatives told me I sounded like a foreigner. They weren't wrong—I was a foreigner. Although I had been born in Tehran and lived there for the first few years of my life, Tehran was no longer a part of me, and I was no longer a part of it.

I received similar reactions when I went to the grocery store or tried to catch a cab. Everyone seemed to comment on my accent. Some people lost patience with me because of my inability to speak the language well. And, due to my darker skin, most Iranians considered me a member of a minority group, likely from India, and were angry that I had not taken the time to learn Farsi.

After only a week in Iran and my desperate attempts to share the gospel, I realized how weak my Christian vocabulary was. I read the Bible in English, not in Farsi, and that made it extremely difficult for me to share about Christ with family and friends. I learned the hard way how important language is on the mission field.

When I shared the gospel with my relatives, they responded with aggressive hostility, and they even kicked me out of their house. So, not only did they not become Christians, but they now also hated me and wanted nothing to do with me.

Although it was difficult for me to share the gospel in Iran, I learned that a number of Iranian Muslims were coming to Christ. This was just the beginning of the revival that was to come. In the 1980s and 90s, Christian leaders in Iran were hunted down and executed in some of the most brutal ways, and their blood was watering the seeds of the church. This persecution was a major factor that led believers to eventually take the church underground.

In the 1980s, well-known pastor Mehdi Dibaj was arrested for preaching the gospel and imprisoned for nine years. When the international community called for his release, the government freed him in January 1994. Yet, less than six months later, his body was found in a park; he had been tortured and killed. I wept as I read Dibaj's testimony from when he had stood before the Ayatollahs defending his faith. Among his many moving words, he declared,

> I have been charged with "Apostasy."…
>
> They say, "You were a Muslim and you have become a Christian." No, for many years I had no religion. After searching and studying I accepted God's call…. People choose their religion but a Christian is chosen by Christ…. "You have not chosen me but I have chosen you."[5]

Pastor Haik Hovsepian Mehr, who had denounced the persecution of Mehdi Dibaj, was also murdered. This persecution, instead of silencing the church in Iran, emboldened many Christians. And with every Christian martyr, the church in Iran grew. For every new believer who was arrested and thrown into prison, a new convert took their place.

---

5. Dibaj Mehdi, "The Testimony and Defence of Mehdi Dibaj," Banner of Truth, January 5, 2015, https://banneroftruth.org/us/resources/articles/2015/testimony-defence-mehdi-dibaj/. See John 15:16.

One church in the center of Tehran that played a key part in the explosive growth that was taking place was Central Assemblies of God. Only able to hold about seven hundred people, it was the largest Protestant church in Iran. The church was located near Tehran University, which made it ideal for reaching young people.

I attempted to attend one of the church's weekly services, but I was stopped by a guard. The guard was screening newcomers to adhere to governmental regulations against proselytizing and to prevent spies from entering the church. Since they didn't know me, I wasn't allowed in.

My inability to speak the language correctly, my failed attempts to preach the gospel message to my own family, and, finally, this rejection at the entrance to the church were enough to convince me that I didn't belong in Iran.

I thought I was a complete failure, and I felt lonely, isolated, and miserable. I questioned whether I had really heard from God.

"Okay, I am done with Iran," I said to myself. "I tried to do what God called me to do, but it clearly didn't work out."

After only six months, I bought a plane ticket and flew back to the United States.

12

GOD'S PERSISTENT CALL

When I returned to America, I threw myself into ministry work. I connected with Calvary Chapel in Boise, and the senior pastor, Pastor Bob, who had prayed for my mother when she suffered from depression, got me a job as the church receptionist. I absolutely loved it! After my experience in Iran, it was like a refreshing drink of water.

The people in Iran hadn't liked me, but I felt loved by the people at Calvary Chapel. My Farsi had not been adequate for sharing the gospel in Iran, but my English was perfect for answering the phone at the church in Boise. In Iran, I couldn't seem to connect with anyone, but at Calvary, I was connecting people to each other. I went from having no friends in Iran to having so many friends at church that I couldn't find time for them all.

Although being at Calvary Chapel was therapeutic after my loneliness and isolation in Iran, my longing to be involved in missions work resurfaced, and I became restless. After Pastor Bob preached one Sunday, my father and I went to talk to him about my interest in missions.

"Well, we have missions work in India," he began, apparently struggling to think of any other missions work that the church was involved with.

"Just India?" I accidentally said out loud, thinking that it sounded strange for a church so large to only have an outreach to India.

Pastor Bob seemed taken aback by my response. "Well, we have several projects there that are having a massive impact. We really try to focus on doing intentional missions," he said, seeing that I was trying to figure out their missions strategy. Then, he added, "You should join us, Naghmeh!" and invited me to accompany him and his wife on the next missions trip to India.

I happily agreed, and, a few short months later, I was with Pastor Bob's wife in a location just south of Mumbai. At first glance, missions work in India appeared to be as far from missions work in Iran as I could get. But, after only a few hours in that booming metropolitan region, I realized that I was closer to Iran than I thought.

Mumbai is one of the most populated cities in the world, and it is full of tens of thousands of idols dedicated to the Hindu gods; these idols may be found in its temples and tourist attractions, and even in the little trinkets sold in the small shops on every corner of the city. There is something for every religion, but among all those statues and makeshift altars was one element that brought me back to Iran: Zoroastrianism. Charshanba Suri, the fire-jumping ceremony that my family would participate in each year in the backyard of our home in Tehran for the Iranian New Year celebration, is a practice that dates back to Zoroastrianism, Iran's ancient monotheistic religion.

Zoroastrian priests had to flee after Iran was conquered by Islam, and the majority of them found shelter among the Hindus in India. Today, more than half of all practicing Persian Zoroastrians live in the city of Mumbai. Many Zoroastrians believe that their founding prophet, Zoroaster, did not initially come to Iran to start a new religion but instead to bring people back to the faith of their ancient fathers.

Cyrus the Great, the founder of the Persian Empire, is mentioned in the Bible more than thirty times, and his life was prophesied by Isaiah more than a hundred and fifty years before he was born. He was called by God and was used to set the Jewish people free from their Babylonian exile and help rebuild the temple in Jerusalem.[6]

With God ordaining the steps of the first kings of Persia—Cyrus, Darius, and Xerxes—it may not be a mere coincidence that Zoroastrianism contains many elements that are similar to the beliefs of Judaism and Christianity, such as the concepts of heaven, a judgment day, a virgin birth, a resurrection, and eternal damnation in hell for the souls of the wicked. Although I had traveled to many countries across the world, I had now somehow ended up in the one city that reminded me the most of Iran.

Yet, amid the seemingly endless number of Hindu idols in Mumbai, it wasn't a Zoroastrian idol that captured my attention. It was a different idol, one that I had unknowingly allowed to supersede God in my life—it was the idol of comfort.

---

6. See Isaiah 45:1; 2 Chronicles 36:22–23.

I had been chasing security, ease, and acceptance by others instead of wholeheartedly pursuing Christ. I had been bowing at the altar of comfort instead of at the feet of God. I hadn't fled Iran to save my children from death, as my parents had done. I had fled Iran because living there had been difficult, and I hadn't felt comfortable in the culture, which had become foreign to me. I realized that I had been burning incense as an offering to my idol of comfort ever since I had left Iran.

"I am called to Iran," I said to myself. "I must go back. No matter what it costs me, I must go back."

When I returned to the United States, I immediately bought airline tickets for Iran, and I was scheduled to depart in early October 2001. As if I needed another reason not to go, the September 11 terrorist attacks by al-Qaeda took place at the World Trade Center buildings in New York City and the Pentagon in Washington, DC, as well as the thwarted attempt against another target by a fourth terrorist-hijacked plane that crashed in a Pennsylvania field.

Consequently, Osama Bin Laden, al-Qaeda's leader, became enemy number one in America, and President Bush called for action against al-Qaeda in Afghanistan, while at the same time declaring the countries of Iran, Iraq, and North Korea an "Axis of Evil."

When my parents saw the news, my father canceled his trips to the Middle East. He asked me to do the same because it was clear there was a war brewing. To put him and my mother at ease, I changed my flight from October to November. Yet, when I saw President Bush in tears on television, saying that the United States would be sending troops to the Middle East, I became emotional, too, and sensed myself going to Iran as a soldier. The major difference between the soldiers that President Bush was sending and myself was that I was not going to engage in a war to take lives—I was going to battle to save lives. My battle was not with *"flesh and blood, but against the rulers, against the powers, against the world forces of this darkness, against the spiritual forces of wickedness in the heavenly places."*[7]

I was a scrawny, weak girl—but isn't that the description of what God uses? I had no idea that I was about to become part of the fastest- and largest-growing house church movement in Iran.

---

7. Ephesians 6:12.

When the time came for me to fly to Iran, I was both excited and anxious. Uncertainty about the future of the Middle East was at its highest level in decades. The drums of war were beating more loudly every day. Europe, America, and the Islamic nations were all saber-rattling and making threats back and forth. The entire world was on edge; it was like a powder keg ready to explode with the slightest spark.

On my flight, the plane was practically empty. After September 11, not only had many people in the United States cancelled their scheduled flights to various destinations, afraid to travel by airplane, but it was unthinkable to most people to consider flying to the Middle East at that time. Yet, here I was—traveling in the midst of an explosive political situation between the United States and the Arab world, still afraid of airplanes because they reminded me of the Iran-Iraqi war and bombs being dropped on my family, and journeying by myself—embarking on a flight to Tehran.

Even before I arrived in Iran, I faced my first major battle. I stared at the immigration form that was handed to me by the flight attendant. I had never seen it before. When I had flown to Iran previously, Baba had filled it out for me. I began to fill in the blanks with all my personal information, and it felt very routine until I came to a section that I hadn't expected.

"What is your religion?" the question asked.

The pale, bubbled section of the immigration form stared back at me, demanding an answer. I skipped it and filled out all the other questions, half-hoping that this question would have disappeared or the answer would have become more apparent to me by the time I came back to it.

It was a very simple question, but my answer could determine whether I lived or died. I was using an Iranian passport. It would not have been possible for me to gain entry into Iran with my American passport unless I had been on a special tour. One glance at my name, and the immigration officers would know that I had been born a Muslim and was a descendant of Muhammad. I could not therefore be a Christian in their eyes without having committed the crime of apostasy. Writing "Christian" on the form meant that I was telling them I was a convert from Islam at a time when the Iranian government was murdering Christians.

Debating within myself, I thought about an incident that had recently happened to my parents. In the year 2000, only a year after they had both become Christians, Baba and Maman had traveled to Iran with a suitcase full of Bibles to distribute. Baba was a known businessman in Iran, and no one ever checked his suitcases, so they thought they would be safe. However, one of our Muslim family members learned Baba's flight information; this individual knew that my father was carrying Bibles, and they tipped off the authorities. When their flight landed in Iran, my parents were detained and separated.

All of their bags were opened and emptied. Every item was shuffled through and tossed about. The officers knew they were looking for Bibles, but none of the bags seemed to have any in them. Baba clearly remembered packing one of his bags full of Bibles, but the Bibles were simply not there. He assumed that he must have accidentally forgotten that particular bag at home, which would have been a miracle in itself, because this was the only time he had ever been searched.

After an hour, airport security finally allowed my parents to leave. When they arrived at their home in Tehran, they called and asked me to look through their house in Boise for the suitcase that Baba had put all the Bibles in. He could not remember where he had left it.

I went and checked in every room of their house but couldn't find a suitcase of any kind. I called them back and told them I was not able to locate it.

While I was still talking with them on the phone, I heard my mother shriek. As Baba had started to unpack the luggage, he had found the Bibles! One suitcase was just as he had remembered it looking—much of the bag was filled with Bibles. Not only had God blinded the eyes of the customs officials as they were checking my parents' belongings, but He had also blinded the eyes of my parents.

"How did you not see them?" I asked.

"Maybe we didn't see them because God didn't want us to be afraid," my mother replied.

Now, as I sat on the airplane headed for Iran, although I knew that my parents had been supernaturally shielded by God, I still could not bring myself to write "Christian" as the answer to the question on the immigration form. I recognized that God could perform miracles to protect me if I believed in Him, but if He did not spare me, I did not have an overwhelming desire to be a martyr on my first day back. I felt alone and scared, trying to make this decision by myself.

"Ahhh…it's not a big deal," I justified to myself, and I quickly scribbled in "Muslim."

I thought that I would forget my internal conflict over the immigration form question by the time I passed through customs, but I didn't. I was able to make it through without the immigration officers asking any questions—but I did so with the realization that I had just denied Jesus Christ.

Writing down the truth on that form had been such a simple task, but I had failed at it. Once again, when given the choice between Jesus and the idol of comfort, I had chosen comfort. I had chosen safety.

After I made it through customs, the entire weight of what I had done fell heavy on my chest. I cried out to God for forgiveness. "Lord, please forgive me. I will not deny Your name again. Please give me another opportunity."

13

MEETING SAEED

I snapped back into working at the medical company as if I had never left. The staff didn't have a lot of experience with foreign accounts and still lacked proficiency in English. I had my work cut out for me. I created a department of international relations with about five employees and trained them how to connect with foreign clients and partners, negotiate international contracts, and maintain relationships.

I also had a team of female associates with whom I built strong relationships, and we went to international business fairs in Dubai together. I took them shopping and taught them simple things, such as how to find the best business attire for boardroom meetings. Knowing what to wear in such settings was a problem for women from Islamic backgrounds because men usually set the rules for what women were and were not allowed to wear.

One employee named Mona, with her petite frame, was not used to looking at clothes in a size that would actually fit her. She had spent her entire life wearing block-shaped garments that might be draped over a person or a kitchen table alike. Another staff member, Bahar, was excited to shop with Mona, but she became more anxious when we looked at clothes for her. When she pulled her hair back, it exposed her plump face, which was greyish white from rarely having been exposed to the sun.

Neither Bahar nor Mona chose to wear a covering over their head in Dubai, confirming my suspicions that the majority of women in Iran do not wear the hijab out of conviction but rather out of force.

Once they looked the part of businesspeople and bounced with the confidence of women who feel pretty, I showed them the proper way to hand out their business cards, how to introduce themselves, and how to communicate with multiple people at the same time without making anyone feel left out.

For women, it is often a struggle working in the business world, especially in the Middle East, and this struggle goes beyond knowing the proper business attire. These women on my staff had to learn to be firm and strong negotiators in the face of great pressure.

The staff knew that I was a Christian and that I read my Persian Bible every morning. I was growing more confident in my Farsi language skills by the day. One morning, an employee named Mahsa joined me, and she began faithfully studying the Bible with me every week. My Bible study gatherings grew bit by bit until, after I had been in Iran for a year, there were five in the group!

One day, one of my cousins asked me, "Why don't you come and join us at the church downtown?" This was the Assemblies of God church in central Tehran that had already turned me away once. My cousin was a new believer who had come to Christ when my parents gave her one of the Bibles they had smuggled into the country. She often attended my Bible studies.

"I would love to join you, but that church has been watched very closely by the government lately, and I don't know if I want to highlight myself," I answered. I wanted to have longevity to minister in Iran, and I had no desire to be put on a government watch list by attending the fellowship there. However, she was not deterred by my explanation.

"But you are going back to the US for medical school, and it is highly likely that you will never return to Iran, so the risk is minimal," she urged. "Even if the government learns who you are, what good would it benefit them if you are no longer in Iran?"

I had made myself a commitment to attend medical school the following year. Her rationale seemed legitimate, and she knew it.

"You don't have to come to a Friday service," she continued, in reference to the main service. (In Iran, the primary day of rest is Friday, not Sunday.) "Come to our Tuesday morning Bible study instead. I am going to be sharing, and I would love it if you could be there to support me. I have not shared my testimony in our group before."

"Okay, I'll do it!" I cheered, letting her know that I was excited for what God was doing in her life.

On Tuesday morning, my cousin shared an amazing testimony about how God had taken her from being suicidal to having hope everlasting. God had supernaturally brought her out of depression.

There were about thirty women in the Bible study, and they would all take turns sharing on alternating weeks. At the study, I met a young lady my age named Leila. She attended the Tuesday morning service because it was easier for her to slip away from her parents that day than on Fridays. We quickly became good friends, and she asked me to help her find a way to attend the Friday service. I agreed.

"Great news!" Leila exclaimed. "My parents love you. If they know that I am going out with you, they will not even question where I am going."

I was happy to help her out. She had been wanting to attend the main church service ever since she first became a believer. The next Friday, we met at her house and traveled together to the service. Now that I knew a few people from that church, getting in wouldn't be a problem.

The Central Assemblies Of God Church of Tehran was a brown urban sandstone building with a large wooden cross on the front announcing that it was a church. The church had not put the cross on top of the building for fear that it might stand taller than the minaret of a mosque. In Muslim nations, no other religious building or symbol can be erected higher than a mosque.

To the right of the massive cross were four small windows that were square at the bottom but came to a curved point at the top. Below the windows was the main entrance. A wall outside the church wrapped around a hidden courtyard. The building was not massive or impressive by any means. It was as drab and boring as all the other two-story structures in central Tehran. Most Americans would not have recognized it as a church building. The large cross was only thing that distinguished it as a church.

In front of the main entrance stood a designated gatekeeper—the person who monitored which people were allowed into the church and which were not. I was now included in the number of individuals who were permitted to enter. The gatekeeper was a man who went by the name Brother Johnny. I had gotten to know him in the short time I had been with the women's study group. If Brother Johnny didn't know you, then you could not go into the building. Often, the way to get through the door was to know someone whom the church trusted. If Johnny didn't personally know you, then you would have to say the name of the person who had invited you.

Brother Johnny also had to watch out for radicals and terrorists who might try to get in. The church was a target for many Muslims who wanted to kill the pastor. Additionally, the Iranian government was looking for any reason to shut down the church, so it would send spies to see if unbelievers were being screened before they were allowed in. Iran has very strict rules against proselytizing. In order to stay open, the church had to show they were actively not allowing Muslims to come in.

Once you walked inside, the church felt and looked much bigger than it seemed from the outside. There was a massive cathedral ceiling, which delivered flawless acoustics that reverberated from wall to wall. The balcony on the second level wrapped around the sanctuary on three sides. The sanctuary was constructed from a classic varnished brown wood, with an altar area that was just large enough to hold the twenty-person team leading worship. On the wall behind the team was a thirty-foot wooden cross that was illuminated by lights hidden behind the brick background.

When the service began, I felt a tangible energy flowing through the room, like water in a wave pool, and it was being propelled by the worship team. One particular member of the team caught my eye. A young man wearing a bright, all-white suit was in the back, passionately jumping up and down during worship, driving the enthusiasm level through the roof. He was lost in the moment and giving it all he had. Although he was not front and center on the stage, it appeared that everyone's focus—including mine—was on him. He was the center of attention even if he didn't mean to be. All the other members of the worship team seemed faded or fuzzy, as if they were on the periphery.

"That's Saeed," Leila whispered as she leaned toward me and spoke into my ear. I nodded in acknowledgement but then pulled back and looked over at her in surprise, wondering how she knew who I was looking at. She glanced back at me with her chin tucked down into her chest and her eyes lifted to meet mine; then she shot me a mischievous grin as if she knew a secret about me.

I smiled back and shook my head.

After the service concluded, many people went to the front of the sanctuary to be prayed for, and I saw the young man in the white suit again as he came and prayed for people. He moved with a special authority as he placed his hands on each person. As soon as he did, it was as if there was a transfer of supernatural energy that sent people to the floor in convulsions. I had never seen anything like it. He seemed to be gifted with some kind of spiritual superpower.

"Wow," I said as I watched him, then covered my mouth with my hand, not realizing my reaction had been audible until it was already spoken. I looked around, but no one had heard me.

Saeed spoke with a commanding voice that boomed more loudly than the voices of the others who were praying. I perked my ears and stood on the tips of my toes, leaning in, as if this would help me hear him better.

As he prayed for the last person in line, I went to talk with him. Shuffling around some people who were headed in the opposite direction, I nodded my head and gave a courtesy smile to each one, as if I knew them personally. I wanted to grab this young man's attention before he left the room from the other end of the sanctuary. Leila had told me that he was discipling new believers, and I thought it might be a great idea to introduce him to the five young believers I had been teaching. I was heading back to America, and they wouldn't have anyone to teach them after I left. He could be the perfect person to continue discipling them.

Standing in front of the stage, I reached over and touched his arm to get his attention. With a slight grimace, he peered at me through his round, wire-rimmed glasses, giving me the look that a pastor gives to someone who wants to be prayed for.

"Oh, no, I don't have a prayer request," I said putting my hand in front of my face as if to wave him off. "I have a different kind of request."

"Okay, sure, what is it?" he asked in a kind and attentive way, like a doctor practicing a good bedside manner. His eyes engaged mine directly in a way that implied he was willing to take all the time I might require. He was not going to rush the conversation or hurry through my request.

I had been watching Saeed throughout the service, but now that I was closer to him, I could see that he was in his early twenties, younger than I by a couple of years. His round, youthful face, with a goatee, was accented by his wispy hair, which was slightly mussed at the top in what seemed like a playful way.

After he heard about the new believers I had been working with, he immediately agreed to invite them to join his Bible study group so he could disciple them. Following this meeting, I felt a release. Now I could leave Iran knowing that those I had been discipling would be left in very capable hands.

14

FALLING IN LOVE

Oh, my gosh, Naghmeh, Saeed is so amazing!" my cousin Foad said, shouting over the phone. "I mean, if you could hear his testimony, it is just like the apostle Paul."

Foad emailed me almost every other day to give me updates on the church in Iran, but he spent most of the time talking about Saeed. "You wouldn't believe it, Naghmeh," he wrote. "You simply wouldn't believe it, even if you were here. That is how amazing it is. He prayed for me the other day, and I have to say, I really experienced the presence of God come into the room."

He shared the remarkable story of how Saeed, at the age of fourteen, had been recruited by Hezbollah, the infamous pro-Iranian paramilitary militia. Hezbollah had been attracted to Saeed's dedication to Islam, and they had trained him to be a sleeper terrorist agent against the nation of Israel. After his training with Hezbollah, Saeed was introduced to a Christian church in Tehran where the pastor told him about Jesus. Saeed set in his heart to murder the pastor for saying that Jesus is Lord and not just a prophet.

The night Saeed was planning to murder the pastor, he was tormented in his spirit. He began to weep uncontrollably, debating the fundamentals of Islam. He cried out to God in prayer, begging, "God, just show me which way is true."

Saeed held the Koran in one hand and the Bible in the other as he knelt down and once more cried out to God, "Just show me!"

After Saeed fell asleep that evening, he heard a voice saying, "Saeed, Saeed, I'm coming back soon. Go to preach My gospel." Saeed woke up and looked around, but no one was there. He thought he had been having a dream, so he went back to sleep. Two hours later, the voice again called out, "Saeed, Saeed,

I'm coming back soon." This time, he woke up thinking he was going crazy. He fell back to sleep again but was awakened a third time to the same voice calling his name: "Saeed, I am coming back soon. Go to preach My gospel."

This time, Saeed saw a strong light and felt the presence of the Lord in a way he couldn't deny. When he looked at the light, he saw Jesus. Saeed fell down and cried out to Him, giving his life to Jesus.

When I heard this story about Saeed, I was filled with excitement and wonder. I took all the stories that I had heard about Saeed, pieced them together with all of the new information I was receiving about him, and attached them to my image of him from that day in church.

When my cousin Foad emailed me and told me about how Saeed had prayed for him, I could imagine what it had been like from the way I had seen Saeed pray for people at the church—how he squinted his eyes when he prayed, how he flipped his hands outward before he placed them on someone's head, and how his smile grew out of the side of his mouth when he met someone new.

I didn't know Saeed, but I was smitten with just the memory of him. From the snapshot of a single moment, I was able to create entire conversations and scenarios with him.

This was the first time I had really been attracted to a man. I had gone through my entire college experience without having "boy fever" like many of my classmates. At one point, one of my male friends proposed to me, but there was never anything romantic between us. I had never even held hands with a guy before. I was beginning to think something was wrong with me because I had simply never met a man I could see myself marrying.

With Saeed, however, I was feeling things I had never felt before. With his glasses and goatee, he had a soft look about him. He seemed like a gentle, humble man with whom a woman could find rest and protection. But, more than anything, I was attracted to his passion for and devotion to Christ. The way he shared the gospel message with dedication and authority drew me to him. Even though I didn't know him personally, I felt that I was getting to know him better from everything I was hearing about him.

I spent the entire winter studying for the Medical College Admission Test (MCAT) to get into medical school at the University of Washington so I could start the program in the following year, but I was quickly losing interest in it. Iran was calling me back. The church was experiencing a kind of growth that hadn't been seen there in hundreds of years. I felt like I was missing out.

"I think I need to return to Iran," I said to my father one day out of the blue. "I know you would like me to attend medical school, but there seems to be something big happening that has never happened before. What if I am supposed to be there and not here? What if I go to medical school and miss out on the timing of what God is doing?"

"Well, that is something that you have to decide," he replied. "You have to do what the Lord is calling you to do."

By the end of February 2003, I was back on an airplane, sitting beside Baba, flying into Tehran.

I had not told anyone about the feelings I had developed for Saeed. I kept them to myself because it felt premature. I didn't know anything about him other than what people were telling me. I didn't know if he was engaged, had a girlfriend, or would even be interested in me.

Like a little girl dreaming about the man she would marry one day, I found myself daydreaming about life with Saeed. I fantasized about what it would be like to share ministry with another person. It was absurd; nonetheless, I seemed incapable of stopping these daydreams.

Not long after our flight touched down, I made my way to the church, excited to see Saeed again—but he was not there. Something seemed a bit odd about it. He was no longer participating in worship or attending church services.

Nobody seemed to know what had happened, but I soon discovered that Saeed had started his own fellowship. He had begun to disciple believers at his house, and his teachings were popular among the young people. His study group had already grown to fifty or sixty attendees, and it was limited to those numbers only because his parents' house could not accommodate any more people. The college-aged students loved his way of preaching. A fire was catching on, and Saeed's home group grew so large it had to split into two groups.

Once I learned that Saeed was teaching at his home rather than at the church, I began to attend his group. The energy was completely different there; in many ways, it felt more spontaneous and relaxed. The Central Assemblies of God Church, like most official churches in Iran, was run by Armenian believers, and the worship was more formal and structured. Armenians have a very long and proud Christian history. Frequently, in Iran, if you say that you are Christian, people assume that you mean you are Armenian. However, unfortunately, Armenian believers often assume a superior attitude toward the Iranians because most Iranians are Muslim at birth rather than Christian.

With Saeed in his home fellowship, there was a kind of free flow when we prayed together, and we were not limited by an official schedule; we would alternate worship and prayer for hours. Although we sang many of the songs that we had learned in the official church, the worship also had more of a Persian feel to it. We used instruments such as the sitar and incorporated some Middle Eastern tunes. Children also participated in the home fellowship, whereas at the official church, they had been separated from the adults, attending children's programs or youth groups. Additionally, we didn't feel the need for new visitors to be screened, and because everyone knew everyone else, there was less fear of government spies. And Iranian believers were not banned because of their Muslim background.

The way the home church fellowship naturally knitted with worship and ministry—without the need for projectors, sound equipment, flyers, announcements, or schedules—felt powerful and right to me. It seemed personal and intimate. In my first moments of sitting in the house church meeting, I felt that I might be in Iran for a longer period this time. The idea of attending medical school started to become a distant memory, as if the goal had never been mine but belonged to someone else.

Although there was a general starting time for the fellowship at Saeed's home, the time was not fixed. We couldn't have fifty people show up at the house at the same moment—that would be a problem for security. So, people generally trickled in one or two at a time over an hour or two.

We would often begin by singing songs, and people would simply join in as they arrived. The order of the songs was from inspiration, instead of having a set program, but the songs were ones we all knew from the Central church in town. When new believers would come who were not familiar with the songs, we would print up the words so they could follow along.

Something was clearly happening with the house church. It was hard for me to put into words, but whatever it was, I wanted to be a part of it, and so did everyone else who experienced it.

No doubt, one of the major attractions for me was that the meetings were primarily made up of people my age. The Holy Spirit was moving among the new generation, and it was making sweeping changes. More than two-thirds of Iranians were under the age of thirty, and they were at odds with the older

Islamic leadership. The young people were looking for answers that were not found in Islam. The vibrant believers filling Saeed's home night after night were young professionals, college students, and idealists who had seen the aftermath of Islamic rule and were disgusted with it. They were the "ABI" generation: anything but Islam.

A generational shift was taking place, and the government knew it. That is why they were so eager to violently crush anything they perceived as a threat. The Ayatollah had come to power by inspiring young intellectuals like my father to overthrow the government. They were not going to allow the same thing to happen to them.

At only twenty-five years old, I was one of the oldest people in the fellowship, and many of the believers looked to me for spiritual guidance—but I looked to Saeed. Even though he was younger than I, he was confident and exuded leadership qualities we were all looking for during those uncertain times. We felt he was the one to lead us into this new era—and he was the one who I wanted to lead me through life.

15

THE HEARTBEAT OF CHANGE

Saeed was doing things that gave me the impression he was in some small way attracted to me. I genuinely sensed that a chemistry was sparking between the two of us. Without words, things were happening that we could both feel. We were experiencing a courtship of secret gestures that had the sweet aroma of innocent and not-so-innocent flirting. And there were layers to the meanings of the words we were speaking to each other. We exchanged laughs at things that were not funny, found urgency in telling each other things that were clearly not important, and accidentally touched in ways that weren't really accidental.

Saeed asked me to be part of his inner circle of leadership, which came together on Tuesday mornings to pray. This opportunity to minister together with Saeed was exhilarating, and everything felt like it was going in the right direction. Ideas of a future with Saeed soon occupied my every thought.

"Let's do ministry together," Saeed said the next time we met. Although I knew what he meant on a pragmatic level, I read so many different things into that statement. I believed he meant it on a different level, as well, but we both pretended it was purely for Jesus.

"You know that a lot of young women are coming to our home group, and they desperately need someone to lead and guide them. Would you consider discipling them? Would you be the women's group leader? I feel that we could make a good team in this way."

I nodded as if I were thinking it over, but there was nothing to think over. My answer was an emphatic *yes*, but I wanted to deliver a reserved reply. I wanted to pretend that his question was solely about ministry and that my answer was solely in response to ministry, but I think we both knew otherwise.

When new women joined the group, I instantly connected with them and ensured that they were engaged. Initially, I gave them a curriculum from the Central church that Saeed used, known as "The ABCs of Christianity." Although the course taught the basics of Christianity, I was not exactly satisfied with the material. I felt that it skipped around too much.

Over the years, I had grown comfortable using Calvary Chapel's systematic approach to the Bible. Calvary Chapel is a network of churches found mostly in the Western part of the United States. They put a strong emphasis on going through the Bible progressively—not jumping around from subject to subject according to the feeling of the speaker but instead going through the Scriptures book by book and chapter by chapter. Additionally, during my time at the University of Puget Sound, when I was active in InterVarsity Christian Fellowship and leading small groups, I had used the OIA (observation, interpretation, and application) method of teaching Scripture. The Calvary Chapel approach and the OIA method were a perfect match, reinforcing one another, and helped to establish my own teaching method.

When sharing with new believers, I liked the systematic approach best, and Saeed allowed me to implement this program for everyone. It seemed that we were quickly becoming a "power couple," an unstoppable dynamic duo. We were doing things that had never been done before and seeing amazing growth among the Iranian young people. College students were bringing their friends, and the word was making its way through the city.

The believers in our fellowship spent hours together in prayer. There were no time limits on our gatherings. It was as if we had no other obligations in the world but to be with Jesus. Not even the need for food interrupted our time together. Instead, it enhanced it. We ate together and prayed together, and it felt like we were a real family. Our fellowship was only briefly interrupted by sleep and work.

Saeed had dropped his ties with the official church and was devoting his entire time to the house church. Years later, I would learn that the Assemblies of God leadership in Iran had noticed something in Saeed that had caused them concern. Brother Edward, the church's former pastor, had seen Saeed interact with women in a way that was not appropriate, so Saeed had been put under church discipline and not been allowed to attend church services or have any interaction with other church members. There were also concerns about Saeed's pride and cultish behavior. But all of this was unknown to me at the time.

Brother Edward had taken over leadership of the church after Pastor Haik Hovsepian was murdered. When Brother Edward's wife passed away, he remarried, but his new wife was Iranian. This was a problem for the church because Brother Edward was Armenian. In the Iranian-Armenian culture, Armenians can only marry Armenians; to do otherwise is considered to be unequally yoked. It is a completely unbiblical and prejudicial custom, and Brother Edwards confronted it in the church. When he left the church, a man named Pastor Aram took over as interim pastor, and there was apparently not a lot of discussion about Saeed's discipline.

While Saeed had been temporarily banned from the church, he had used the time to develop the house church under his own leadership without connection to the official church. Saeed used the formula he had learned from the leadership training he had been given by the Assemblies of God.

Things were going so well with the house church that Saeed had more reasons not to return to the Assemblies of God church than to return, but he took things one step further. He didn't allow the members of his house church to connect with the official church. The future was with the underground house church in Iran, and Saeed knew it. The official church was clinging to a methodology that was not going to work in Iran's future. Persecution was increasing, and brick-and-mortar churches were too easy for the authorities to target. Christians were being hunted down like wild animals and killed.

Saeed knew that he no longer needed to be associated with an official body and didn't need the approval of the church leaders. He had tasted the freedom of doing things on his own and in his own way. He was now leading a movement. There was excitement among the young people about having such a young leader. Saeed was not an old clergy member with outdated ideas. He was not an Armenian Christian, patronizing the Iranians. He was one of them, and he was a visionary. We all intuitively knew that this was the beginning of something huge. We could taste it. Saeed had told the young believers not to connect with the official church, and they didn't because, deep down, they didn't want to.

Iran's future was going in a new direction. Saeed monitored the heartbeat of this change, having his fingers on the pulse. Old methods that had worked for hundreds of years were not going to work any longer. The new methods would have to go back to the first-century church found in the book of Acts— and a first-century church is exactly the strategy Saeed had in mind for the house church in Iran. Most important—and likely the most deadly part of what we did—we focused our services specifically on evangelism for Muslim converts. We would have to flourish during times of persecution and thrive without organized religious controls.

16

A PROPOSAL?

During prayer time, we need to refrain from speaking in the name of God as if He is speaking directly to us," Narek said. "Only Saeed has the ability to hear directly from God."

I pulled back. This was something that was happening more and more often. Narek was Saeed's right-hand man, and he was growing very protective over Saeed's power and prestige in the group. I might have understood Narek's actions more if he were a new believer, but he was not. He was one of the leaders.

I looked around the room, wondering if any of the other leaders were going to challenge him, but they didn't.

I, however, couldn't let this statement go unchallenged. I had to say something. "No, no, no. We all can equally hear from God, Narek. We cannot say that one person in our group has exclusive access to God, because that is simply not true," I protested. "We all have the Holy Spirit."

"Saeed is the number one apostle of Iran," Narek shot back. "We are the apostles of Iran. We are needed because the original apostles didn't do their job. We are called to complete the task that the first apostles didn't do."

"What are you talking about? We are here today because of the work of the first apostles." I didn't back down, and I talked to Saeed about it.

Saeed just smiled. "Oh, he means well," he said, shrugging it off.

"This is dangerous," I protested again. Eventually, I was able to make my point, and Saeed assured me that he would not let it go too far. So I let it go.

I spent a lot of time around Narek, and we butted heads from time to time, but he was part of the leadership team, so we had to "make nice" to allow the team's plans to run smoothly. We didn't have a choice. We spent most of our waking hours together.

I went to Saeed's house every morning for prayer, and then I headed to work until it was time for the evening house church meetings. In order to keep a low profile, we were meeting in a different home every evening. We tried not to meet in any location more than one day in a row so our gatherings would not draw very much attention.

The church was all-consuming for me. I didn't want to do anything else but worship and minister among the believers, and I didn't want to spend my time with anyone else besides those in the church and others we were ministering to. The funny thing is that I had the impression the same thing was true for others.

I was in awe of how God seemed to be using Saeed in such a powerful way in Iran. I was becoming more and more intrigued by what appeared to be Saeed's passion for God and evangelism, a passion I shared and that I hadn't seen much in the young Christian men with whom I had attended university. And I was falling more deeply in love with Saeed. We had never really talked about our relationship, but I had the impression he had feelings for me too.

If I had any doubts about that, they were dispelled one day when he invited me to go on a trip to the train station with our friend Azim to pick up Azim's fiancée.

Azim was a gifted musician and one of Saeed's converts; Saeed had shared the gospel with him and led him to the Lord. Ever since that day, the two men had been nearly inseparable; they were always hanging out together. Azim was almost like one of Saeed's groupies—following him everywhere.

Azim didn't have a car, and his fiancé was arriving that day, so Saeed had agreed to drive him to the train station so they wouldn't need to use a taxi. Saeed gripped the top of the steering wheel with one strong, square-knuckled hand and held the gearshift with the other. Sitting beside him, I experienced a sense of security. It felt like we were a couple, and the feeling was addictive.

Azim was silent in the back seat, gazing out the window and not engaging in any conversation. No doubt, he was imagining reuniting with his fiancé after a long period of separation. All of a sudden, without looking at me, Saeed slowly slid his hand over to me and placed it in my lap; he then moved his fingers across my thigh like the legs of a spider until he found my hand. He did it so naturally and emotionlessly, and he was behaving so normally otherwise, that I didn't know how to react. I wondered if it was really happening.

I went stiff, not sure if I should be happy or shocked. I wasn't certain if I should hold his hand back or just pretend I hadn't noticed. I closed my eyes and hoped that he could not feel my entire body trembling. I didn't want to do anything that would make him move his hand away from mine. I had never held hands with a boyfriend before.

After a few minutes, Saeed firmly gripped my hand and pulled it toward him. My heart raced. I closed my eyes again. Then I glanced over at him—but he didn't look back at me. His eyes looked determined and were focused on the erratic changes of the Tehran traffic.

My limp hand was a willing victim. I was happy that he was taking the initiative. I hadn't had what it took to do it.

Then, without warning, he pulled my hand straight down into his crotch and held it there. I felt that this most definitely had to be an accident, but Saeed made it clear that it was not.

I didn't move. I was afraid to cause any extra movement that might draw the attention of Azim in the back seat.

"You feel that?" Saeed whispered with a slight grin as he lifted his hips and pushed my hand down into his pelvic area. I hoped that Azim could not hear him.

I didn't respond. I forcefully kept my head looking straight ahead. This was the first time that I had ever felt a man's penis, and it had all happened so fast that I was not certain how to feel about it. It was something I had never seen coming.

When we arrived at the train station, I was a bit shell-shocked. Like a zombie, I emerged from the car and blindly walked toward the train station. I had forgotten what we were doing there or where we were going.

"We still have another hour before she gets here," Saeed said to Azim, to which Azim nodded.

"I will wait right here for her," Azim said, indicating that he would stay outside by the main exit.

"Okay, then. I think that we are going to stroll in this direction," Saeed responded, pointing his fingers the opposite way. Taking my hand in his, Saeed turned and walked toward the nearby park.

I aimlessly paced behind him until, suddenly, he turned and grabbed me firmly around the waist, swinging me off balance; he pushed me behind a tree and, without warning, kissed me on the lips.

I didn't think I could be more shocked than I had been in the car. I was wrong. For the second time that day, I didn't know what was happening until it was already happening. I had never kissed a guy before—or, rather, had a guy kiss me. I was part of the purity movement that adhered to the biblical teaching of sexual abstinence until marriage. I had taken a "purity pledge," promising to abstain from any sexual contact—including kissing—until I was married. I had made a promise to God that my first kiss would be on my wedding day.

I don't think that Saeed realized it then, but when he kissed me, it wasn't just a kiss. The kiss signaled my eternal devotion to him.

"Shhh," Saeed said to me after pulling his head back. "I had a vision that you are to be my wife."

Frozen in the moment and not wanting to move, I felt like I was floating outside of myself, not watching Saeed through my eyes but watching both of us from a third perspective. I wanted to bite my arm to see if I was in a dream or experiencing real life. My brain was caught in a foggy tailspin, trapped in the clouds and not knowing if I was corkscrewing through the air up, down, or sideways.

Marriage had been the number one thing on my mind for the last couple of weeks, and now, without my saying a word, Saeed was talking about our marriage as if it were an inevitable fact—as if it were God's will.

This was everything I wanted, but I had never envisioned it happening like this. I tried to look around the tree to see if Azim could see us or hear what Saeed was saying, but I wasn't able to lean far enough to see.

"God gave me this vision," Saeed continued, lowering his voice so no one besides me could hear him. "There was a woman who was coming off a plane with her father. The father had brought his daughter from another country, and as I watched her walking down the stairs from the airplane, I knew that God was telling me this was the woman that I was supposed to marry. And do you know who that woman was?" he asked.

I slightly shook my head as if I didn't know because I wanted to hear him say it. I wanted to hear him verbally tell me who that woman was who had been brought by her father.

"That woman was you. She looked exactly like you in my dreams. Naghmeh," he said, emphasizing the moment by using my name, "I am supposed to marry you. God wants us to be married."

When we returned to the car with Azim and his fiancée, Saeed and I were more than just a couple—we were engaged. Saeed had never asked me to marry him, and I never had the opportunity to accept or reject his proposal. However, it was clear that he felt sharing his vision with me was a type of proposal. He wasn't simply telling me the vision; he was telling me that it was God's will for us to be married, and I succumbed to the destiny of it all. He was so convinced that I was supposed to be his wife that I didn't dare disagree.

This may be hard for many people who have never been part of the purity movement to understand, but even Saeed's kiss at the tree made me feel that the sexual boundaries between us had been breached. I later learned that pushing those boundaries is something male abusers often do, pressuring women to go beyond what they are comfortable with sexually, sometimes taking them by surprise in order to do it. With that kiss, I suddenly felt like damaged goods according to the purity movement and theology because, again, I was supposed to wait until my wedding day to kiss my husband for the first time. Saeed's claim of having received the vision from God that we were to be husband and wife, my feelings of distress that I was now trapped without any other marital options because of our shared kiss, and Saeed's earlier inappropriate sexual advances when we were in the car made me think I was obligated to marry him.

After we kissed behind the tree at the train station, our relationship progressed quickly. Our kiss rapidly turned into much more. There were times when we were simply unable to keep our hands off each other. All of my purity promises were thrown out the window—and I was not alone in that. Many Christians in the house church were promiscuous, and from that day onward, the way Saeed continued to push the boundaries of physical contact between us, we did not lead by example.

Saeed and I were doing things that are not allowed according to Christian standards, but we justified it to ourselves until it was okay in our minds. Our prayer meetings ended late at night, and Saeed would rationalize that it was too late for me to go home. I would fall asleep on the couch as he prayed with people into the morning hours.

Saeed's mother, who was not a Christian, began making a bed for me in Saeed's room so I would not have to travel late at night. After the last person returned home, Saeed would slide in beside me, and we would sleep together. We didn't have sex, but we did everything else. We would often lie together in the night with no clothes on, exploring each other's bodies. Anytime we were convicted of our sins, we would both find ways to explain them away. It became our little secret that we didn't share with others. It was something we were confident we could contain. We didn't need to go all the way and could somehow find salvation by only indulging in "little sins," not realizing that sin always starts off small and innocent. It never declares its real intentions. It whispers to us, "This is okay. It is not really that bad. *You will not surely die.*"[8] Sin shrouds itself in the bright lights of pleasure and joy. It announces its arrival with innocence and promises unending bliss.

"We are going to be married anyway," I told myself. "Adam and Eve didn't have a ceremony. Their union before God was when they became 'one flesh.'"

The fear that haunted me, however, was the unshakable nagging voice in the back of my head that didn't care about any of my excuses and explanations but told me that I would have to stand and face all the young new believers the next day. I would have to pray with them, sing with them, and read the Word with them, pretending to be a leader who was in love with God. I would need to play the part of a good Christian even with the raunchy stench of the sin from the night before still traipsing around the room.

"Just for now," I told myself. "Once we are married, then all of this will be over. This sin is only temporary."

I didn't look for all those excuses and explanations merely to make myself feel better. The deeper reason was far easier to correlate with the Bible: the reason was love—at least, on my part. Saeed had actually told me he was not in love with me because he was still not over his ex-girlfriend. I convinced myself that I was okay with this because I was seeing God do so much in the house church, and because Saeed and I worked so well together in ministry.

But there was an additional element at work that caused me to ignore the warning signs of sin and make excuses for the problems in my relationship with Saeed, and it may have been the biggest reason of all. It wasn't just that I had fallen in love—I had become emotionally attached to Saeed in an unhealthy way. There were times in the following weeks and months when

8. Genesis 3:4 (NKJV).

I sensed I was continuing to fall into a snare because Saeed was treating me badly, calling me names and putting me down. Twice, I had emotional breakdowns and tried to break off the engagement, but I had become so attached to him in my soul that I kept moving forward with my wedding plans.

17

PUSHING THE BOUNDARIES

First of all, congratulations!" cheered Pastor Aram, the interim pastor at the Central church. "This is a big day. You're selecting the person that you want to commit to for the rest of your life. This is no small thing. The person sitting next to you is the owner of the face that you will see every day for the rest of your life. You will buy a house, have children and grandchildren, and, most important," he said putting his finger in the air as if making a profound point that no one had ever thought of before, "you will serve the Lord together."

Saeed and I wanted to have Pastor Aram's approval. Although it was clear that Saeed was leading his own ministry, we had a strong sense that the official church still thought of Saeed as their shepherd. He had been trained and supported by them, and they considered the growth of his house church to be a result of their efforts. As we sat in Pastor Aram's office to secure his sanction of our marriage, Saeed did little to dispel any of those ideas.

"I want you to know that, here at the church, you have our support. Your engagement and marriage will have the full support of myself as your pastor and everyone here at the church. We all want to see you succeed in life. We want to see you do well. That is why I want to give you a list of rules that you must abide by until you are married. These rules are very important. They are the key to a long and healthy marriage. They need to be taken seriously, and you need to do everything in your power to make sure that you do not break them. Do you understand?" he asked.

Both Saeed and I nodded in unison before saying yes. Sitting in Pastor Aram's office, it was easy to feel like we were two young students who had been called to the principal's office. The pastor's caring eyes and warm words were tempered by his strong jawbone, which lined its way down to his pursed lips as he began listing off the rules.

"You cannot be alone," he said, shaking his head. "This is of supreme importance. You can never be alone together without someone else around. This rule is above all else and lays the foundation for all the other rules," he continued, again throwing his finger in the air. "Before you are married, it is important that you don't kiss, hold hands, or have any resemblance of even the slightest physical relationship. This is easier if you are never alone, so, from this day until the day that you are married, you need to have someone with you at all times if you are traveling together."

Then, his voice boomed as he added, "And the person with you should be an older adult—not one of your friends. Friends do not look out for us as much as we would like them to."

Shame washed over me as I thought about Saeed's mother making up a bed for me in her son's bedroom.

"Finally," he said, letting us know that he was coming to a conclusion, "you need to set up a time for your parents to meet each other. They are family now and will forever be a part of each other's lives through you. Two families are now uniting and becoming one. You need to be the ones to put this together."

Again, we nodded in agreement. We both knew that the final part of Pastor Aram's instructions was going to be easier for us to follow than the previous set.

Although Saeed's parents were not Christians, they made it clear that they loved me. They considered me to be a huge benefit to their family because my parents were well-known, well-connected, educated, and wealthy by Iranian standards. Saeed's parents came from a very simple background and had not expected Saeed to do well. He didn't have a job, hadn't graduated from high school, didn't own a car, didn't have any money in his bank account, didn't have any ambition to move into his own house, and didn't show any desire to truly advance himself in a career or trade.

Saeed liked to stay up late and sleep until the afternoon. At one point in his younger years, he had been depressed and suicidal. His parents had often worried about him, and when they learned that he had become a Christian, their concerns had only increased. But now he was marrying a woman from America from a stable family who was a college graduate and a medical school candidate. Both of Saeed's parents went out of their way to make me feel comfortable, loved, and accepted into their family.

I would like to say that Saeed and I listened to Pastor Aram's advice, but we kept barreling down the same road we had been racing down for months. It was the same story every night. By the end of our evening Bible studies, I was drained from the day and ready to fall asleep. But Saeed would come and join me, and we stayed up late into the evening adoring one another. Every morning, I would awaken to a feeling of extreme exhaustion, while Saeed would continue to sleep. I had to be at work at seven o'clock in the morning, but he had no morning obligations. He slept until noon and would be fully recovered by the time I returned home from work.

I thought about quitting my job so I could provide more help to the church, but Saeed didn't want me to. I was the only one of us making money. He was no longer bringing in an income from the official church, and the house church wasn't well funded. Almost all the people attending were either university students or lived with their parents and, like Saeed, didn't have a job. "I only have one desire," he would often tell me, "and that is to build the church of the Lord. I can't take any job that would interfere with that single goal in my life."

I loved that Saeed was so passionate about building the church. Unfortunately, I was not completely convinced of his real desire to strengthen the church. He was ardent and firm about not allowing any outside job to interfere with his spiritual obligations, but he didn't seem as concerned about our unbiblical premarital relationship hindering anything. Every night, we pushed the sexual boundaries further and further.

I was growing increasingly concerned about our behavior and the influence it was having on our testimony to both believers and unbelievers. Several times, after it had grown late, I told Saeed that I didn't want to stay at his house but preferred to return home. Saeed would drive me home but then insist on coming to my room. He didn't want to go home. He wanted to hang out longer and talk into the night; he was unworried about my concerns or about my early-morning work schedule.

At that time, I was living at my uncle's house. He had given me a room that was separate from the main house and was connected to the outside garden area. He and my aunt had prepared the room to be a private suite, with its own kitchen, living room, and rear entrance.

Saeed liked that arrangement because we had more privacy there than at his parents' house. But, in the morning, I would be hit with extreme feelings of shame when my aunt would come to check to see if I was okay, only to see Saeed in bed with me.

My aunt and uncle were Muslims. I was supposed to be a Christian witness to them, but I was not. I was confirming all of their suspicions about Christians being immoral. My aunt and uncle never said anything to me about this, but I felt the agony of having failed them.

"I don't like what is happening right now," I told Saeed early one morning.

Saeed was still sleeping and didn't want to wake up to discuss it. I shook his side. I knew that he was tired, but I didn't feel guilty about waking him up. I had to wake up every morning for work, but that never stopped him from keeping me awake late at night to talk.

"Hey, can you hear what I am saying?" I said again in frustration. "They know that I am coming home with you and that we are sleeping together."

"Who?" Saeed asked in a groggy morning voice muffled against his pillow.

"My aunt and uncle. We are not showing the light of Christ to them right now. We can't do this, Saeed. We are breaking all the rules that Pastor Aram gave us." I listed them off one by one on my fingers. "We are not supposed to be alone together. We are only allowed to be together in a group setting. We are supposed to slowly introduce our families to one another—your introduction to my family is you sleeping in my bed!"

"We will be married," Saeed shot back, aggressively covering his head with his pillow to shut me out.

He hadn't heard anything I was saying. That night, we went right back to life as normal, continuing to digress from maintaining sexual boundaries between one another. Sadly, it seemed that Saeed didn't care about this. It was scary how easy it was for him to justify what was happening. What we were doing did not seem to torment his conscience at all.

In the sober light of day, I clung to Saeed's words about our upcoming marriage as a refuge. They were the only thing that offered me enough comfort to live with my conscience while I wrestled with the sin in our relationship and worried about how it would affect the calling on our lives.

Saeed was right. We were engaged, and our wedding would be held soon. I would only have to hide our sin for a little while longer, and then it would all be made right in the end.

18

REVIVAL IN THE
HOUSE CHURCH

I continued to have reservations about my engagement to Saeed, feeling extremely convicted about our habitual sinning. I also felt hurt by the way he was treating me. He would make fun of me for having darker skin because of my Arab blood. "You are related to Muhammad," he would say, referring to my complexion in direct contrast to his lighter skin tone.

Saeed's family was proud of the light hue of their skin. Their light complexion confirmed to them that they were members of the Aryan race, which is actually where the name *Iran* comes from. The word literally means "land of the Aryans." Iran is called Persia in the Bible, but in the 1930s, during the rise of the Third Reich in Germany, Hitler and Reza Shah, the leader of Iran at that time, built an extremely strong alliance. Hitler was one of the first leaders to refer to Persia with the official title of "Iran." After hearing the ideology of the German leader, many elites and intellectuals in Iran clung to ideas of Aryan superiority. Germany soon became Iran's number one trading partner, built libraries in Iran and filled them with books about the Aryan race, and even made special laws exempting Iranians from the Nuremberg Race Laws. An obsession with racial superiority dominated the national dialogue during this time, and some of those ideas still linger.

Saeed would often tell me that he was more attracted to girls with lighter skin than those with darker skin. I pretended it didn't bother me. When we would travel together or go to a restaurant, he would stare at other women without any concern about whether I noticed. The women he stared at inevitably had light skin, light hair, and light eyes. They reminded me of what I was not.

"That is why no one wanted to marry you," he would joke, referring to both my darker skin and my "advanced age," because I was in my mid-twenties. One time, he said, "You are a fermented pickle"—a Persian phrase for women who are older and unmarried.

In these and other ways, Saeed had been slowly stripping me of my self-confidence. He would tell me I needed to color my hair blonde or have plastic surgery to raise my eyebrows or alter the look of my nose and cheeks. He would criticize my weight and my taste in clothes. Because of the emotional bond I had developed with him, Saeed's comments caused me to become even more reliant on and attached to him as I sought his approval.

Despite the hurt I felt at Saeed's put-downs and criticism, I was encouraged to witness the house church multiplying as the Spirit of the Lord continued to move in Iran. There were so many people who were hungry for the message of the gospel, and somehow they were miraculously finding our home church.

We didn't advertise our meetings on billboards, and we had no event page about "revival" posted on social media, but people still found us. Sometimes believers discovered our fellowship through a friend, and sometimes God told them about it directly.

I am unable to explain what was happening from a theological perspective. I can't say that God was moving because of anything Saeed and I were doing. In fact, I had evidence that He was moving in spite of us, not because of us.

Revival fires in Iran started in 2003 and 2004. That is when we saw things really start to take off. No one single ministry or person was in control of it. God was independently working through so many different factors to create the "perfect storm" for revival. When Saeed and I compared notes with other believers in Iran, it was clear that we had the fastest-growing house church network in the country; we were at the tip of the spear.

The number of Christians in Iran was clearly increasing in a way that hadn't happened prior to the Revolution. After more than thirty years of Sharia law, the country was going in the opposite direction than had been intended by the Ayatollah. The Iranian government was doing everything in its power to stop Christianity, but anything it did only seemed to make the problem worse. We were living in one of the most inhospitable nations for Christians in the world, and yet we were seeing an explosion of growth like never before.

I realized how little we really know about the omniscience of God. Understanding His plans for the church in Iran can be like trying to give someone directions to find a shop in the Grand Bazaar in Tehran. The church is messy but vibrant. It is chaotic and unorganized, but it is contagious and exciting. Church growth in Iran, like the Grand Bazaar, is initially dizzying because it is confusing, endlessly zigzagging, and seemingly without order. And it carries the daunting mystery of the new things God is doing.

Revival in Iran has not followed the same pattern as other modern revivals. The revival is not taking place in tents or modern church buildings. Camera crews are not standing by ready to document every service and post it online. The leadership is not writing books or teaching seminars about how to have a revival. Instead, the awakening is taking place in homes, as it did in ours. The churches are set up in a series of networks like the ones Saeed and I established.

The Christians that we were seeing in our home church were not looking for organized religion. They already had that. They were not looking for programs or financial support. They were not looking for a political group to overthrow the government. Of all the hours I spent in fellowship with our house church, I never heard anyone discuss how to take power from the Ayatollah. They came for one reason: to fall in love with Jesus.

Day after day, I was witnessing characteristics of a growing, thriving church—although one that might not appeal to many Christians today because it probably wouldn't look like what they are used to. Every day, we were singing, praying out loud, and even dancing in the Spirit. We couldn't have done any of this ourselves; we didn't have the energy or the capacity to depend on our own logic and cognitive reasoning to build the church. And we couldn't have gone even one day without a strong reliance on the work of the Holy Spirit.

19

PLANTING CHURCHES
AND EVANGELIZING

We had seen our small group of fifty double to a hundred believers in only a few weeks. We had gone from having a house church in Tehran to planting house churches in other cities as well. As soon as we traveled to a new location, we would meet with a few believers there, and, within a week or so, we would see the number of attendees double and triple. It was happening without any effort on our part, and it was happening in spite of our failures.

The primary factor fueling the revival in Iran during that time was the college students as they became spiritually fired up in our home group meetings in Tehran. Saeed and I took the time to train and disciple them. Then, when they graduated from college, we sent them out, often back to their hometowns. Our fellowship stayed in a perpetual state of rotation. As soon as one university student left to return home, their vacant spot was filled by at least two more eager students ready to be discipled.

After graduation, before the students left, we loaded them up with ministry materials to take with them. The materials were a kind of ministry starter kit, with electronic Bibles, discipleship teaching, music, and *The Jesus Film*. These young students were fearless and energetic. They were bright-eyed and ready to share the gospel message in the most unreached areas of Iran.

After a graduate left to return home, Saeed and I would arrange to travel to their area and help disciple their new home group. In the beginning, after we had planted three or four churches in other cities, it had all seemed manageable—but it soon turned riotous. After only a few short months, there were more students returning home than we could keep up with, and each of them was planting churches in cities throughout Iran. The church was multiplying at such an astronomical rate that we were simply not able to keep track of it.

We would also travel to visit with other believers. In the summer of 2004, we went on a road trip to the city of Shiraz in the south of Iran. Saeed and I took the lead in one car, and my father followed in his car, along with two other believers from the Tehran house churches. With all the stops we made, it took us close to fourteen hours to get to Shiraz. One of the main reasons for the trip was to visit a family that had recently converted to Christianity after learning about Jesus through a Christian satellite television program. We wanted to meet them, encourage them in their faith, and also provide them with some Bibles and discipleship material.

When we walked into the home of these believers, we could smell the enticing food aromas specific to that region. The mother, Shirin, made the most amazing Persian rice covered with saffron water, pistachio, and fried shrimp. She also made many other delicious local dishes. Over the next year, we visited them often and always looked forward to Shirin's cooking!

The city of Shiraz is Iran's ancient city of love and literature—two things that go with red wine, which is perhaps why one of the world's best wine-producing grapes is called Shiraz, named after the city. For thousands of years, Persians have been cultivating love, poetry, and wine.

Make the mistake of calling any Iranian an "Arab" in the city of Shiraz, and you might find yourself ejected from the country. Iranians are not Arab; they are Asian. If you ask someone from Shiraz what the difference is between Persians and Arabs, they are likely to respond with one word: *culture*.

Persians are cultured and don't relate well to the nomadic, goat-herding heritage of the Arabs. No home in Iran is complete without two books—the Koran and a book of poems. One of the books, Iranians are required to own, but the other owns the Iranians. Iranians live and die by poetry. Bits of prose and psalm pepper almost every conversation, and even the most uneducated taxi driver can recite these words from Iran's most famous poet, Abolghasem Ferdowsi:

But all this world is like a tale we hear—
Men's evil, and their glory, disappear.[9]

---

9. Abolghasem Ferdowsi, *Shahnameh: The Persian Book of Kings*, https://www.goodreads.com/quotes/59092-but-all-this-world-is-like-a-tale-we-hear.

Shiraz, in Fars Province, is a city that reminds us that Islam is not the ancient religion of Iran. Islam was forced upon the people and only continues by force today. The Persians (including the Parthians, Medes, and Elamites mentioned in Acts 2:9) had been among the first people groups to become followers of Christ.

Fars Province also contains the tombs of kings from the vast ancient empire of the Medes and the Persians, such as Cyrus the Great and Xerxes I, who are mentioned in the Old Testament. Reportedly, at the time of its greatest strength and reach, this empire ruled three million square miles over three continents and oversaw 44 percent of the world's population.[10]

On our first visit to Shiraz, a ten-year-old girl came up to me and gave me a hug. Her name was Maral, and she was the youngest of Shirin's three daughters. She had become a follower of Jesus and was eager to learn more about Him. She had so many questions. When I would answer one question, she would ask another. It was wonderful to see her love and passion for Jesus.

We had brought children's books with us, and Maral was eager to read all of them. She soon became the children's leader, teaching other children about Jesus. As she grew older, she led the youth group and later was a leader in various underground house churches. I could not have imagined when I first met beautiful little Maral that, years later, she would suffer much for her belief in Jesus.

It wasn't long before Saeed realized that the underground house church he was leading was now larger than the largest brick-and-mortar church in Iran. With the momentum we were experiencing, it was obvious something was playing out on a greater scale than we had ever seen before in Iran, and there was no way Saeed was going to stop now and go back to submitting to the leadership at the Central church.

The church may still have had visions of imposing spiritual correction on Saeed and bringing him back, but it was now clear that he had broken free. He had not been rehabilitated. He had been unleashed.

Saeed's gifting was his singular focus. He thrived off the thrill of sharing the gospel with unreached people and thought about nothing else until he was able to do it. His drive, ambition, and passion for preaching the gospel—and

---

10. "Map of the Persian Empire," Bible History, https://bible-history.com/maps/persian-empire; "The Tombs of 4 Biblical Persian Kings," Biblical Reading Archaeology, October 1, 2018, https://biblereadingarcheology.com/2018/10/01/the-tombs-of-4-biblical-persian-kings/.

the unique way in which he did it—was one of the things that made him attractive to me. He wanted to reach more people, obtain more Bibles to distribute, pass out more tracts, launch more churches, train more disciples, and see more sick people healed. He was obsessed with preaching; he was addicted to planting churches in closed cities, and I was addicted to him.

So many of the church members in our fellowship were individuals whom Saeed had met on the street and just spontaneously begun sharing the gospel with because the Spirit had told him to. Saeed would tell others how to do the same, mainly leading by example.

One night, after we attended the wedding of one of Saeed's cousins, we were driving back home with two of Saeed's sisters. It was about two o'clock in the morning, and all of us were exhausted after the all-day celebration. Suddenly, Saeed whipped the car around and, without warning, pulled into a back alley. I had been half asleep, but I sat up straight and tried to see what the emergency was that had caused Saeed to drive so erratically.

He pulled the car up beside a young woman who was obviously a prostitute. Prostitutes will often wear their *chador*—a black covering—inside out so that the seams are showing while they wait by curbs in back alleyways.

This woman had a line of cars in front of her, full of people waiting to negotiate prices. She had been holding out for the customer with the highest bid. Saeed rolled down the window and told her to jump into the back seat. Before she could answer, he shouted, "I'll pay whatever price you say; just get in."

Confused, she opened the back passenger car door and jumped in, and Saeed pulled away from the alley. When she saw three other women in the car, she was as shocked as we were. All the other cars with waiting customers had only one man in each vehicle and no other passengers, but Saeed already had three women in his car. It surely had to be one of the strangest things she had ever seen.

Now that she was in the back seat, we were able to see her more closely. She was wearing heavy makeup, old high-heeled shoes, and worn, tattered clothes. Her cheekbones were weathered, telling a story of a hard-lived life.

"Do you want out of this lifestyle?" Saeed asked her. "You don't have to do this. There is another way to live that you can have right now."

Before she could answer, a police car pulled up behind us. It was clearly a bust. The police had been watching the prostitute and wanted to see if anyone would pick her up. Prostitution was illegal in Iran—but preaching the gospel was a far bigger crime.

Saeed pulled his car over to the side of the road, and a police officer grabbed the prostitute and put her into the police car. One of the officers told me to get into the back seat of Saeed's car, and then he told Saeed to get into the front passenger seat. The officer then proceeded to drive the car to the local police station. Other police vehicles followed, creating a small convoy behind us as we drove through the streets of Tehran.

On the way to the police station, the officer began to question us. The first thing he asked was who we were and how we knew each other. When he heard that I was Saeed's fiancée, he jerked his head back to look at me and almost crashed the car. Confused, he asked, "And the other two in the back? Who are they?"

"They are my sisters," Saeed said with a sly smile, knowing that this was going to be an interesting night for the officer.

"No way!"

"No, it's true," I chirped.

The police officer shook his head in disbelief. "I have been doing this job for many years, my friend, and I have to tell you, I have never heard of anyone picking up a prostitute with his fiancée and sisters in the car. Why in the world would you do that?"

"Because she needs help. She is not getting help from the system in Iran. In Iran, she knows that her body is the only commodity she has to survive with. She has been reduced to a price. You guys can keep arresting her, but she is going to keep doing it because she needs the money to survive. Your way is not going to help her."

"Well, what would help her then?" the police officer asked.

"Jesus!" he said.

The officer swerved the car, almost wrecking it for the second time.

At that point, against his better judgment, Saeed started fearlessly sharing about Jesus with the police officer. After only a few moments, the officer pulled the car over to the side and stopped at the entrance to an alleyway. "You realize that you are evangelizing to me right now, right? We are now looking at charges for prostitution and proselytization. Do you want to go to jail for one or both?"

When the officer pulled his car over, all the other police cars pulled over as well. In the back seat, I was having an anxiety attack and silently praying, "Dear God, show me a sign that everything is going to be all right. Please help us and protect us."

As soon as I prayed that silent prayer, a little six- or seven-year-old boy opened my door on the back passenger side. He held up part of my dress, which had apparently been hanging outside of the closed door. I drew my body away from him, further into the backseat. I had no idea what he was doing. He handed me my dress, placing it in my lap. "Your dress, miss," he said in the sweetest little voice. "It was sticking out of the car." Then he looked up at me, and his eyes caught mine. "And I want you to know, everything is going to be all right."

He shut the door, and as quickly as he had appeared, he disappeared.

An unexplainable peace like I had never known before descended on me in that moment.

Almost immediately afterward, and without explanation, the police officer, breathing heavily through his nose as if he were about to say something he couldn't believe he was about to say, stated, "You know what? I am just going to let you guys go."

He called the other police officers in their vehicles over the radio and told them the same thing he had just told us.

This type of situation was normal life for Saeed. He was always preaching and sharing the gospel. He didn't have a manual, a special tactic, or a teachable system of evangelism. He just did it.

When I attended university, I had been considered the most evangelistic of the students in my fellowship group, wanting to reach the unreached, but now I felt so small in Saeed's shadow. My ability to preach the gospel to unreached people paled in comparison to his. I had never met anyone as bold as he when it came to sharing the gospel message. This is what attracted me the most to him and caused me to see past his flaws and, at times, the dark moments in our relationship. There was nothing I idolized more than seeing Muslims reached for Jesus.

Observing Saeed's focus on sharing the gospel, and witnessing his ability to do evangelistically what no one else was able to do, confirmed to me that he was the one I was supposed to spend the rest of my life with. I didn't want to do anything but stand by his side and help serve on the mission field of Iran. I knew that, together, there was nothing we could not do.

I became more resolute in my desire to marry him than I had ever been before. I lost all desire to do anything else in life. I didn't have time for friends, frivolous shopping, meticulous grooming, or extracurricular hobbies. I only had one thing on my mind, and that was to see the kingdom of God spread in Iran during our lifetime.

I no longer even had time for the job at Baba's company. Before Saeed and I were married, I stepped down and handed my position over to someone else. I wasn't saddened by this change. I knew it was time to move into what God had for us next.

20

ARRESTED AND TESTED

I am really scared. There are people surrounding my house. I think I am about to be arrested." It was early 2004, and Azim's voice shook in a quiet whimper on the other end of the phone. Azim was not in the habit of imagining dangerous situations. Because of his training with the terrorist group Hezbollah, Saeed knew that this could be a group of assassins sent by the government to murder Azim. Christian leaders had a history of being mysteriously murdered.

We knew that Azim was in serious danger and was looking for us to help him escape.

"Okay, stay there," Saeed said. "We are coming to bail you out."

"What can we do about the situation?" I asked. "Wouldn't it be easier for him to try to escape from his home when no one is looking?

"We have to try something," Saeed shot back. "We can't just leave him there! He is our friend, and he might die tonight. We have to do everything we can to get him out of there."

Saeed understood the danger more than anyone else. The time he had spent with Hezbollah had taught him how the group thought and how they operated on missions. If Jesus had not reached him, it is possible that Saeed would have been a trained killer with several dead pastors already as his trophies.

Saeed felt it would be better to try to rescue Azim at night rather than in the morning. At about midnight, we arrived at Azim's house in my car, which Saeed drove. I had just bought a new cheap Iranian-built vehicle, and when we pulled up to the curb and stopped the car, its brakes gave out a slight squeak. The sound seemed magnified in the dark night. We both sat motionless. I didn't know exactly what we were waiting for; I was just following Saeed's lead. He wasn't moving, so I, too, wasn't moving.

"Okay, let's go," he whispered. "Open your door slowly," he added as he cautiously pulled back on the latch. When we opened our car doors, they made a definitive clicking sound that echoed through the quiet. We gently closed the doors again.

The glow of the dome-shaped streetlight illuminated the cold night air and temporarily blinded us in the darkness. As we approached Azim's building, Saeed tiptoed swiftly to his front door and lightly rapped on the metal frame, in hopes that Azim would be able to hear the knock. We waited for a minute or two and didn't hear anything. Saeed looked back at me, and I shrugged my shoulders as if to say, "Now what?"

Saeed lifted his hand to rap on the door again, but before he was able to, we heard the sound of metal clicking on the other side of the door. Then there was silence again. Slowly, Azim opened the door a slight crack, and the whites of his eyes peered through it.

I instinctively gave him a happy wave, but as quickly as I did, I regretted it and pulled my hand down again, awkwardly putting it into my jacket pocket, feeling like a tourist. This was a situation where life and death possibly hung in the balance, not one that called for happy waves.

Azim opened the door wider to let us in.

Crack! Car doors slammed, and I heard the sound of loud, indiscriminate shouting. Before I had time to react, someone grabbed me and lifted my body off the ground.

"Saeed! Saeed!" I screamed—but there was no answer. All I could hear was my own voice and the voices of several unknown men telling me to shut up. Within seconds, they had put me into a car, and the tires screeched as we took off.

"Cover yourself up!" one man with a long beard as black as pitch yelled at me.

I could hear other tires squealing. I assumed they must be from additional cars that were following us.

"Saeed!" I yelled again, hoping he was nearby.

"Shut your mouth, or I will shut it for you," the voice of a strange man snarled.

Suddenly, my head was jerked back by someone's hand on my forehead, and a cloth was tightly wrapped around my head. We drove fast and erratically, and I was tossed around in the back seat like a rag doll, but I wasn't going anywhere. I was sandwiched between two mammoth-sized men sitting by each door, their muscular shoulders blocking any escape. Though they were deliberately not touching me because I was a woman, they made it clear that they wouldn't hesitate to hurt me.

Without warning, I was flung forward as the vehicle came to a screeching stop. The man to my right dragged me out of the car with such force that I wasn't sure where the ground was, but someone grabbed my other arm and stabilized me. My legs collapsed underneath me, but adrenaline kept me going until I was able to regain my footing.

The man on the right side removed my blindfold, and the one on the left shoved me in the back, throwing me forward, saying, "Move!"

"Saeed!" I yelled as soon as my eyes came into focus. I could see that he and Azim were being led out of two separate SUVs.

"Shut up!" yelled one of the men while jerking my arm as a warning not to speak again.

"Don't look around! Don't talk! Just move!" they commanded us.

We were being scuffled into a dirty white brick building that looked abandoned. As they steered us in, I could see that there were several rooms inside. They took me to a room on the right and plopped me into a lonely chair in the center, then began to pepper me with rapid-fire questions.

"How do you know this person? What were you doing at this house? What was your purpose of meeting tonight?"

Spittle saturated my face as the interrogator shouted question upon question without pausing for breath. All the questions were chained together so that they were almost indecipherable. Sounds were coming out of my mouth in response to their questions, but they were little more than grunts and groans mixed with tears, mucus, and slobber. I had nothing to offer but blubbery answers. My bladder was the only measurement of time as we moved into the early-morning hours. I needed to go to the bathroom, but they would not let me.

After they had turned my mind into a floppy noodle, one of the guards dragged me to another room, where I found myself sitting on a bench in front of a man wearing a tailored black suit with a finely pressed, white button-down shirt. All the guards spoke to him with a high level of respect. They snapped to obey his commands precisely when he ordered them to. It was unmistakable who was in charge.

Azim and Saeed were also brought in and ordered to sit on the bench on either side of me; we were flanked by masked guards armed with rifles, ensuring that we didn't try to escape. In front of us was a large wooden desk where the man in charge stood.

"Azim?" asked the man in the fine black suit. He peered over the paper he was reading and looked at all of us until Azim nodded in acknowledgement of his name. "Stand up, please, and come here." He pushed a piece of paper to the edge of the desk and repeatedly pounded it with his right index finger, hitting the desk with a loud thud each time.

"What is your religion?" he demanded.

"Shia," Azim responded without delay.

"Write your religion," the commanding officer said, pushing the paper toward him.

Azim got up, approached the desk, and stood still for a moment before bending over and writing down what he was instructed to write.

From the vantage point of my seat, I could see that Azim was writing the word "Shia."

"Shia?" I thought to myself. As if he could read my mind, Saeed leaned over to me slightly and whispered, "He's writing Shia Muslim."

I gulped so hard in the back of my throat that I was certain everyone in the room could hear it. I could see a dark replay of what had happened that day on the airplane when I flew into Iran. I had denied Christ once before on a simple immigration form. There was so much more at risk this time. Was I going to do it again?

"Okay, you can take a seat," the man said to Azim. "Next," he said, glancing over at me. "What is your religion? Come up and write your religion here on this paper."

I shuffled over to the desk and grabbed the pen, but before I started to write, the man interrupted me. "Now, you might say that you are a Christian, but if you write anything on this paper other than Muslim, you will be going to jail tonight. And let me tell you, you will not be going to jail with your fiancé over there. No, you will be going to a women's prison," he said with a bit of a nefarious cackle in his voice. "Do you know what they do to women in prison?" he asked rhetorically. "A girl like you, well, they would rape you and then leave you for dead. And, I promise you, if they don't kill you in prison, the government of Iran will. The punishment for apostasy in Iran is death. So, I would advise you to choose your words carefully."

Three years earlier, on a flight to Tehran, I had denied Christ on the immigration form in fear of possible arrest, imprisonment, and death. Now I was surrounded by radical revolutionary guards with guns pointed toward me and promises of rape, torture, and execution. What I feared was no longer a possibility—it was right in front of me.

"Jesus, please help me not to deny You again. I am so afraid," I prayed.

Everything within me wanted to do whatever I could to escape rape and torture, but I could not deny the precious name of Jesus a second time. With a shaky hand, I began to write. This one single word would decide my future. Would I be a denier of Jesus or an apostate of Islam?

I wrote my answer and placed the pen on the desk. My fate had been sealed. I had written what I had written. I couldn't take it back.

The interrogator looked at the paper and exhaled. "Okay," he said. "Your testimony is your death sentence. You have testified against yourself." He shook his head before looking up at me. "How? How did you become a Christian?"

I told him how my family had moved to America, how my brother had received a vision from Jesus, and how, from that, we had become Christians. The more I talked, the angrier he became.

"You were brainwashed by the Americans!" he shouted. "You were only nine years old; you didn't even know what you were doing," he said. "Your brain was not fully developed. You changed your religion before your brain was fully developed! Go and sit back down on the bench," he demanded.

I turned and sat down. As I sat there, his words about my being brainwashed in America were going through my head. The incongruity of his statement was not lost on me: he and several men with guns were threatening to have me raped and killed if I didn't write down that I was a Muslim, and yet he was angry that Christians in America had brainwashed me.

After I sat down, the man motioned for Saeed. Saeed walked over to the desk, picked up the pen, and confidently wrote the word that none of the interrogators expected him to write: "Christian." Saeed later told me that seeing how I stood up for my faith had given him the courage to write "Christian" as well.

The interrogator was taken aback. "How can you be a Christian?" he demanded.

"Let me tell you," Saeed replied. If Saeed was going to die, he was going to die giving everyone in the room that night the best presentation of the gospel they had ever heard. He wrapped his testimony in one of the most moving messages about Christ that I had ever heard. It wasn't a confession—it was a sermon.

When Saeed got to the part of his testimony where he said that he had been depressed and contemplating suicide, the senior officer behind the desk began to cry. He tried to stop crying but couldn't. The guards grew noticeably uncomfortable.

"Let's go to the courtyard," the officer said abruptly, trying to suppress the crack in his voice as he motioned to Saeed with his hand.

Azim and I had to remain seated while Saeed and the officer went into the back courtyard. We could see them through the window as they entered the yard and could hear part of their conversation.

Azim leaned over to me and whispered, "I really hope that Saeed is not evangelizing him. Let's pray against that, because we will die. We will die!"

We closed our eyes to intercede for Saeed, and I heard Azim praying, "Oh, God, please close his mouth. Don't let him get us killed."

I couldn't help chuckling to myself at Azim's prayer. He didn't realize that I kept peeking at what was happening in the courtyard, and I could see Saeed talking passionately with the officer, who was listening intently. I knew full well that Saeed was indeed evangelizing!

When Saeed and the commanding officer returned, the officer was in tears, and the guards had a look of shock on their faces.

"You guys just go," the commander said, waving his hands for us to leave. "Just go. Get out of here and go back home." He turned away and covered his face. "Call your parents or friends or whoever and have them come pick you up."

As we were leaving, the officer asked, "Can you guys get me a Bible?"

Saeed paused, made eye contact with him, and said, "Sure thing."

21

THE WEDDING

Our wedding was planned for June 30, 2004. I had wanted it to be on July 3—the same day as my parents' wedding anniversary—but it didn't work out because local holidays interfered with the scheduling.

The explosive church growth we were seeing was garnering international attention, and large international ministries around the world were suddenly curious about Saeed's work with the underground house church.

Baba invited the Christian Broadcasting Network (CBN) to our wedding, and they jumped at the idea. No one had ever filmed a Christian wedding in Iran, and CBN decided they could do a story on the revival in Iran in connection with our wedding.

CBN had front-row seats to one of the most fascinating stories in modern-day Iranian weddings. When we applied for our marriage license, the Iranian officials knew by looking at our names alone that we were born Muslim, but we applied as Christians, and the certificate was approved. We were among only a very few couples in Iran that we knew of who were given this right.

We also applied for permission to have a Christian wedding instead of an Islamic wedding at the local mosque. I couldn't imagine being forced to be married at a mosque. Again, our application was miraculously approved. The Iranian government had not only recognized our conversion from Islam to Christianity, but they had also approved us to be united under the name of Jesus. This was indeed a miracle. We never believed we would see the day in Iran when we would be approved for a Christian wedding in a church, but we had the certificates in front of us, and we were ecstatic.

It was clear that God was doing a new thing in Iran. It was a new day, and we were a new generation of believers.

Saeed and I didn't want our wedding day to be just about our relationship with one another. We wanted it to be a day of celebrating our love of Christ for the nations. We wanted to see the country of Iran transformed, and we wanted our wedding to be a part of that effort.

The celebration lasted for two days. The night before the ceremony, we invited the CBN crew and other believers to join us for a house church meeting, where we worshipped together into the night. My parents hosted the meeting four floors underground in the parking garage of their apartment building, and the room where we met was filled with house church members who had slowly arrived throughout the day so as not to draw the attention of the Iranian revolutionary guards. Some of the guests had arrived early in the morning and had waited in the underground garage until others from the house churches arrived later in the evening. Everyone was standing shoulder to shoulder as we sang, danced, and prayed together.

Wearing khaki pants, a short-sleeved white shirt, and light-brown suspenders, Saeed paced back and forth under the round, golden ceiling lights preaching a message of salvation and victory. He often had to dodge the raised hands of someone who was lost in prayer, but he kept his cadence and stride.

With hands lifted high, Baba was emotional, not just because I was getting married but because he, too, could see that God was doing something new in Iran.

That night, it felt like the worship could go on forever. We couldn't turn it off. There was no switch we could flip or button we could push to make us all more palatable for the public when we left the next day after the time of worship at my father's house. The excitement lingered in our spirits and teased us endlessly with the idea of having more—more of His grace, more of His glory, more of His presence.

Saeed and I arrived at the church next day in a sleek, nickel-colored car with an array of roses on the hood and green branches knotted together with white ribbon on the door handles. I stepped out of the car feeling like a princess in my modern strapless wedding dress. Although it was the most illegal dress I had ever worn in Iran, it had actually been made in Iran. Women can get away with a little more on their wedding day, but my dress pushed the limits. The banded bodice neckline featured detailed touches of elegant grandeur, and the dress dropped down from a flattering tight waistline into a flared skirt that went all the way to the ground. The dress designer spent a lot of time on a vertical pattern from the waist to the top of the bustline that wrapped around under my arms and then dropped in the back in a plunging V. My bare shoulders would have been scandalous to any dress code enforcement officer in Tehran, if he had seen me.

My veil was traced in sparkles of silver, which I accented by wearing classic pearl earrings that dangled above my dainty necklace, which was only visible close-up. My hair was parted on the side, and I wore it up with a tight bun in the back. I carried a bouquet of white flowers to signify purity as I walked down the aisle.

Saeed was right in step with me—his shirt, jacket, pants, and shoes were all white. The only thing he wore that was not white was his vintage black bow tie.

The church was packed with our families and church members. Pastor Bob from Calvary Chapel in Boise, Idaho, was there and spent time with us in prayer. During the wedding ceremony, he asked Saeed and me to get on our knees as he prayed over our lives and dedicated our marriage before God.

Azim, who had become a famous music composer in Iran, wrote original music for our wedding and led an accompanied choir. Their angelic voices filled the room as they sang songs of praise during our procession.

Some of the guests grew restless when they heard that the Iranian Revolutionary guards were gathering outside. There was a rumor that they were going to raid the church at any moment, but the Spirit of the Lord had fallen so strongly that I didn't care. If we were arrested for praising the Lord too loudly on our wedding day, then that would be a great way for Saeed and me to start our life together.

The guards outside continued to grow in number, but they were not showing any signs of raiding our wedding, so we didn't stop the ceremony. The more guards that gathered outside, the more the Spirit poured out on us inside.

At the reception, as gifts to our guests, we passed around both wrapped Bibles and *The Jesus Film*. Even if every guest already had a Bible or had seen *The Jesus Film*, the idea was that they could take them and pass them on to others. We wanted everything about the wedding to be about the Great Commission.

With the level of excitement people were feeling, things soon grew out of control. Someone hung up a disco ball and flashing lights in the main hall of the church, which had never been done before. People started dancing, and we all demanded that the music be turned up to full volume. We wanted the guards outside to hear us. If they were going to storm the church, we didn't want them to find a scared and shivering group of believers. We wanted them to arrest the most joyous group of offenders they had ever encountered.

Bubble makers were passed around, and the entire place was filled with glistening, bouncing spheres that floated in the air until they burst under their own weight. As the bubbles drifted, the wedding guests started to do the train dance, in which guests hang on to the hips of the person in front of them and parade around, dancing together in a long line.

The pastor of the church made an early exit. It was clear he was not comfortable with some of the activities he was seeing. The church elders did not approve of the lights, disco ball, and dancing.

The guards never raided our church that night, but there might have been some elders of the church who wished they had. That would have been easier for them to explain to the congregation than why there was dancing.

After our wedding, the church posted a sign with an updated list of guidelines those holding weddings should follow. The list said, "No dancing allowed."

22

HONEYMOON FROM HELL

After the wedding, Saeed and I flew to western Turkey for our honeymoon. We had thought about going on a European cruise together, but we couldn't get a visa for Saeed to enter Europe. Due to the numerous sanctions against Iran, there were many countries where Iranians could not travel, but Turkey was one of the few nations that was willing to give him a visa. I had much more leeway with my American citizenship.

As a wedding gift, Baba had arranged with a travel agent for us to go on a five-star tour of the sites of the seven churches of Revelation.[11] The two of us were going to have a weeklong biblical pilgrimage. The agent had booked the best hotels along the way that were set in the middle of the ancient cities we would visit, overlooking Roman amphitheaters, temples, and baths.

As soon as we arrived in Turkey, I could tell that something was off with Saeed. We were on our honeymoon, yet he brooded, moped, and indicated he wasn't excited to be with me. I knew he felt out of place not being able to speak the language or understand what was happening around him.

In Iran, he was the confident leader. He knew the people, understood the culture, and was respected among his peers. But, in Turkey, he was just another foreigner from Iran. I spoke English, and everywhere we went was set up primarily for American tourists, so English was the main second language that many of the local workers spoke. From the very beginning, it was clear that Saeed didn't like to be dependent on someone else, so I decided to be gentle and try to encourage him.

Our first night in Turkey was not passionate at all; we didn't touch each other. I chalked it up to exhaustion. Saeed had preached for hours the day

---

11. See Revelation 2–3.

before our wedding and had spent more time ministering than paying attention to the ceremony. I was emotionally drained from all the excitement that had taken place over the course of our forty-eight-hour wedding celebration.

We were both running on empty; still, I was concerned that Saeed's lack of interest in me was something more than fatigue or the discomfort of being in a different culture. Something was wrong that went deeper, although I couldn't fully identify it. I had never seen him in this state before, and it was alarming. It's true there had been some dark moments during our courtship, but I had kept pushing them aside. Seeing so many Muslims become followers of Jesus was most important, and Saeed and I worked well together. But now those dark moments were coming back to me.

The next morning, when the tour started, we saw that about twenty other tourists would be joining us. They were all English-speaking Europeans and Americans. The tour guide spoke only in English, so I translated for Saeed.

Throughout the day, I kept secretly reminding Saeed that our first night of being man and wife would be a special one that neither of us would ever forget. I hoped it would cheer him up and make him happy, but it didn't. He shrugged it off as if it didn't matter to him at all.

When we returned to the hotel, I tried to set the mood by flirting with him, but from the moment we entered our room, he started to do things that physically hurt me. He had never grabbed me hard, as he did that night. At first, I was confused and thought that maybe he hadn't meant to hold my arm as tightly as he did, but after a minute, I realized he wasn't loosening his grip.

He pulled me over to the bed and shoved me down onto the mattress. I was confused as to what was going on until I saw that he was getting undressed.

I thought, "This is the way we are doing this?" Of all the ways I had imagined our honeymoon would play out, this was not one of them.

Saeed proceeded to push against me as he pulled off my clothing in a painful manner. "Saeed, that hurts," I protested playfully, hoping he would be more gentle, but he only grew more aggressive.

"Seriously, that hurts," I said again, this time less playful, in hopes that he would understand I was not joking—that he would realize he was stronger than he thought and what he was doing was really hurting me.

His eyes burned with anger as if he were about to enter a fight. I was instantly terrified. "Saeed, please, you are scaring me. Stop being so rough. Please."

His response was that maybe I needed a drink so I could relax.

The more I begged him to stop being so rough, the more aggressive he grew. I tried to wriggle free, but he pinned me down, completely restraining me.

Then he forced himself on me.

There was nothing about what he did that felt romantic or loving. I didn't know this Saeed. This was not the Saeed I had slept beside and shared foreplay with night after night in Tehran.

I lay on the bed, crying. Saeed was emotionless. His face was stone-cold, showing no remorse or empathy for me.

The next day, Saeed and I continued the tour, but our arguments grew. No one else in the group spoke Farsi, but they could tell we were not having friendly conversations. Our negative interactions were impacting the entire group. I could see that people were growing impatient with us.

For one of the legs of the tour, I had booked a special cruise aboard a small vessel that would take us to some of the most remote islands in Turkey. I figured that, since we hadn't been able to book a European cruise, this would be the next best thing. We shared the ship with some other tourists from Europe.

The Turkish cruise vessel was nothing fancy, but it had small rooms onboard for us to sleep in at night. Soon after we boarded, Saeed started yelling at me, calling me names. Because the boat was small, it was obvious everyone could hear him. No one could understand what he was saying, but they could tell the tone was not good.

During the lulls in his tirades, no other sounds could be heard. I strained to hear if the other guests were talking with one another, but it seemed they had all been disturbed into silence by Saeed's fits of rage.

"Excuse me," a kind lady with a German or Swiss accent said to us at one point, interrupting Saeed mid-insult. She had come down from the upper deck, obviously bothered by the shouting.

I was unable to look her in the eyes, but I tearfully glanced in her direction with shame on my face. I knew we were ruining her vacation time.

"Excuse me," she said again, trying to get my attention directly. Although she was a petite woman, she didn't seem afraid to confront Saeed. Standing firmly, with her feet shoulder-width apart, she didn't tell him to shut up, but her mere presence communicated to him that she was not the kind of person who could easily be pushed around.

"Do you need help?" she asked me. Her delivery was firm, direct, and without fear. For a moment, she reminded me of my mother. I looked up, and her caring eyes connected with mine.

I shook my head no, unable to speak.

"Are you certain?" she persisted, knowing I was not telling the truth. She knew I needed help. The entire boat knew I needed help.

"I don't know what is going on here, but if you need any help, we are here. We are not going to spend this entire time on this boat listening to someone be treated like you are right now." When she finished speaking, she stared at Saeed. It was almost as if she were daring him to say something. She was visually holding words back.

Saeed got the point. He never raised his voice on that trip again, not on the boat and not anywhere else. Yet when I tried to reach out to him and reconcile with him, he rejected me. I tried hard to make some kind of connection with him, but he was completely removed emotionally. He showed no affection.

When we would board a bus or a ferry with the other tour group members, he would purposefully take a seat away from me. When I tried to talk to him, he would ignore me. There was just no reaching him.

At night, when we retired to our room, I would again try to talk to him and ask what was going on. I was seriously lost and confused. If I had done something wrong, I wanted to fix it, but I couldn't fix it if I didn't know what needed to be fixed.

"Please talk to me," I begged.

"I just need to be left alone. Can you understand that? Can you just give me a break?"

I didn't say anything in response, but I thought, "A break? On our honeymoon?" We remained strangers during the remainder of our time in Turkey.

"It'll get better when we return home to Iran," I thought to myself.

23

BEGGING FOR LOVE

As soon as we got off the plane in Tehran after our honeymoon, Saeed pretended that nothing had happened in Turkey. When our friends asked about our trip, Saeed smiled and told them how great the experience was. I smiled with him and repeated the story.

Saeed and I had rented an apartment of our own in the middle of Tehran, not far from the official church. We wanted to be close to the university campus so the students wouldn't have to travel far when they came to our home for discipling. Baba had helped us secure a location that was perfect for our ministry. We had shopped for furniture before our wedding, and the furniture was waiting for us when we arrived home.

I wanted to discuss with Saeed what had happened on our honeymoon. I needed him to know that the things he had said to me were hurtful and had wounded me in a deep way, but he just wanted to move on. I realized that if I continued to bring up the topic, I would be dragging him into a conversation he didn't want to have. I convinced myself that forcing Saeed into a discussion like that would only be counterproductive.

So, I started to suppress what I was feeling. I persuaded myself that his verbal attacks on my character and looks were not hateful; they were just his way of communicating. I satisfied my thoughts by arguing against the need for romance in my life. "I don't need to fall in love like they do in the movies. I need a partner to serve with on the mission field, someone I can build a life with in preaching the gospel to the unreached." I looked for inspiration in Amy Carmichael, an Irish missionary to India who never married and launched a ministry that is still operating more than a hundred years after she started it.

Saeed was not perfect, but, in my eyes, his passion for ministry and talent covered a multitude of sins. He was the man I had chosen to be with for the rest of my life, and I was not going to give up on our marriage.

With all the problems we were having in our relationship, I was able to find ongoing comfort in the fact that the church continued to grow. New believers were joining the fellowship from every walk of life. There were former Muslims, like Saeed and me—even children of mullahs and other Islamic leaders. There were people from the Baha'i faith, a religion that started in Iran and essentially teaches that all religions and all people are united in purpose. There were doctors, professors, businesspeople, and former prostitutes.

After we returned from Turkey, I took a short trip to the United States to meet with potential supporters who were interested in partnering with Saeed and me in our work in Iran. Thousands of Iranians were watching Christian programs by satellite and getting saved, but they didn't know where to go for fellowship or discipleship afterward. This was a growing problem for Iranian ministries based in the UK and the US. Although they were seeing people respond, they were unable to provide them with practical help on a local level. One ministry in particular that broadcast Christian programming in Iran via satellite was keen to work with us. Saeed and I agreed to partner with this ministry by connecting their viewers with people on the ground in Iran.

Saeed and I were good at connecting with people and could lead an effort to bring new believers into the fellowship. I had an incredible feeling of being connected in Iran—where my life was now firmly planted. The nation from which my parents had fled was now the nation I called home and where I would one day raise my own children. My parents had left as Muslims, but now I had returned as a Christian missionary.

It was not long before I discovered I was pregnant with twins. I was thrilled about this news because I was also a twin. Unfortunately, I lost the babies at ten weeks. I was told they hadn't attached well to my uterus.

After that, I lost a lot of weight and was skinnier than I had ever been. All the work I was doing in ministry, the fast pace of my life, and the absence of a real relationship with Saeed contributed to a lack of appetite. It didn't help knowing that Saeed and I might be arrested at any time for our ministry activities. But, more than anything, it was losing my babies that contributed to my weight loss. I could feel myself slowly descending into depression. Food just did not appeal to me, and I wasn't able to sleep well, even though I was always tired.

Saeed still did not express any excitement about being with me. He wasn't romantic in any way. He would regularly leave for long mission trips to other parts of Iran. To him, it didn't seem to be a big deal to be away from me for weeks. There had been a time during our courtship when he would have protested at being away from me for even a few hours. Now, several weeks could go by without his appearing to notice my absence. He had seemed infatuated with me when we were dating, but now almost nothing I did could grab his attention.

I noticed that I wasn't the only thing Saeed was losing interest in. Activities that had previously excited him no longer appealed to him. At the beginning, he had seemed enthusiastic about our recently launched small-size house church structure, but after we had held several meetings in our home with only about ten people in attendance, his enthusiasm declined.

I hadn't realized it when we first initiated the idea of running smaller home groups in a greater number of locations, but I soon understood that Saeed had no interest in leading only small groups of people. Every month, we would hold larger meetings where we would have approximately a hundred people come together. Those were the meetings he was excited about.

With a small-group setting, the work was more personal. Students and others would often come to our house by themselves or in groups of two or three to be trained in discipleship, which is what we had hoped would happen when we rented our house in the middle of the city. But, after a few months, Saeed was no longer attentive to this type of ministry either.

As his interest level in these activities was decreasing, my workload was growing bigger. New believers from various areas would show up at our door for training. At these times, I would often be cooking, cleaning, or working around the house, so I would welcome them in and go tell Saeed, but he would not be concerned enough about training them to even get out of bed. So, I would host them and conduct their discipleship training myself.

When I had first come to Iran as a single woman, I had been taught by the church that a woman was not permitted to lead other believers unless she was teaching women. One of the reasons I had felt that I had to get married was so I could legitimately do house church ministry. Because Saeed had little interest in discipling or teaching the house church members and leaders but only wanted to be involved in the larger gatherings where he could pray for people and see dramatic results, I ended up teaching the members of the house churches using the same discipleship methods I had used with the women I had first taught. And, I was not only discipling leaders but also managing the finances and structure of the house churches. Although, as a woman, I was afraid to be in a position of authority in the church, thinking that God would be angry with me if I did, in reality, I was already leading the churches under the name of "pastor's wife."

I have since found it interesting that in a culture heavily influenced by Islam and male dominance, the majority of house church leaders in Iran are now women—and the men have no problem with that. This is truly a miracle. It has drawn many Muslim women to the house churches—and to Jesus Christ—because of their high regard for women.

The visitors who came to our house for discipleship were perplexed by Saeed's indifferent behavior. He would sleep until the afternoon. Then, when he would stumble into the living room from the bedroom and see them for the first time, he would not engage with them. He had lost all motivation and ambition for ministering in this way.

I finally told him I was tired of doing all the cooking and cleaning plus the training. I asked him to get out of bed so that our guests could at least see him from time to time. "These people are here to be trained, and then they are going to go back to their city. This is not fair to them."

He merely grunted in response.

I was starting to recognize that Saeed liked shiny new toys, and once they were not new anymore, he would merely set them aside. It was the same with both people and things. I was an old used object, of little value or importance to him.

The most torturous thing Saeed did to me was to continue ignoring me. He was a master of giving me the silent treatment for days and acting as if I didn't exist to him at all. When I crawled in bed next to him at night, he would not acknowledge I was even alive. I grew incredibly lonely and vulnerable and would have done anything to have a conversation with him.

"Please talk to me, Saeed. I am begging you," I said to him one day, trying to break the ice after a long period of being ignored. "I am literally begging you. What do I need to do to end this? You name it—I will do anything."

"'Begging'?" he inquired without looking at me.

"Begging," I answered, happy to at least have received some kind of response. I could see that the word had gotten his attention. It was powerful enough to break the silence.

I smirked. It seemed good that he was at least being playful with me again, but when I looked at his face, I realized he was not joking. He liked hearing the word *begging*. His expression communicated that begging would be a form of penance that would satisfy him.

I immediately scoffed to myself at the idea of actually begging. "There is no way I am getting on my knees and kissing the feet of any man," I thought. "That will never happen! I am not a beggar."

Then, almost immediately afterward, a wave of insanity wafted over me, and I saw a demented opportunity to show Saeed how much he meant to me. In that glimmer of a second, in terms that no feminist would ever understand, I saw a window of openness in his eyes. What he was requiring went against my whole being, but I was desperate. If I could do something small, no matter how psychopathic, to show him how much he meant to me and win his affection, then I was going to do it.

I could either spend several years of misery in our marriage arguing with Saeed about how wrong he was to even insinuate that I should beg, or I could close my eyes, indulge this one maniacal request for only a few moments, and bring everything back to the way it had once been between us. If humiliating myself before him by getting on my knees and kissing his feet was symbolic of the begging he was looking for, and if it would give me what I wanted, then I was more than willing to do it.

When I understood that Saeed was serious, I didn't hesitate. I dropped to my knees, crawled over to him, and began kissing his feet. From the floor, I looked up at him to see if my penance was acceptable to him. I don't know what I expected his reaction to be. I think part of me half expected him to finally recognize the love I had for him and quickly lift me off the ground and tell me how much he loved me and how moved he was by my devotion to him—but that is not what happened.

Instead, he remained standing. I could see a gaze of satisfaction on his face as he took delight in watching me grovel. He showed no empathy for my humiliation. In fact, there was an air about him that seemed to indicate he was finally getting what he was entitled to. In that moment, I realized I had taken on a role he had been expecting of me all along. It was a role in which I didn't care anything about my own happiness but was completely focused on his. I realized he had not been punishing me for anything I had done. He was punishing me for *who I was*. He needed to break me—like the breaking of a wild horse so that it could be trained to do what he wanted.

He walked away, leaving me on my knees. He didn't open up to me as he had indicated he would do. He didn't even acknowledge what I had done for him.

I swore to myself that it would never happen again.

I was wrong.

24

FALLING APART

After much prayer, we decided to go to ten cities in only ten days and to start ten churches. In most of the cities, we had no contacts, no plan, no strategy, and only about the equivalent of a hundred US dollars with which to conduct our ministry over those ten days. We didn't even have money to stay in a hotel in each city, but we knew the Lord would provide for us. We were following the leading of God's Spirit to visit the believers in these cities and disciple them. The cities we focused on were Qazvin, Rasht, Ardabil, Tabriz, Urmia, Sanandaj, Kermanshah, Khoramabad, Arak, and Hamedan.

Each day, Saeed would drive the ministry team to a new city. We would go to the highest point of that city, where we could view the entire area, and we would pray over it and bind the evil spirits there. After taking the "high ground" of the city, like a military commander, we would pray for the Lord to lead us to divine appointments. We would pace the city together, silently praying for the people and their salvation until God would speak to us about whom to approach.

Saeed's method seemed simple, but following it took an extreme faith that some people were not comfortable with. We had to put our trust in the Lord, and that is what we did. It was a true joy to watch the various ways in which He supplied what we needed.

In the city of Urmia, about halfway through our trip, Saeed did have a contact, so we didn't think we would have to worry about finding accommodations there. We arrived in Urmia late at night. It was raining very hard, making it difficult to drive. The visibility was poor, obscuring the road ahead, so we ran over a rock and got a flat tire. The person we were supposed to stay with ended up backing out at the last minute. On that portion of our trip, we had to spend our full budget of hundred dollars on two hotel rooms, fuel for travel, and fixing the flat tire. The one city where we had relied on ourselves—trusting in having somewhere to stay lined up ahead of time, and not feeling the need to depend on the Lord for our provision—was the only city that cost us all the money we had brought with us. This was a lesson that we learned the hard way, and the team often talked about it afterward.

But every time we stepped out in faith, we would see God work. He never left us alone, in the cold, homeless, or without food. We were supernaturally guided and provided for. Without fail, God would lead Saeed to speak with someone, and, before long, he would be praying with them and leading them to Christ. The new believers in the city would immediately become disciples, and a fellowship would be launched. One time, an entire group of young college students gave their hearts to Christ at the same time.

Saeed's actions were in line with his idea of what an apostle would do. He truly believed that he was the apostle of Iran and trusted that he could simply be led by God's Spirit.

Our ministry trip of planting ten churches in ten days with only a hundred dollars in our pocket caught the attention of international ministries. No one had heard of such a thing being done before, and they were blown away by Saeed's church-planting efforts.

My uncle in California, who had baptized me when I was a little girl, loved what God was doing in Iran, and he provided a salary to sustain the church-planting work. His ministry in the US started to give us regular financial support. In the beginning, this seemed like an answer to prayer. We didn't realize then how damaging this financial support from outside Iran would be to the house church.

The nature of the outside support ultimately led to one of the two biggest challenges resulting in division within the house church: greed. We implemented a discipleship program called the G12 Vision. The G12 Vision is a Christian evangelism and discipleship strategy based on a system of hierarchy. The program is founded on the idea of systematically multiplying disciples and creating a pay structure according to the number of people being discipled. It quickly became the largest discipleship program in Iran.

The way it works is that someone in a similar role to what the apostle Paul had in the first century would essentially choose twelve "Timothies"[12] to

12. See Acts 16:1–5.

disciple, and those twelve Timothies would plant churches and raise up twelve more Timothies who would do the same.

Both the "Pauls" and the "Timothies" in the program would be paid for their work in the ministry, but the Pauls would be paid a considerably larger amount of money than the Timothies—until the Timothies had their own mentees and became Pauls themselves.

Thus, your pay would increase depending on how big your network was. This idea of increased pay according to your number of followers provided an incentive for people to skew numbers, double-claim members, and incorporate members who were not even Christians. The system soon caused splits among the fellowships, with leaders fighting over which members belonged to which fellowship. This changed the entire dynamic of the house church.

The second challenge that began to split the church was Saeed's pride. He grew to be self-destructive. He was an emotional wrecking ball. He would get in an angry mood, and everyone who strayed in his path was subjected to his outbursts. He interacted with his leaders as if he were a ticking time bomb. He would deal harshly with appointed leaders and assistant pastors, often lashing out at people for no reason, and he would kick individuals out of the fellowship. It seemed that Saeed was butting heads with his own leaders every other week. Several people who had served with us left the fellowship; they had been loyal to Saeed, but they had their limits. It was hard for them to stay around and allow themselves to be treated badly for reasons that were not understandable or explainable.

I tried to serve as a buffer between Saeed and these leaders, attempting to both calm Saeed down and persuade him to treat people in a nicer way. I knew this was needed, and I sought to convince him of it for his own sake.

When Saeed treated a leader badly, I would approach the leader privately and try to persuade them to stay, telling them how much Saeed *really* loved them and how we needed them.

Cleaning up Saeed's relationship messes turned into a full-time job for me. Sometimes, I was not able to intervene in time to do damage control, such as when Saeed would perform church discipline on one of the leaders in front of the entire fellowship. There were times when he would publicly call people names in front of the entire group. At one point, he shamed a brother in our fellowship for allowing his wife to wear clothing Saeed felt was too revealing. It was a shocking moment that could not be covered up or made better in any way.

Perhaps the saddest fallout of all was with our longtime friend Azim. Saeed never let him live down the time when he had written "Shia" as his religion during our interrogation. He talked about it every opportunity he got.

Azim was one of the top leaders, had been tremendously loyal to Saeed, and would do anything for him. He was an extremely effective evangelist and brought many young people into the church. When Saeed put Azim down in front of the people who were loyal to him, many of those people broke their bonds with Azim.

After that first interrogation, Azim had been arrested many times, thrown into prison, beaten, and even given the death sentence, but he had never again denied Christ. Yet Saeed would not allow him to forget the one time when he had denied Christ. He was always shaming him for it, so, eventually, Azim left the fellowship.

The house church in Iran continued to grow, but we never fully recovered from these two splits.

25

THE BEATING

My relationship with Saeed was still going badly. He had largely continued not to show any interest in me. He ignored me more often than not and seemed to prefer being away on trips to staying at home.

Added to this, Saeed was being arrested by the police more and more, and he was even jailed a number of times, although he had not yet been put into prison. I had been detained with him on more than one occasion, but most of the time when he was arrested, I was not with him. We didn't want to be paranoid, but it was clear that our increased church activity was prompting the government to monitor us more closely.

Toward the end of 2005, we received a notice from the court saying that Saeed had to appear before the magistrate in person on November 19.

The letter didn't say why he had to appear, and we knew that it might be for anything. It didn't necessarily mean that he needed to stand before the court because of something he had done while engaging in ministry.

We decided to show the letter to Pastor Aram. He would have a better idea about what it meant.

"This is a big deal," Pastor Aram said after taking a look at it. "It is from the Revolutionary Court, which means that you are being summoned for religious crimes." He exhaled out of his nose and then glanced back down at the paper again. Shaking his head, he blurted out, "Saeed, I am sorry to say this, but you are most likely going to be arrested."

"No!" I shouted. I couldn't imagine Saeed in jail. "Pastor Aram, what should we do?"

He looked at me and then back at Saeed. "Have you considered leaving Iran?" he asked. "It might be time, because if you wait until the court date, it could be too late. They might not have any travel restrictions on you yet. Your name might not yet be on the blacklist in the immigration system, which means that you should be able to travel. If there was ever a time for you to leave Iran, it is now. This window will surely close after your court date."

We had known the time might come when we would need to leave Iran, but we hadn't thought it would come this soon. We had so much more ministry to do, and the church was growing in ways we had never imagined. It was a nightmare for us to think about leaving when things in the fellowship were developing so fast.

After meeting with Pastor Aram, we decided that one thing we could do was to ease up on our interactions with the believers. We needed to protect them and the network of churches that had formed in the various cities, and we needed to protect ourselves. We knew things overall were getting more intense with security in Iran. More believers were being arrested than previously, and, because of our role in the church, we were being watched more than ever and were being followed by the police. Our partners needed to know what to do in our absence if we were to leave the country, which meant we were going to have to take some risks to prepare others for our departure.

I was not feeling well, but I had blamed it on the stress of the letter and the events that were transpiring because of it. My stomach was constantly in knots, and I hadn't been eating well. I felt sick every day. I began to suspect that I might be pregnant again.

We decided that the best thing to do would be to fly to Dubai, wait for Saeed's American visa, and then fly to the US. It felt like a good plan—one that might be good enough to keep Saeed out of jail. My uncle in California knew some Southern Baptist missionaries who had an apartment we could use during our time in Dubai as we waited for the visa.

We weren't completely certain we could make it out of Iran. There was a very strong possibility that the immigration officers would see Saeed's name show up in their database with a travel prohibition and prevent him from leaving the country.

When we arrived at the airport in Tehran, we silently prayed the entire time we were standing in line at the immigration area. We knew many of our church members were praying for us, as well as our families, and their prayers were answered because the immigration officer who processed us didn't even flinch when he stamped our passports and allowed us to go through.

When our flight landed in Dubai, I was exhausted. A beautiful young woman was waiting at the gate to pick us up. She was an American missionary and would take us to the apartment where we would be staying.

"The Internet service is not working right now," she said as she drove, pulling her hair behind her ear so that it would not block her view of me as we talked. "But I will return in the morning to have it turned on. You are free to live at the apartment for as long as you need, but, during your time, please be certain to pay the fees for the Internet, gas, and electricity." She paused for effect and continued, "And be sure to feed the pet iguana...everything else is paid for, so you don't have to worry."

Her non-melodic, Midwestern American accent instantly brought me back home to Idaho in a way that I had thought only a familiar song from my youth or the smell of certain American foods could do. I had not heard an American voice speaking English for a long time, and I didn't even know I had missed it until that moment. Something about the woman's presence immediately made me feel like I was at home. I wanted to hug her for simply being an American—and I might have if she hadn't been driving.

"You might want to get a Dubai SIM card so that you can use your phone without paying high fees for international roaming. There is a little shop down the road from the apartment that has SIM cards you can purchase. I can help you find it if needed." I nodded with a smile, barely remembering anything she said because of my fatigue.

When we arrived at the apartment, I just wanted to go to bed, so I put my suitcase on top of the bed to look for my pajamas. Saeed had packed our suitcases, as he usually did. We had needed to fit as much as possible into each bag, and he was more efficient at packing than I was. Everything that we now owned was in those suitcases. Not knowing if or when we would ever return to Iran, we had given away everything in our apartment to the house church members. I had told people to just come and take anything they wanted, and they did. We had almost nothing left.

Since Saeed had packed everything, I didn't really know where anything was, so with the suitcase on the edge of the bed, I rummaged through the layers inside looking for my pajamas.

"You are making a mess," Saeed protested, upset that I was disheveling his neatly packed bags.

"Who cares?" I said in a tired, flippant voice.

Bam! A hard blow hit my face from out of nowhere. I fell to the floor and lay there, limp. Looking up, not yet knowing what was happening, I suddenly felt feet kicking my head and stomach and anywhere else I could not manage to cover with my arms and hands. I realized Saeed had flown off in a rage of unbridled anger.

He paused his kicking only to pound me with his fists, while I crawled into a fetal position, trying to protect myself. I instinctively screamed out, begging him to stop, but he was in a blind fury. He couldn't seem to hear a thing. He didn't say anything to me; he only grunted in anger. He was like a wild beast with swinging fists.

After a few moments of fury, there was a lull. I didn't know why he had stopped hitting me. Was he stopping altogether, or was he just pausing long enough to grab something to beat me with further? Either way, I was desperate to get away from him. Like a panicked, wounded animal, I pulled myself along the floor to the bathroom, digging my fingers into anything that would allow me to have enough grip to drag my body forward.

I was convinced I was going to die. I wasn't thinking of anything other than survival. Every cell in my body was telling me to hang on for my life—and to hang on for the life I now knew was growing inside me.

I made my way to the open door of the bathroom, pulled myself across the threshold, slammed the door shut, locked it, and sat up with my back against the door. Then I yelled for help and screamed as loudly as I could, hoping that someone, somewhere, would be able to hear me.

I called my mother—the only person I knew who would understand my pain. She immediately began trying to think of ways she could help from a distance. Since she was currently in Idaho, there was not much she could do. She was several thousand miles away, with an ocean between us.

Hearing her voice made me wish she were with me at that moment. If she were there, with her military training and extensive experience in martial arts, I knew I would not have to be a victim to Saeed. But my mother was not with me to protect me, and I was not my mother—I was me.

However, speaking with her helped to calm me down. My mother agreed to call Saeed and try to talk to him. She wanted to settle him down, not knowing what he would do to me in a country where men had a great deal of power. After we hung up, I could hear Saeed talking on the phone, and I assumed he was speaking with my mother. The air around me seemed to become lighter as I heard his voice soften after only a few moments.

Then the bedroom became quiet. I still didn't want to come out of the bathroom. I continued to lean against the door, trying to hear any kind of movement, but I heard nothing. I finally drifted off to sleep listening to the silence.

After what felt like a couple of hours, I awoke and reached up to the sink to pull myself to a standing position and look in the mirror. I needed to get a visual of where all the throbbing pain on my face and head was coming from. When I looked into the mirror, all I saw was a deformed monster staring back at me. In that moment, I remembered the *Tom and Jerry* cartoons I had watched as a child, in which Tom would get hit on the head, and a large lump would appear. It had seemed so funny when I was little, but now I was watching actual lumps extend from my face and head.

I slumped back down onto the bathroom floor, sobbing. I called my mother again. I didn't know what else to do. After several hours, my mother convinced me to leave the bathroom. She had talked with Saeed and promised me that it would all be okay.

I slowly opened the bathroom door and crept into the bedroom. I saw Saeed sitting on the side of the bed with his head in his hand. Without looking at me, he said, "It was a demonic attack."

I froze. I didn't answer; I just listened to him as he talked. "It wasn't me that did that. It was demons, but you started it. You made me do it."

I still didn't move or respond.

"This was your fault," he said. As the words came out of his mouth, I understood again that he felt inferior outside of Iran. In Iran, he was the man; he was in charge. But in other countries, like Turkey and the United Arab Emirates, he was dependent. I was the international traveler. I understood the language and the systems of getting around. He needed to rely on me instead of the other way around, so he needed to put me in my place. He needed to show me that I was not as powerful as I thought I was.

It worked. From that day on, I was truly aware of what Saeed was capable of. I promised myself that I would never again talk back to him or say anything that might upset him. I knew that I could have reported Saeed to the police in Dubai, but I had to do everything I could to protect the precious life growing inside me. After the beating, a war had raged within me. To really protect myself and the baby would mean walking away from my marriage. But I could not walk away. I was damaged goods now, as Saeed would often remind me, and no one would want me. In addition, I could not imagine my child growing up without his or her father. I did not want to go to America without the father of my baby. I wanted to keep our family together. I resolved that the only way to maintain peace and safety was to obey Saeed at all costs.

From that moment on, I was a different person. I became a submissive wife. And I still had hope that Saeed would get better.

In the following days, when people came to the door to see us, Saeed would tell them I was not feeling well. He told them I was resting and couldn't see anyone.

I was unable to eat for days. I was vomiting, and I was panicked at the thought of losing another baby. Saeed wouldn't talk to me for several days. I had no one else to talk with. My parents were in America, and I had no friends in Dubai. And I couldn't go out in Dubai because my face was so black and blue.

It took my body several weeks to fully recover, but the emotional wounds lingered for much longer.

Saeed never apologized.

26

CHURCH SPLIT 2.0

W hat's going on?" I asked. I was straining to hear Saeed's voice on the other end of the phone. He was calling from Turkey, and there was a bad connection.

Saeed's visa to America had been approved. I had immediately flown to Idaho to spend the rest of my pregnancy with my family, while Saeed had flown to Istanbul to spend time with some Iranian house church leaders who had gathered there for a special conference. My uncle from California, who was financially supporting the ministry, was also in Istanbul.

"Your uncle is trying to screw me over and steal my church, that is what is going on!" Saeed lamented. "I have my network leaders here from Iran to attend this conference, which I never would have done if I had known that your snake of an uncle was going to take this opportunity to steal them away from me."

"I am certain it is a misunderstanding," I said, forgetting my place but quickly readjusting by covering it up with, "But you are there; I'm not. You have a better understanding of the situation."

I knew the meetings in Turkey were not going to go well. Before Saeed flew to Istanbul, we had already decided that we no longer wanted to work for my uncle's ministry. Saeed had the feeling that he could do better in the US conducting his own fundraising than he could by relying on another ministry. He strongly believed that his influence as a pastor over the house church leaders in Iran would continue even while he was in America. He could run the Iranian ministry from outside of Iran and raise funds for it directly. He didn't need to submit to the leaders of an organization that didn't know anything about the Iranian house church. He could connect with supporters and donors himself, and he would not have to watch all his efforts benefit another ministry.

When Saeed arrived in Istanbul, he met with my uncle, along with several other ministry leaders. My uncle asked Saeed where he expected to live in the US and what his plans were. When Saeed told him that he planned to branch out and work independently, my uncle was shocked. That was the first time he had heard that Saeed no longer wanted to work with him.

"I have invested my life in these Iranian leaders," Saeed continued over the phone, "and we have grown our house church network to over two thousand believers, and now your uncle is just trying to waltz in here and take over the whole thing."

"Tell me what happened," I said.

After the meeting with my uncle, Saeed had retired to his room and gone to sleep. While he was sleeping, my uncle and several other ministry directors had called an urgent meeting with the Iranian pastors and shared with them how Saeed was leaving the ministry and how it was breaking the unity of the fellowship.

"I heard he was speaking to them with tears in his eyes," Saeed reported with disgust. "He was pretending to be the victim, and he painted me as the big bad villain, and they all completely bought it."

The uphill battle that Saeed was fighting was that so many of the Iranian leaders had seen Saeed's harsh side. They knew how angry he could get. When my uncle came to them crying, they were quickly able to recognize the scenario that he was describing. Over the years, the Iranian pastors had known my uncle to be a softer, gentler leader. He did not exude the harsh, emotionally bruising character that Saeed did.

When Saeed went down to the meeting room, he was surprised to see the Iranian pastors in tears.

"Why are you crying?" he asked.

"We were just told that you are breaking away from the fellowship," they answered.

Saeed went into a rage and pulled my uncle out of the conference room. "Why would you tell them about this behind my back?" he demanded. "This should have been talked about as a group when I was here, not behind my back."

The foreign pastors who were there, mainly from America, saw Saeed's reaction and felt that they were witnessing some sort of demonic influence, and they began to pray over Saeed. It became a circus, and the Iranian leaders watched it all. They witnessed with their own eyes something that had come full circle: Saeed was now reaping in Turkey the public correction that he had imposed on his own leaders in Iran.

The international ministry leaders, together with my uncle, were able to convince Saeed to go back to his room and not return to the meetings until he had calmed down.

Afterward, my uncle called me in Idaho and asked me to arrange for Saeed's flight to the US as soon as possible. He wanted to manage the disaster that was unfolding as best he could.

The house church ended up splitting right down the middle, with half of the believers sticking with Saeed and the other half going with my uncle's ministry. My uncle had finances, and Saeed had nothing. Saeed was not ready to support the churches. Those who stayed with him remained because of their loyalty to him.

After Saeed arrived in America, Pastor Bob of Calvary Chapel Boise reached out to us. We shared with him about the events in Turkey and why we had had to leave Iran. Pastor Bob wanted to invest in our family and support the church in Iran, so he offered Saeed a position on staff at Calvary Chapel Boise to run the Iranian ministry from the US. Saeed took the opportunity to help develop the house church in a new way online.

The online Iranian fellowship grew, and, the following year, Saeed returned to Turkey with Pastor Bob. Together, they baptized a hundred and twenty leaders. However, Pastor Bob had concerns about Saeed. During the first year that Saeed was on staff at Calvary Chapel, Pastor Bob had witnessed his anger issues as he worked with other leaders. He provided Saeed with private council, but Saeed was never fully receptive to it.

On one occasion, Pastor Bob witnessed Saeed berating his leaders online in a way that is just not acceptable at Calvary Chapel. Pastor Bob did not understand Farsi, but he understood the tone, volume, and anger in Saeed's voice.

"Saeed, this is not the way to treat people," Pastor Bob told him. "You are attacking your own sheep. You are like a shepherd attacking the sheep instead of protecting them from the wolves."

Usually, someone saying something like that to Saeed would have triggered him and put him in a rage, but Saeed never got physical with Pastor Bob. Perhaps it was because Pastor Bob was bigger, stronger, and seemed to not mind physical confrontation if the situation required it. Saeed only liked to get physically aggressive with those whom he thought couldn't or wouldn't fight back. On several occasions, he thought Pastor Bob was being too physically threatening to him and wanted to go to the police and report it!

Pastor Bob didn't just help provide a purpose for Saeed and finances for our family, but he also helped to reveal something about Saeed's behavior that I had not recognized before. Before and after our marriage, I had witnessed a pattern that I had refused to accept: Saeed had a problem with the leadership at Central Assemblies of God Church in Tehran, he had issues with those who served with him in the house church, he had a falling out with my uncle, and now he was experiencing issues with Pastor Bob. He had problems with those in authority over him, as well as with those whom he had authority over. Unfortunately, Saeed would continue to reject the wise counsel and legitimate authority of others, while also battling with those under his authority.

Maman in her army uniform

Maman and Baba in Iran

Baba, Nima, and me in Iran

Maman, Grandma, and me

Naneh, Nima, and me with Maman
and her sidearm

Maman, Grandma, Nima, and me in our backyard

At school in Iran (back row, wearing glasses)

Summer at the Caspian Sea

Naneh in the kitchen

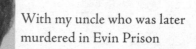

With my uncle who was later murdered in Evin Prison

Baba, Nima, and me in Iran

Maman, Nima, my sister Nazanin, and me, the night we left for America

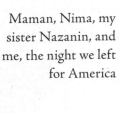

Nima and me in America

The Panahi family

Nima and me with Baba at
our college graduation

Baba and me on my birthday

Worship service on the eve of our wedding

Saeed and me and the children in
Boise, 2011, just before leaving for
Iran to work on the orphanage

FOX NEWS 1:45 PT — WIFE OF AMERICAN PASTOR HELD IN IRAN PLEADS FOR HIS FREEDOM — JUSTICE with Judge Jeanine

...ISTS HAVE SEIZED GOVT BUILDINGS AND DECLARED INDEPENDENCE... THE

THE WORLD LEAD — THE LEAD WITH JAKE TAPPER

THE LEAD — AN AMERICAN PASTOR JAILED IN IRAN — Saeed Abedini sentenced to 8 years — CNN

Prayer vigil for Saeed at the state capitol building in Boise, ID, September 26, 2013

Prayer vigil for Saeed and the persecuted church, Washington, DC,
September 25, 2014 Photo credit: *The Christian Post*

Skype call with Saeed from prison

Meeting with Donald
Trump at Trump
Tower, 2014
Photo Credit: Courtesy
The American Center for
Law and Justice

Meeting with President Obama
at Boise State University,
January 2015

Photo Credit: Courtesy Barack
Obama Presidential Library/Photo by
Pete Souza

Meeting Mariam Ibraheem for the first time with Tony Perkins

Photo credit: Courtesy Family Research Council

Me without makeup, accepting God's unconditional love

Mariam Ibraheem, Anne Basham, and I establishing the Tahrir Alnisa Foundation, June 2019

Mariam Ibraheem being rescued from domestic abuse, with Anne Basham, 2018

Mariam Ibraheem and me Photo credit: Courtesy of Christian

27

A BABY BORN IN CHAOS

It was hard to see the giddy smile on Saeed's face upon arriving in America disappear after he realized where we would be living. He had wanted to live in the United States for most of his life, but he had no idea what it would really be like. When he thought of the US, he imagined what he had seen on TV—programs set in New York or Los Angeles. Boise was a far cry from those huge metropolitan areas.

When I introduced him to my hometown, he kept waiting to see where the main area was, even when we were driving through the heart of the city.

"Where's the rest of it?" he asked. "Is this like a suburban area or...?"

Living in Boise was not an easy adjustment for Saeed because he could not speak the language. He was also limited in what he could do. He was used to the big-city nightlife of Tehran. Boise had only 220,000 people. Tehran had almost nine million—more than forty times larger than Boise. In fact, there are more people in the single Iranian city of Tehran than there are in the states of Idaho, Montana, Oregon, and Wyoming put together. Saeed felt that he was in the middle of nowhere, and in many ways he was.

However, there were certain things in Boise that had given him a soft landing after fleeing Iran. My parents had provided us with food, a car, and a place to live. Our church had given him a salary to continue shepherding the church in Iran. He had an office, status as a pastor, and the ability to continue walking in the calling God had given him. In addition to offering him a salary to lead the churches in Iran, Calvary Chapel had also asked him to use this time to write his story. Pastor Bob felt that his testimony was one that should be shared with the world and wanted the church to invest in it.

To get things started, the church made a dramatic testimonial video of Saeed's conversion. The video motivated many people to pray for Iran and only highlighted the need for a book about Saeed's story.

Even though Boise was not exactly Saeed's dream, things seemed to be turning around. Our ministry in America was starting to take shape. Saeed seemed more focused than he had been in months. He had a passion for learning English and sharing his testimony with others.

Saeed represented the church in Iran and raised awareness about the persecution that believers there suffered every day. The people of our congregation loved Saeed and were so excited that the church was connected to his work—but there was a side to him that no one knew about. Something was growing inside him that I had not even seen in Tehran. Apart from his responsibilities at the church, he had a lot of free time on his hands, and he began to develop certain habits.

Because I was pregnant, I found myself having to go to the bathroom much more often. One night, I woke up and walked into the living room, where I caught Saeed watching porn on television. He leaped up to quickly shut off the TV, but it was too late. I had already seen what was going on. He was embarrassed.

I was confused, because he used to yell at me for watching television programs depicting couples merely kissing. It seemed to be a very large jump to go from being offended by watching people kiss to watching people having sex.

"Are you watching porn?" I asked.

"No! No! No!" he exclaimed, trying to cover the television screen with his hand. "I didn't know what channel it was. You know I can't speak the language."

There was a part of me that didn't believe him, but I desperately wanted to trust that he was telling me the truth, so I went along with it. However, as time went on, things progressed. I would wake up late at night to go to the bathroom and would keep catching him watching porn. Each time I caught him, he was slower and slower to turn off the television or change the channel. Eventually, it grew to where I could walk in on him, and he no longer cared—he kept watching.

On occasion, I would travel to the church to have lunch with Saeed, and he would be watching porn at the church office.

He told me pornography is what he used to satisfy his urges because he didn't find me attractive as a pregnant woman. He often called me "fat" and "gross," saying that he could not stomach the idea of lying with me during the pregnancy.

In my mind, I made excuses for his behavior, thinking that he was a man with needs, and since he could not be intimate with me, then it was natural for him to find other outlets. But I hurt inside because I knew that physical intimacy was the only way I could get to his heart. People often say that the quickest way to a man's heart is through his stomach, but I believe the real target is a few inches lower than the stomach. A man opens up his heart to a woman to whom he is sexually connected, and a women opens up sexually to the man who connects with her heart. It is a balance between lovers that causes mutual dependence. When the cycle is broken by the needs of the man (or the woman) being met through pornography or an affair, then an estrangement naturally follows.

That is where Saeed and I were—that cycle had been broken. We were two strangers living in the same house, not really knowing each other. Over time, Saeed's pornography habit grew to the point where he would watch hard porn in front of me with no shame. When he didn't even attempt to turn off the pornography when my parents came into the room, I realized that we needed to move out.

After months of living with my parents, we found a house of our own. My father paid the down payment and helped us to move. Even though he and Saeed were often at odds with each other, and Saeed had said many hurtful things to him—calling him ugly names, accusing him of being a traitor by conspiring with my uncle to take his churches—that did not change Baba's commitment to us.

The move into our own home did not come a moment too soon. Saeed's problems with my father had only been escalating. It bothered Saeed that Baba was still supporting my uncle, even after the church split. Saeed felt betrayed.

I could understand why my father stayed in contact with his brother: they were family. Even though there had been a falling out between Saeed and my uncle, my father could not disown his own brother. Saeed didn't see it that way and believed that my father's continued support of my uncle was the reason why our house church was facing challenges.

It seemed suicidal for Saeed to go after my father, his character, and his company, considering that Baba was helping us get on our feet and financially supporting us. Practically everything that we owned had been given to us by him. I felt that we were indebted to Baba. Attacking him was like shooting ourselves in the foot. Even though Saeed and I had not been married for very long, in the time that we had been together, my father had gone out of his way to help us. He was truly the one person we could rely on. He had paid for our wedding expenses, our car, our first apartment, and our plane tickets to America. He had also just helped us buy our first house. Even though I, too, felt somewhat betrayed by my father because of the situation with my uncle, I could see that he always took care of me.

Once we were in our own home—which Baba had helped us buy—Saeed took his vengeance against my father further. He told Baba that neither he nor my mother would be allowed to be present for the birth of our first child. Saeed knew this would really cause Baba pain, and indeed, the news was devastating to my parents. I wanted to believe that Saeed would not be so cold as to keep them away from the birth of their first grandchild.

Toward the middle of September, I gave birth to our daughter, Rebekka. At the last minute, Saeed relented and allowed my parents to be present for the birth; but, afterward, he banned Baba from seeing me or our daughter. Although my mother was allowed to come once and a while to visit with Rebekka, it would be almost a year before my father had an opportunity to spend time with his granddaughter.

While Saeed continued to spiral completely out of control, I tried to hold everything together. I was committed to our marriage and wanted to see a transformation in our family. I continued to believe that I could "fake it until I made it." I convinced myself that "no one is perfect" and that "we all have our problems." I went to church with a smile and returned home in tears. Our pot was starting to boil over, and I was trying to keep a lid on it so no one would see. I was attempting to change our chaotic private lives while maintaining a calm appearance in public. It wasn't working.

Saeed fought with the Iranian leaders online, he argued with Pastor Bob, he was keeping my family from seeing our daughter, and our marriage was in the tank. There was never a day without drama with him. He spent every day unnecessarily fighting with people over the smallest things. He would go into a rage over the slightest comments.

One Sunday morning, before church, he was chatting with his parents and sister online. (He was allowed to talk to his family, but I was not allowed to talk to mine.) While they were talking, he told them that I was causing problems between him and Pastor Bob.

I heard them talking from the other room, and I shouted, "Not true!" I said it loudly enough for Saeed's family to hear me.

Saeed snapped. I saw him come after me with the same look in his eyes that he had exhibited in Dubai, and I was afraid for my life. I tried to run away, but he caught me. He grabbed me by my shirt and slammed me against the wall, pinning me so that I couldn't escape.

"Saeed!" screamed his family. Saeed had left his computer open, and while his family couldn't see us, they could hear everything that was going on. Hearing their voices screaming shook him out of his state of rage. He rotated on his right heel, stepped away to grab his computer, walked into his home office, and shut the door.

Saeed's family had saved me in that moment, but I was certain he would emerge from the room in a matter of minutes angrier than when he went in. I called my sister, who still lived in the area, but she was at church and wasn't answering her phone. I tried to call my parents, but they were also at church.

I hung up the phone. Was there anyone else I could call? I glanced over and saw Rebekka sitting on the floor across from me. The only thing I could think is that I could not allow what had happened to me in Dubai to happen again in front of her.

So, for the first time in my life, I did the only thing that I knew to do—I called the police.

It did not take long for the police to come. When they arrived, I rushed to them with Rebekka. They were such a welcome sight. Instantly, I felt the security of being in a safe environment, and the emotions that I had been holding back came flooding out of me as I felt I had finally gotten my daughter and myself to safety.

"What is wrong, ma'am?" one of the tall, broad officers asked as they approached the house.

"My husband. He is in a rage. He grabbed me and threw me up against the wall. He is on a Skype call now, but I know that when he is finished with the call, he is going to come after me again."

I explained what had happened in Dubai and told them I was afraid for my safety and for the safety of my daughter. I didn't know it then, but I was also pregnant, just as I had been during the incident in Dubai.

The officer nodded to his partner, and, without saying another word, they went into the house and arrested Saeed.

Seeing Saeed in handcuffs sent my mind racing with emotions because, for the first time in our marriage, he was not being arrested for preaching the gospel in Iran but for domestic abuse in the United States. When I saw them put him in the police car, I was flooded with extreme guilt. I had put everything at risk, including his immigration. He was being arrested for domestic abuse, and if he were found guilty, he might not be allowed to remain in the United States and could be sent back to Iran. It would no longer be only myself against Saeed but the state of Idaho against Saeed. The state would remove the power from my hands because they had seen it too often: a victim of domestic abuse calls the police, the police arrive and arrest the perpetrator, the victim feels guilty, and then she drops all charges.

When I realized the possible damage I had done, I immediately went to my parents and asked for their assistance. After all that Saeed had done to hurt them, I still begged them to help us. Saeed would need a lawyer to help him plead down the charges, but we couldn't afford an attorney. The fees to try to plead down the charges for domestic abuse amounted to more than three thousand dollars. My parents agreed to pay the full fee for us.

Eventually, our lawyer was able to get him out of jail, and we rejoiced, but our marriage was worse than it had ever been. He never became physically violent with me again, but he channeled his anger toward my golden retriever. Soon after I had arrived in America, I had bought a playful golden retriever, one of the most loving dogs for young children. I have always loved golden retrievers and was so glad to have one in our home. He was the sweetest dog and loved everyone, but Saeed would go into fits of rage and begin beating the dog. When I would scream for him to stop, he would respond by accusing the dog of trying to bite him.

Our dog would never have bitten anyone. After a while, I knew that I could not subject an innocent animal to that kind of constant abuse, so I gave him away. I cried and mourned how empty the house felt without my dog, but I was thankful that he was now safe and in a good home.

Although Saeed had not physically threatened me since he went to jail, I noticed a growing aggression in him. He had further altercations with Pastor

Bob at Calvary Chapel, and he eventually left the church. Pastor Bob reached out to me, saying he felt it was no longer safe for me or my daughter to stay in the same house with Saeed, especially since I was pregnant.

I didn't want to believe it, but somewhere deep inside me, I knew the pastor was right. I needed to look out for the safety of my children, so I moved back in with my parents.

Saeed was no longer working at Calvary Chapel. And, due to Saeed's poor treatment of them, the house church pastors had all left him over time and joined other house church networks, so he was also no longer pastoring believers in Iran. He grew restless and concluded that he needed a change of scenery and that getting away from Idaho was the answer. He borrowed three thousand dollars from Baba to help him get on his feet, took our only car, and left Idaho to go stay with one of his aunts, who lived in California.

I put our house up for rent so I could pay the mortgage and keep up with the bills, and I went back to work for my father. I didn't want to admit it, but life calmed down without Saeed around.

28

AN ALTERNATE UNIVERSE

I want to come back home," Saeed said in a deep, loving voice over the phone. "I really miss you and the kids. I want to put things right and bring our family back together."

I knew the story. I had seen it before: Saeed would go into a rage, blame it on a demonic influence, and then eventually seem to change, saying he wanted our family together again. I should have known things would not go well. But I was pregnant and wanted my family reunited. I didn't want to be a single mother. I didn't want to be a lonely ex-wife. I wanted to be with my husband and serve the Lord. I knew the chances that Saeed would change were slim, but I believed in miracles. I had faith. I knew that God could do the impossible.

Since Saeed had always loved the nightlife, California suited his lifestyle a lot more than Boise did. Unlike in Tehran, everything in Boise starts to shut down around nine or ten in the evening. In Tehran, most restaurants do not even open up until that time. Like a true Iranian, Saeed enjoyed late-night dinners, long conversations that lasted into the morning hours, and waking up late in the afternoon. Idaho was not Iran, and Boise was not Tehran, but Saeed didn't have money, a job, or a support system in California, and he wanted to return.

Saeed's call made me excited. I knew that, most likely, he had been involved in the club scene and some other seedy activities in California, but I was willing to put all that behind us and move on. I told myself that what I didn't know wouldn't hurt me.

When Saeed returned to Boise, he really did try to make a go of it. He wanted to be a good father to our two children, and he wanted to refocus on building the house church in Iran. He was passionate about getting back into ministry, and we both agreed that online ministry was the best way to connect with the house church for the short term but was not a substitute for face-to-face interaction. If we were serious about restarting the ministry, Saeed was going to have to begin traveling back and forth from the United States to Iran.

While working for Baba, I received stock options in his company, and the options were worth several thousand dollars. Saeed and I prayed about it and decided that the best way for us to get involved in Iranian ministry again was to sell the stock options and use the money to launch an orphanage in Iran.

When we lived in Iran, we were constantly exposed to street children who didn't have a home. I always had a feeling that God would one day use us to minister to such children. Saeed said the Lord had shown him a vision of how we were to start an orphanage that would bring in children from the street and give them a loving home.

Watching Saeed pray about this vision, passionately dig in to the planning stage, and make calls in Iran to get things rolling filled me with excitement and contentment. I had my husband back. I had my family back. I had my life back on track to serve the Lord.

The gratitude that filled me every morning was almost more than I could contain, but it didn't last long. After a few months, Saeed grew restless again. His mood swings increased, and a darkness seemed to follow him. He was becoming both irritable and irrational. He grew impatient with everyone around him and picked fights about everything.

We were living with my parents again, and, one day in early July 2009, I saw him sitting in the living room and knew that he was in one of his dark moods where anything could go wrong. Like an old farmer predicting the weather from the look of the clouds, I knew Saeed's signs well. There was a storm brewing, and we needed to seek shelter.

"Let's go somewhere," I suggested to my parents.

"Why?" my mother asked.

I nodded my head toward Saeed without saying a word.

My mother looked over at Saeed and realized my implication. "Oh," she said.

"Ummm, yeah..., so maybe we can go out for some ice cream with the kids," I suggested while pulling our one-year-old son, Jacob, into my arms. My parents and I went out with the children in my car, and I allowed a few hours for the storm clouds to blow over before returning home.

As soon as we pulled into the driveway, we saw that something was wrong with my mother's car, which was parked in the driveway. She owned a brand-new Lexus, but the hood and sides of the car had been battered with some sort of blunt instrument like a hammer, and the windows had been smashed.

"What happened?" I yelled. We jumped out of my car and walked around the Lexus, evaluating the damage. It looked like someone had come by and just randomly attacked the car and nothing else. The outside of the house and yard weren't damaged in any way.

"Who would do something like this?" Baba asked.

"We need to call the police," I said. "Maybe Saeed saw what happened."

We sprinted to the front door to ask Saeed if he had heard anything, but when we walked through the door, we saw that the inside of the house had been trashed. There were holes in the drywall, curtains had been torn down, and knickknacks and decorations had been thrown all around. The house looked destroyed.

I walked into the middle of the living room with my mouth gaping open, shaking my head, unable to comprehend what had occurred. Had we been attacked and robbed? Was Saeed still at home? I didn't have a clue what was happening.

Every room we walked into seemed worse than the previous one. I turned on the lights in my parents' bedroom and saw the same level of destruction. I didn't even enter. "You don't want to go in there," I said to my mother, which made her want to go in to see the damage.

Back in the living room, I saw that my father's large flat-screen television had been destroyed. It looked as if someone had taken a big knife and cut it from corner to corner, across the middle of the screen.

My eyes scanned from the TV to the sofa, where Saeed was sitting calmly, as if everything was normal. The moment my eyes came into focus and saw him, I knew.

He knew that I knew.

"What happened? Was there a thief?" I asked, with a small sliver of hope that he had not done all this.

With a stern look in his eyes, he solemnly told me that he had done it in order to make a point: the next time I wanted to leave the house with the children, I had to ask him for permission.

"I am calling the police," Baba said.

Within minutes, the police arrived at the house and were flabbergasted by what they saw.

"You want to file a report?" the police officer asked.

Baba pulled at his hair and looked up as if searching for an answer in the ceiling. He put his head in his hands and shook his head back and forth.

"Sir? Would you like to file a report and press charges?" the officer asked again.

"No," he finally answered in a muffled voice, his mouth covered with the palms of his hands.

"Sorry, sir, we didn't hear you. What did you say?"

"No," Baba replied, pulling his hands away from his face and looking up. "No, I do not want to file a report or press charges. I am sorry to have wasted your time, gentlemen."

Baba cared more for me and his grandchildren than he did about his house and his flat-screen TV. He knew that pressing charges against Saeed would only create problems with immigration for Saeed.

"Can we talk with you outside?" the officer said to my father as he waved his hand toward the door. I went outside with them, and when we were a safe distance from Saeed, the officer shut his notebook and said, "We are seeing a progression, Mr. Panahi. He has assaulted his wife. He has abused their pet. He has destroyed your property. It is only going to get worse if he continues to get away with these things. The next time, someone might lose their life."

My father assured the police officer that he was certain he did not want to press charges, but I could see reluctance all over his face. He seemed to be internally debating whether he was doing the right thing.

Shortly afterward, about mid-July, Saeed and I returned to Iran with the children for a two-week family vacation. This trip had already been scheduled, and although I was reluctant to go after the latest incident with Saeed, I didn't want to cancel our plans. Rebekka was excited about the trip, and I also thought it might help Saeed if he could visit with his family and be back in Iran for a little while. We wanted Saeed's parents to be able to see their grandchildren again, since they didn't have that opportunity very often (we had previously met them a few times in Dubai and Turkey so they could meet the children). This would be the first time Saeed and I had returned to Iran since our escape from persecution in 2005; however, we believed that enough time had passed—especially since the house churches we had worked with were essentially dispersed—that Saeed would not be in danger of being arrested.

Yet, at the conclusion of the two weeks, when we arrived at the airport to return home, Saeed was arrested as we went through immigration. I was filled with anxiety as I held two screaming children who didn't understand why their father was being taken away from them. I didn't know whether I could board the long flight back to America without knowing what was happening to Saeed. But there was little I could do, and it seemed safer to return home with the children. I felt devastated as I left the country, not knowing when or even if I would see Saeed again.

The authorities put Saeed under house arrest because of his prior activities with the house churches and for having missed his court hearing when he'd fled Iran in 2005. He remained under house arrest for almost two months, which was the longest the government had detained him to that point. At that time, Saeed was not yet a naturalized US citizen, which meant he would be tried as an Iranian citizen. This made it difficult for us to assist him from the outside. Fortunately, I was able to stay in constant contact with him through Skype and phone calls. I prayed, fasted, and held on to hope that they would let him go.

At the end of September, the authorities returned Saeed's passport to him. However, they released him only after he had signed an agreement promising to focus solely on the orphanage and other humanitarian projects and not have anything to do with the house churches. When Saeed arrived home in Idaho, we gratefully celebrated Rebekka's third birthday together, a celebration I had delayed until the end of the month, hoping that Saeed would be released by then so he could share that day with us.

Even after the distressing experience of being under house arrest, in the months that followed, Saeed frequently traveled back and forth to Iran. Everything appeared calm, and Saeed seemed happy to be able to spend time with his family and focus on setting up the orphanage. I thought our turbulent times were over. Yet, in the summer of 2010, the police officer's warning from the previous year that Saeed's violence would escalate seemed to turn prophetic.

One Tuesday, my grandmother was at our home for a visit. She was playing the typical Persian mother role, guilting her son by telling him that she didn't get to see him often enough.

"Don't I come and get you and bring you here each week? Aren't you here now? Mom, I own my own business. I am not able to see you more than I do. You know this."

They were talking more loudly than usual, each one trying to get their voice heard over the other.

I jumped into the middle of the quarrel. "Come on, guys. We are all here now; let's not ruin our time together. Let's not argue today."

"This is between my mother and me, Naghmeh. You can butt out," Baba protested.

The words had no sooner came out of Baba's mouth than Saeed started punching him in the face repeatedly.

I leaped back and screamed. My grandmother's face was frozen in shock, turning shades of grey and off-white. Saeed kept punching my father relentlessly. Blood spattered everywhere. Baba's face bounced back and forth as it absorbed each heavy blow until he fell to the ground, where he tried to crawl away. I saw flashes of what had happened to me in Dubai.

"Stop!" I screamed. "Saeed, stop!"

As Baba was crawling away, Saeed was kicking him in the side while simultaneously aiming for his face with his fists.

I pulled on Saeed to try to get him to stop. When he finally ceased, I could see fury filling his eyes and curling his lips.

"What are you doing?" I screamed. "Baba didn't do anything."

"I thought he was going to hit you."

"What are you talking about?"

"I thought your father was going to hit you," Saeed said again between heavy pants.

"No! My father has never touched me!"

His insinuation that my father would hit me was outrageous. Saeed knew that. Unlike Saeed, my father had never done anything to cause harm or pain in my life.

I rushed over to Baba and dropped to my knees to see what I could do to help him. His face was covered in blood, and he wasn't able to move.

I called the police. Then I called my mother, who was out, and told her she needed to come home right away.

When the police arrived, my father, again trying to help my family, told them he did not want to press charges. However, his injuries were serious, and he needed to go to the hospital.

The police were in complete disbelief. As they had predicted, the number of violent incidents was increasing. Again, they told us that it was only a matter of time before something worse, possibly even death, took place.

After that day, things continued to deteriorate. Saeed would travel back and forth to Iran to try to win back the house church leaders who had left, as well as to work on plans for the orphanage; but when he was home in Boise, he had no local ministry or job. He grew more dissatisfied with his life. I was working all day and coming home to clean and cook. In order to ensure the children were taken care of, I hired my pastor's daughter-in-law as a nanny.

I discovered that Saeed was filling his days in Boise meeting and chatting with girls online. At night, he would go to clubs. Some of my family members saw him at clubs with different girls. We began to get phone calls at our home from local massage parlors banning him for sexually harassing their staff.

Saeed had also started to use the Bible as justification for watching pornography. One day, he sat me down and explained how it was God's plan for a woman to sexually please her husband, and watching porn with him would be the best way for me to please him. Not only did he want me to watch porn with him, but he also argued that it was God's plan for our marriage. He wanted me to recreate some of the scenes that were his favorite to watch. Some of the things he was asking me to do in reenactments were humiliating, rough, degrading acts that were not about making love but about something far different. I loved Saeed, but I could not do what he was asking me to do.

We were living in an alternate universe where sin and the divine coexisted. Saeed seemed to be both a sinner and a saint, and I was a contributor to this perplexing dichotomy. My family and I were enablers. We were supporting him during his times of ministry, knowing that Saeed was not fit to lead a ministry.

Saeed was on the road six months out of the year for ministry trips to Iran, as well as to speak, preach, and raise funds in the United States to support the work. Instead of feeling obligated to warn people about his behavior, I felt relieved that he was not at home causing fights, getting arrested, going to clubs, watching porn, or trying to talk me into doing something debasing.

After Saeed put my father in the hospital, I thought that our marriage was over and any chance of our working in ministry together was gone for good. It seemed that I would lose all hope, but every time I felt like giving up, another event would happen that would breathe life back into my relationship with Saeed. Just when I thought he had crossed a line from which we could never return, another opportunity would present itself that made me think things would be different. Now, the orphanage ministry was taking shape and beckoned for us to go back to Iran. In an attempt to bring us closer together, I decided to take the children with me to Iran for six months so we could be with Saeed as a family.

29

ATTEMPTED ESCAPE

The city of Rasht, the site of the planned orphanage, is a four-hour trip from Tehran. It is a beautiful drive to the Caspian Sea, which is the same area that Saeed's family is from. The full spelling of Saeed's last name is Abedinigalangashy, indicating it is connected to the Galangash region of Iran in the north.

When we arrived at the plot of land set aside for the orphanage, Saeed jumped out of the car and began to walk around the property to help me visualize where each building would stand. I realized that it would be more than just an orphanage but rather a type of compound. Saeed's family owned the property, so we had not needed to purchase the land. In fact, everything that we built would add value to their property.

"This here," Saeed said, pointing to the location where he intended to build, "can be used as an orphanage for children, but we can also use it for vacation rentals to bring in money. It can be used as a wedding venue for people to come and get married. This will be a side income for the property and a self-sustaining project."

Saeed wanted to build an orphanage for children that didn't need continual donations to keep it going. He feared that a heavy reliance on donations could spell disaster for the children if the income ever stopped coming in, which was a very real concern with all the economic sanctions being imposed on Iran.

"First things first," he said. "We need a place to live while we oversee the construction of the orphanage, so we will use the money that we have from your stock options to build a home for ourselves. As we are building that structure, I will continue to fundraise to obtain the money we need to continue."

I nodded in agreement, only half understanding everything he was talking about. He pulled out the plans that he and his father had worked on for the design of the buildings. Since the property belonged to Saeed's family, it was important that they had a say in the way the buildings were designed.

When I looked at the plans, I saw that the concept was not a simple structure that would have served its purpose of housing orphans; instead, every building had a unique design that would be appealing to visitors as well. The structures around the Caspian Sea are distinct, more like villas than homes. They are not the large, spacious homes you would find in the wealthy suburban areas of Tehran; they are smaller, more manageable beach properties made with cheaper materials.

There was already a small building on the grounds, more like a shack, which had been halfheartedly constructed a decade or two earlier. It was livable, but, without a bathroom and toilet, only barely. I felt that what the building lacked, the isolation would provide. In this remote area of Iran, close to the beautiful Caspian Sea, Saeed and I would have time to build our dreams and work on our marriage.

Saeed had many relatives in Rasht who had not yet met our children. We took the opportunity to visit with them and share the vision we believed God had given us. We spent long days and unending nights sharing about Jesus with his family.

As winter set in, we had to drive back to Tehran. Like many structures built by the Caspian Sea, our temporary abode lacked heat. The simple structure was meant for lazy summers, not for the cold, unforgiving winters that blew in over the black waters of the Caspian on the wings of the northern winds from Russia.

Back in Tehran, we lived with Saeed's parents. The apartment was warm, but the relationships were a bit icy. Now that Saeed and I were married, I was no longer the trophy wife that his parents had always prayed for but a lowly daughter-in-law who was to respect and obey her husband's parents. My relationship with my in-laws was tolerable, but the pleasantries we shared were driven by courtesy rather than by mutual respect or love. That was to be expected. Their thoughts about me were no doubt shaped by Saeed, just as my ideas about them had been shaped by him.

Saeed could not be completely blamed for the slow deterioration of my relationship with his parents. With our family of four, plus Saeed's mother, father, two sisters, and brother, there were nine people sharing a very small apartment. Not even the bathroom was a place of refuge anyone could use as an oasis of escape. The moment someone went to the toilet, it was a matter of seconds before someone would be banging on the door needing access.

For the most part, Saeed escaped this chaos by leaving in the morning and not returning home until late at night. He spent every day meeting with his friends and colleagues. We both agreed that the meetings and the building of relationships were essential for our future ministry, yet I couldn't help but feel he was out experiencing freedom in open spaces while I was in a small box exchanging begrudging grunts, moans, and passive-aggressive sighs with his family. In small spaces shared with multiple people, the most innocent infractions can provoke the most combative responses.

Added to this, in Tehran, I was a bit intimidated to travel by myself because I felt unprotected. It was not unusual, out in public, for men to say lewd comments to a woman and get very aggressive with her when they saw her alone. I didn't want to subject myself to that, so, without Saeed to accompany me, I was trapped in the apartment day after day.

I tried to do things that took my mind off my circumstances. I homeschooled the children and kept them fed and entertained. The kitchen was only really big enough for one person, and Saeed's mother felt it was her domain. If I approached the kitchen while she was in it, her demeanor would change from that of a harmless housewife to a territorial guard dog. In practice, this meant that my children and I would have to eat whatever meals she cooked.

As time went on, the days without Saeed grew longer. I spent my afternoons and evenings imagining what he was doing, who he was meeting with, and when he would return home. I feared for his safety, knowing that he was meeting with house church members while in the spotlight of the secret police.

In the late evenings, when he would stagger through the door, I would pepper him with questions about his day, but he was never in the mood to talk; he would say he was too tired. He would always insist we talk the next day, but when the next day arrived, he would be gone again.

I was growing lonely and isolated. I hated myself for being so needy; I wanted to cut out the part of me that needed Saeed, but I couldn't. I made concerted efforts to be less dependent, making deals with myself that I would not talk to him unless he talked to me first. I hyped myself up to believe that I could wait for him to begin the conversation. I would not be the initiator; I would wait until he was ready.

My plan failed. It always failed. I was so much stronger in my fantasies than I ever was in reality. Saeed was simply better at the game than I was because he didn't play it. When he was home, he wasn't pretending not to care about our relationship—he actually didn't care about it. For him, I was like a gnat that needed to be shooed away.

After receiving the silent treatment for a while, I had to speak up. I couldn't play the game; I couldn't deal with not knowing where Saeed had been.

"You can't tell me you are too tired," I said one day. "You are out all day while I am stuck here with your parents and the kids with nowhere to go and nothing to do. You have a family. You can't just abandon us here every day. I don't have a car. I don't have money. I can't leave this house without you."

"Shhh," Saeed said dismissively. "Let's not talk about it now. Everyone can hear you."

He was right. There was no place in the entire apartment where anyone could have a private conversation. Not only was the apartment small, but its walls were thin. Everyone could hear everything, which wasn't good for communication between us.

Saeed continued to ignore me, but I couldn't endure one more night of not existing in his eyes. I couldn't endure one more night of his not caring.

"I can't take this any longer. You are gone day and night, going wherever you want to go, to God-knows-where with God-knows-who, while the kids and I sit here and wait all day long. We don't know what we are going to eat. We don't know when or if you are coming home. I can't do this anymore."

It was like talking to a wall. The words audibly left my mouth, but they never made it to Saeed's ears. I knew I wasn't getting anywhere, so I said the one thing I knew would get a reaction: "Saeed, I want to go home to Boise *now*."

It wasn't an idle threat—it was an admission of defeat. I had said all I needed to say, so I walked out of the room and started packing. As I packed, I called Baba and asked him to send a driver to take me to his villa. (My parents owned a very nice villa in the city of Karaj, which is about forty-five minutes from Tehran.) My father agreed, saying he would send the driver right away.

"Why do you have to be so dramatic, going to your *daddy's* villa?" Saeed said, stressing the word *daddy* as if it were a dirty word. I noticed the tone in his voice and was no longer satisfied with his finally noticing that I existed.

I knew that Saeed thought of me as a spoiled daddy's girl, but I didn't mind. I was thankful to have someone in my corner because Saeed certainly was not that person. If he had wanted me to run to him instead of to my father, that would have given me hope that there was some kind of love between us, but he didn't. I later recognized that, like most abusers, Saeed wanted me to be completely reliant on him, without being able to turn to anyone else for help; he wanted me to have to depend solely on him so that he could exercise full control over me. Perhaps the one thing Saeed hated more than my turning to my father in times of trouble was when he, also, in desperate times, had to turn to my father for help.

"I'm going to the villa. I'm going home to America!"

"No, you aren't," Saeed replied, switching over to his commanding, authoritarian voice.

I picked up my suitcase to head to the door and immediately had a terrible confrontation with one of Saeed's family members, so that I was forced to stay.

"You aren't leaving," Saeed stated again.

Finding myself outnumbered by Saeed and his family, I was too scared to reply. Slowly, I slunk over to where the children had been sleeping on the floor, crawled next to them, and pulled them close to me. I lay beside them and waited for my father's driver to come pick me up. The driver was a large guy and would help me if I needed it, so I counted the minutes until he came.

As soon as the driver arrived, before anyone else could react, I shot across the room like a cannonball and hit the button to unlock the door. Then, I opened the door so that he could come right into the apartment.

When the driver's big frame filled the doorway, nobody made a move to stop me. Without delay, I ran for the door with the children and asked the driver to grab my half-packed suitcase.

As I made my way to the car with the kids, I realized that I had made it out of the house safely.

The driver came down with my bag and loaded it into the car. As I sat in the back seat with Jacob on my lap and Rebekka beside me, I kissed them both on the forehead and let out a sigh of relief.

Unfortunately, my feeling of liberation at having escaped from the clutches of Saeed's family was short-lived. I realized that I could not leave Iran with the children after all—I had left our passports in Saeed's parents' apartment.

30

TRAPPED IN IRAN

I frantically checked my purse and my jacket pockets. "No! No! No!" I moaned as I rummaged through my belongings in the back seat, praying for a miracle. As we continued driving through the night, I realized the great mistake I had made. However, the truth is, even if I'd had the passports, I would not have been able to leave Iran without Saeed's permission. Both the children and I needed to have Saeed's consent to fly to another country. Saeed knew that.

All night, I anguished over what to do. How would I dig my way out of this? Saeed and his family held all the power, and they knew it.

The next morning, I came to the only conclusion that was feasible: I would have to grovel and make up with Saeed and his family. I would have to take all the blame and absorb all the repercussions. There was no getting back home to Idaho without doing so. I had no other way to leave Iran than to leave with Saeed's blessing.

"Just this one more time, God," I prayed. "Please let me get back home just one more time."

I swallowed the dry lump in my throat, picked up the phone, and slowly began dialing the number of Saeed's family's apartment, pressing each digit slowly and deliberately. As I pushed the buttons, I was trying to work out in my head what I would say.

Saeed answered, and I started off right away eating humble pie. "I'm sorry. I'm sorry I behaved that way yesterday. I was wrong and out of line." I paused to see if he would say anything. He didn't. "I don't think it works for me to be in Iran."

Saeed was unmoved. "You disrespected my family," he said. As those words floated over the line, I bit my lip and said, "I know. I am sorry for that. I never meant to do that. I owe everyone a huge apology."

"Your disrespect brought pain to my family. How are you going to make up for that? I can't help you in this. The damage that you brought is solely on you, no one else. You need to find a way to fix it. My sister was traumatized by the way that you acted yesterday. My father is in a state of grief because of the disunity that you have caused in our family."

"What can I do? How can I make it right?"

"You are going to have to find a way back into this family—if they will even have you back." He paused, then continued, "Yeah, I don't know. I don't know what you are going to have to do, but even if you have to crawl back into the house on your hands and knees, kiss their feet, and beg their forgiveness, that is what you are going to have to do."

I stopped breathing as the reality of what he was saying to me began to sink in. I knew Saeed well. I knew his language. I knew exactly what he meant, and he knew that I knew what he meant. He wanted me to do for his parents what he had made me do for him. He wasn't speaking metaphorically. When he said that I needed to crawl on my hands and knees and kiss his family members' feet, he was being literal, not figurative.

"Well, I just wanted you to know that I am incredibly sorry," I said, breaking the silence. "I am just going to take some time here and work things out."

"No, you're not. I am your husband, and we are going to spend time with family. It is not okay that you go running to your *daddy* every time there is a problem. It is not okay that he keeps putting his nose into our family business. Your place is not at *daddy's* villa. Your place is here with your husband."

I agreed and hung up the phone. I sat there for a moment and prepared myself for what I knew was coming next. I gathered the children and all of our things, got a taxi, and headed back to Saeed's parents' house.

The distance from the taxi to the front door never seemed so long. I stood at the door, paused, and then knocked.

Saeed's mother opened the door. I could see that everyone was standing there with their eyes filled with judgment and their scowls of disapproval. I was drained. I had cried all night, and every ounce of emotion had poured out of me. Now I was on autopilot, my actions mechanical.

Saeed and his family members were stiff and silent, so I broke the silence. "I am sorry for what I did last night. I don't want to give any excuses—"

"No," Saeed said, interrupting me mid-apology. "You can't just come here saying you are sorry this time. It takes a lot to get over what you have done. *A lot,*" he emphasized.

He looked at me, knowing that I knew what to do. His family did not say anything, but I could tell they were expecting me to grovel on my knees.

At that moment, I was willing to do anything to get myself and my children safely out of Iran. I dropped to the floor and got on my hands and knees like a dog as they all towered over me. I started with Saeed's little sister, pulling myself toward her, and began kissing her feet and begging. "I'm so sorry; can I please come back?" I moved down the line of family members, kissing their feet while trying to hold my head as low as possible. "Please let me come back." I kept kissing and begging.

When I finally got to the end of the line at the feet of Saeed's father, the family circled around, motioned for me to stand up, and welcomed me back into their home. They hugged me and told me that my apology was enough to allow me to be accepted back.

"We are not done," Saeed said, breaking up the lovefest of apologies and forgiveness. "We have to address the root issue here. You are sick and need to see a doctor. After what we saw here yesterday, it is clear you need psychiatric help."

My heart sank. He knew what he was doing. He had made me beg and grovel, knowing that I was doing it in hopes of getting back into his good graces so I could make it back to America, but now he was pulling the rug out from under me by telling me that I would be going to see a psychiatrist.

It was code. It meant that he was not going to allow me to go back to America.

I played dumb.

"You mean a psychiatrist in America?" I asked.

"No. You are not going back to America," he said with a smirk.

One of Saeed's family members turned and walked out the front door. Saeed nodded his head toward them and said, "They have your passport. I asked them to take it in case you get the crazy idea of leaving without my permission."

"Please just let me go back to America."

"No," he said firmly. "And that's final. You are not going back until I feel that you are ready to go."

Everything inside me was crumbling. I mustered all my strength just to keep standing. My world was falling apart before my eyes, but I had to act as if it wasn't killing me. I needed to appear strong even if I wasn't. I had to remain strong for my children.

Saeed called my parents and told them that I was crazy and needed medical attention. I knew that my parents were not buying it, although I did start to question my own sanity. When you are living in a small space with people who do not think rationally, you begin to have doubts about yourself.

As soon as Baba learned about my predicament, he immediately went into rescue mode. After learning that Saeed's family member had my passport, as well as Rebekka and Jacob's passports, he called them and played along with the game. He told them he realized I was sick and was so glad I was getting the help I needed.

He convinced them that the passports should be kept in a safe place and told them that his company had a steel safe where the passports would be under twenty-four-hour surveillance. He was able to get them to agree to hand the passports over to the company for "safekeeping." After he had all three passports in his possession, he started to arrange plane tickets to get me and the children out of Iran without Saeed's knowledge.

During the time that Baba was making arrangements for our tickets, Saeed was making arrangements for me to see a psychiatrist. My first session with the psychiatrist lasted about forty-five minutes, and I did not say much. Saeed was there, and he talked for me. For someone who never listened, it was apparent that he had a lot to say. He talked the entire time, answering every question for me and sharing his own diagnosis with the doctor.

The psychiatrist was Muslim and did not find any of the things that Saeed told him about my "disobedience" to be odd in any way. He didn't question Saeed when he shared how he had to "correct" me for being disrespectful.

At the end of the visit, based on the information he had received from Saeed, the psychiatrist wrote me a prescription, and he told Saeed to make sure that I took my medication. Once I had the medication in my hand, I took a picture of it with my phone (thankfully, that hadn't been taken away from me) and sent it to my parents, asking them to connect with my family doctor in the US, who had known me since I was nine years old, to check what the medicine was really for.

My family doctor immediately told my parents that the medication was for schizophrenia. "Your doctor said that these are extremely high doses of strong medication, and they will mess with your mind. Do not take them. They will mess you up," my mother told me over the phone in hushed tones so no one around me could hear what she was saying.

Later, a family member told me that Saeed planned to have me go through electric shock therapy if I didn't take the medicine. This situation was extremely serious. I might never make it out of the nightmare I was in. Committing me to a psychiatric ward would transform Saeed into a victim, someone who had had to deal with an unstable wife. If he wanted to, this would make the transition to his bringing another woman into his life and having full custody of our children explainable to the house churches and also to the people we knew in America.

"Naghmeh, you need to pretend that you agree with them and that you are willingly submitting to the therapy," Baba told me over the phone. "Do not take the medication! We will find a way to get you out of there, but our chances decrease if you are on those powerful drugs."

I acted like I took the medication, but I never did.

My father was able to buy airline tickets for the children and me. He planned it out so that his driver would pick me up and take me to the airport. I packed up only a few small things in a way that no one would notice. We didn't need much. I was okay with leaving everything behind. I needed only to get my children out of Iran and away from Saeed and his family. Everything was in place.

Unfortunately, I was not made to keep secrets. I had so much anxiety the night before we were to leave that I felt sick. I couldn't repress my obsessive thoughts that everything would go wrong. Finally, after I couldn't think of any other option, I broke down and told Saeed the whole plot for the children and me to escape from Iran.

"I can't keep a secret from you. I was working with my father to leave the country," I confessed, wailing and crying.

"You know," he said, "even if you had your passport, I could've charged your dad's coworker with kidnapping." He grew very angry with my father.

"Saeed, I told you the truth, but you have to trust me. I need to be treated in the US. I need to be in a place where I feel comfortable with the treatment. I am not comfortable getting this treatment in Iran. I am not comfortable with a Muslim doctor treating my mental illness. Can you understand that?"

I could see that he needed more convincing. "I need to be in America working in order to sponsor your family to come to America." Something about the way I brought up the subject this time made him come around, and I saw a softness in him.

"I understand," he said. Suddenly, he seemed much more sober and kind, and he agreed to allow me to fly back to the US to be treated for mental illness.

The tension inside me released, and I knew deep down that God had answered my prayer to be able to return to America. It was a miracle that Saeed had agreed to allow me to leave Iran. And he would accompany us back to Boise.

Before we returned to the US, Saeed took the children and me to various locations in Iran, and we spent time together, just the four of us. We hired tour guides to take us to historical sites and went on a family vacation. Looking back, this was one of the best times we ever had as a family. Saeed was kind and sweet, caring and attentive. I was the mother, and he was the father, just as I had always imagined married life would be like.

Part of me felt it was odd that he was so content for me to return to the US.

When we finished our tour of the country, we flew back to America.

31

THE PHONE CALL

We had returned to the US in March, but, by May, Saeed was ready to fly back to Iran. He had grown less agreeable to life in Boise with every passing week.

Because of all that had happened with the Iranian psychiatrist, I made an appointment with my family physician. After examining me, he told me I was *not* mentally ill. During my visit, my family doctor noted only that I had some thyroid issues, and I started taking medication for that condition.

My time in Iran had emphasized to me even further Saeed's apathy toward me and the serious weaknesses in our marriage. Although Saeed would surprise me from time to time with gifts of jewelry, I had largely given up hope of ever having a normal relationship with him. It seemed that our marriage would perhaps always be riddled with ups and downs. I lowered my expectations and increased my resolve to hold on to what we did have.

Saeed appeared eager to return to Iran to oversee the construction of the orphanage. He also wanted to maintain his ties with the house church leaders who had remained loyal to him, and to reestablish connections with other house church leaders that he was no longer in regular contact with. He had been investing more time in trying to reconnect with certain leaders he had formerly worked with. However, he was having little success because these leaders no longer wanted to partner with him. By seeking to work with the house churches, Saeed was exceeding the parameters of his agreement with the Iranian government, and I was becoming anxious about his activities. I asked him to be careful and just focus on the orphanage.

After Saeed left for Iran, I tried to hold things together for our family. He needed me to be solid in his absence. He had to be able to rely on me to raise our two children in a safe, healthy way while he focused on the ministry. He also needed me to continue to work so that I could support our family financially and fund his travels and ministry work.

In July, Saeed phoned and told me he was making plans to take a brief trip to the country of Georgia. He was working to put together a Bible school outside the capital city of Tbilisi. Georgia was easy for Iranians to travel to because it was not far from Iran, and Iranian citizens were automatically granted visas to visit there. Again, this was not the case with some other countries, which often refused entrance to Iranians. It was also not as risky hosting Bible training in Georgia, where Orthodox Christianity was the main religion, as it would be in a Muslim nation like Turkey.

Over the past few months, during Saeed's phone calls from Iran, he had mentioned spending a lot of time with a female member of the house church. Men and women worked together in the fellowships, but I started to sense that something wasn't right with this situation. Just before his trip to Georgia, Saeed talked to me about the woman, saying, "You need to know that she has struggled with depression like you have. Something has happened, and she would like to tell you about it."

"What?"

"I want her to tell you."

"What does she want to tell me? I want to hear it from you first," I said, confused and a bit miffed.

"Look, all I am going to say is that you need to call her. Maybe you can help her deal with it." He hung up after giving me her number.

It felt awkward calling her, and I had no idea what to say over the phone. I was of course willing to help if she was going through a crisis. There were times when I struggled with anxiety and mild depression due to my marriage difficulties, and I had known the stress of being under the watchful eye of the Iranian authorities, so I would try to encourage her if I could.

I called and greeted her in the tone of voice that you use when you are trying to be friendly with someone over the phone whom you haven't actually spoken to in a long time. "I just talked to Saeed. He told me that you are dealing with some issues? I want you to know that I have dealt with the same thing. Depression can be a tough challenge."

"You have dealt with depression because your marriage has had problems," she said, interrupting me mid-thought. "And your marriage has problems because you are married to my husband."

"Your what?" I asked, with a sudden taste of vomit in my mouth.

"You heard me. You are married to the man that I am supposed to be married to. Saeed is my husband. I am mentally struggling, and you are mentally struggling, because you are married to my husband. The best thing that you could do for your mental illness and my mental illness is to divorce Saeed and let him go the way that he needs to go. We need to be together because he loves me, not you, and this situation is bad for everyone's mental health."

After she related some other disturbing details, I hung up and grabbed my chest. A panic attack swept over me, and I found it hard to breathe. I could hear my heartbeat in my eardrums as the blood coursed through my body.

I took a deep breath, picked up the phone, and called Saeed. After a few seconds, I hung up, took another breath, and dialed him again.

"She just told me that you are her husband," I said when he answered.

"Oh, she is crazy," Saeed said. "She is dealing with a mental illness like you have been."

"She told me you have been kissing her."

"Oh, I kiss her in the way that a pastor kisses a fellow servant, as instructed by 2 Corinthians 13:12. You know, like a shepherd kisses his sheep."

"She told me that you told her you loved her."

"I do, the way that a pastor loves his congregants. That's all. Nothing more."

Against everything within me, I believed him. I needed to believe him. If he were lying, I would rather find out later than sooner. I was unable to face it. I felt that I wouldn't survive it if I faced it today.

"Okay, I get this, Saeed, but she obviously does not feel the same way about you that you do about her. She thinks you are husband and wife. Please don't spend time with her anymore."

"What? How dare you! Seriously! Naghmeh, you can't control me like that. I will not allow you to be a Jezebel trying to control her husband. You do not tell me who I can and who I can't hang out with."

"I am not trying to tell you what to do, but, Saeed, I am your wife, and I am begging you to end this."

"I can't talk any longer. I need to go."

I desperately wanted to discuss this further, but Saeed concluded the conversation with a harsh rebuke for me, telling me I was being paranoid and that I should trust him. "I will call you when you arrive in Georgia," I said before reluctantly hanging up.

On the night that Saeed was supposed to arrive in Tbilisi, I called his cell phone, but he didn't answer. So, I called his hotel and asked them to connect me with his room. It was already two in the morning in Georgia, but I knew that Saeed didn't go to bed before three or four. I was certain that he would be awake.

The phone rang one time. "Hello?" came a woman's voice on the other end of the line. It was the voice of the woman who had told me Saeed was her husband.

I immediately broke down crying. Trying to push through my tears and panic attack, I demanded, "Put Saeed on the phone!"

"Hello?" Saeed answered very calmly, as if nothing was wrong.

"You are cheating on me!" I shouted.

"You are crazy. You have mental issues. Nothing is going on."

"Are you two staying at the same hotel?"

"We are sharing a room, but it is only to save money."

"Are you kidding me right now? You two are sleeping together in the same room?"

"I told you, you are crazy.

"Saeed, this is not okay."

"You need to go and see a psychiatrist like I told you to. You are not listening to me, and this is the result."

I hung up, feeling like everything I had believed about our marriage was a sham, everything I had believed about Saeed was just a wishful fairytale. But the most hurtful thing of all was that I now believed that everything bad I had been told about myself was true: I wasn't worthy of happiness. I wasn't pretty enough to be loved. I wasn't good enough to experience loyalty in my marriage.

Panic overwhelmed me once again. Whenever I felt like I was having a panic attack, I would take a hot bath, which always helped me to calm down. I went into my bathroom, closed the door, and turned on the hot water faucet on the bathtub. As the water flowed into the tub, agonized tears poured down my face.

When I was about to get into the bathtub, I caught sight of myself in the mirror. Hollow eyes stared back at me. I looked like I had become a shell of a person. Gone was the strong, confident businesswoman who had entered Iran after college, full of dreams of being a missionary. Overloaded with confusion and stress over my marriage, I no longer felt human; I seemed vacant, void of a soul. I had become like a zombie, lifelessly walking around performing one necessary task after another to provide financially for my family and take care of the children. All I had left in me was the ability to feel pain.

Over time, as my emotions had become increasingly numb, my relationship with God had grown cold, and I rarely prayed anymore. I felt that God was distant and did not care about me. But now, my extreme pain pushed all my suppressed emotions to the surface, and my panic and anxiety burst out in agonized cries to God from the very depths of my being: "Is this the life You want from me? A marriage with an unfaithful spouse? Being in a loveless marriage? Not being loved? Please answer my prayer. Please help me! God, I can't do this any longer." As I cried out, I tried to stifle the sounds so my children wouldn't hear me.

There was still a part of me that wanted to doubt that something was going on between Saeed and this woman. The thought pushed to the surface that perhaps I should see a psychologist after all in hopes that they could tell me if I was reading more into the hotel incident than was really there, and that it was actually an innocent situation.

I cried until I had no more tears left. I prayed until I had no more words to speak. I had reached out to God hoping to find His comfort, but I only seemed to find despair. Utterly exhausted, I fell into a deep sleep.

Four hours later, I was suddenly awakened by my phone ringing. Feeling groggy and confused, I looked at the screen and saw Saeed's name.

I answered and heard his voice on the other end: "I have been arrested."

32

A DIFFERENT KIND OF ARREST

What happened?" I gasped. My entire world suddenly shifted from despair to disaster. I tried to wrap my mind around what Saeed was saying.

He told me he had been on a bus traveling back from Georgia when he had been detained by Iranian officials at the border of Turkey and Iran, and his passport taken. He was told to return to his parents' home and remain there under house arrest.

Saeed had been arrested so many times previously that it was fairly normal, aside from his two-month house arrest in 2009, for him to be stopped, questioned, and then let go after a few hours. I hoped that pattern would hold in this case as well.

"I have been told that I have to wait for questioning and see what is going on. I honestly do not know how long that is going to be, but something feels different this time than the times before."

"Why?"

"I can't say. It is just the way that they had my name at the border crossing. It is pretty remote out there, Naghmeh. It is not the international airport in Tehran where the border guards have access to a lot of information about people who live in Tehran."

Saeed told me he had also recently had a dream in which he was in a cell with a well-known Iranian Christian who had also been arrested, so he had the sense that his present detention might have more dire implications.

While Saeed was under house arrest, the authorities regularly called his home number to make sure he was still there. They also frequently called him in to their offices to be interrogated. During one of those interrogations, a guard secretly told him, "If I were you, I would leave the country. I don't think the government is going to let you go this time." After this, Saeed called me and said, "Naghmeh, I think that you need to contact the Assemblies of God superintendent and ask for his advice. I think that we are going to need help on this one."

I called Dr. George Wood, who was then General Superintendent of the Assemblies of God in the United States, and he suggested that Saeed stay in Iran. He felt it was premature for him to think about escaping from the country since he was not sure what the charges against him were. I remember him saying something like, "If he flees Iran, he will most likely never be allowed to return to minister there again."

I passed along Dr. Wood's advice to Saeed, and he agreed. Since Saeed did not have a passport, getting him out of the country would mean trying to smuggle him across the Turkish border, but we were hesitant to go that route. It would be highly risky—he might get caught and receive a much worse punishment.

Saeed later told me he thought he had avoided being detected when he periodically slipped out of the house to spend time with house church leaders. He also told me he was still meeting with the same woman. His continuing to see her under the circumstances compounded my distress. However, I called Saeed through Skype every day, and we would talk for hours. It felt good to converse with him for these stretches of time.

One of the things that Saeed enjoyed doing with the kids during these calls was to play Iranian music; he would dance or jump on camera from his parents' house, and the kids would dance, jump, and run through our house at the same time. Jacob and Rebekka loved this game. They also loved it when Saeed would play Christian music and sway with them in a form of playful worship.

Soon after his house arrest, Saeed said to me, "I need you to reach out to a woman named Lisa Daftari. She will know what to do to get me out of Iran, in case things get really bad."

"Who?"

"Lisa Daftari." He spelled it out: "D-A-F-T-A-R-I. Call her; she will know what to do in this situation to put pressure on the government."

I called Lisa Daftari, whom I learned was an investigative journalist, and she recommended that I contact a group called the American Center for Law and Justice (ACLJ). The ACLJ listened to my story about Saeed and agreed to help me in any way they could; they immediately involved human rights and advocacy groups such as Middle East Concern to put pressure on international dignitaries working with Iran. The ACLJ didn't want to make the story public to avoid unduly provoking Iran.

Afterward, we wondered whether these efforts weren't creating the opposite effect, because the frequency of Saeed's interrogation sessions with the police increased. It seemed that he was being questioned much more often than before. There was the sense that this was truly growing into a situation that was a lot more serious than the earlier detentions had been.

Saeed told me that the Iranian authorities were asking him about the house church work that he had been conducting in the north. The government was upset because they felt their agreement with Saeed had been that they would let him travel freely if he no longer evangelized, if he severed his ties with the underground church, and if he focused his energies and resources on the humanitarian project for orphans. In their minds, Saeed had disregarded that agreement. They had various pieces of evidence, including photos of Saeed with house church members, showing that he not only had been using his freedom to travel in Iran to meet with members of the home fellowships, but he was also planting churches in the most religious cities of Iran. They wanted the names of all the leaders he was working with, and they wanted details about the church-planting work he had been doing.

When I told the ACLJ about this line of questioning, they saw the storm rising. Saeed had been naturalized in 2010, so he was now an American citizen. Friends and family encouraged me to contact the State Department about his situation. Once the ACLJ had agreed to represent me, I contacted the State Department, and an ACLJ team member was present on the call with me.

The woman we talked with at the State Department, who became our main contact person there, said something to the effect of, "This is not Hollywood, Mrs. Abedini, where the US sends in planes and soldiers to rescue those who violate the laws of other nations." She gave the impression they felt that American Christians went into foreign countries and violated those countries' laws by preaching about Jesus, and then they expected their government to intervene when they were arrested.

"Listen," the woman said before she hung up, "just keep us updated if you hear anything. Other than that, there is nothing that we can do."

I was devastated after that phone call. I believed there was no hope of getting Saeed out of Iran. The State Department seemed to have a clear idea of how things would go: if anything happened, I was to report it to them; but if I needed any help, I was on my own. In their world, I worked for them. They didn't work for me.

I had no idea that things were about to get even worse. In late September, the phone rang in the middle of the night, and when I answered it, I heard a cry of "Naghmeh! Naghmeh!" from the other end of the line. It was Saeed's mother.

"What?" I asked fearfully, knowing that something very bad must have happened.

"They arrested Saeed," she screamed.

"What? Slow down. What are you trying to tell me?"

"They took him. The police! They took Saeed."

"They took him where? Where did they take my husband?"

"I don't know. Police came with guns. They raided our house this morning. They blindfolded him, they took our passports, and now we don't know what is going to happen to him."

In the early-morning hours of September 26, 2012, five members of the Revolutionary Guards stormed my in-laws' home, arrested Saeed, and dragged him out of the house.

For four nerve-racking days, we heard nothing. The government was being totally tight-lipped about his situation, and we began to think the worst, imagining that he might have been executed.

I didn't feel I could tell Rebekka and Jacob what had happened because I didn't want them to go through the pain of not knowing if their father was dead or alive—or, worse, if he were still alive, of thinking about what kind of torture he must be experiencing. They wondered why their father was no longer calling them through Skype to play worship music and jump around together, and I tried to reassure them.

After four days, Saeed was permitted to call his parents. My relief at hearing that he was still alive was combined with alarm at the devastating news that Saeed had been taken to the dreaded Evin Prison—the same political prison where my father's brother had been executed so many years earlier when he was only eighteen. Saeed was in solitary confinement in a detention and interrogation center located within the prison.

When I heard that Saeed had been taken to Evin, memories from my childhood of hearing the firing squad execute prisoners seemed to ring in my ears, and images of visiting my bearded young uncle in that dark prison came flashing back to me: the narrow halls, the look of fear and desperation on his face when I saw him through the glass divider. I could not imagine Saeed being in that prison, and I felt panicked. I had to get him out.

Saeed was now allowed to call his parents once a week. Several times, he called them on their landline, and they would call me from their cell phone at the same time and put the call on speakerphone so we could all talk phone to phone, and I could hear Saeed's voice. The calls lasted for only a few minutes, and the line was faint, so it was very difficult for me to understand what Saeed was saying. However, I cried when I first heard him because I could tell he had been broken, and I could sense the fear in his voice. I kept telling him not to worry and that we would do everything to get him out. I was trying to be the strong one for him.

At the beginning of November, Saeed was moved out of solitary confinement, and he was placed in an isolation cell with another American, Amir Hekmati, a former United States Marine. It seemed that the Iranian government had put Saeed with Hekmati in hopes that the two of them would talk together, and the officials could listen in on their conversations to try to glean important information from them.

We were shocked when Saeed told us he was sharing a cell with an American. We told the State Department about it on our next phone call with them, and they seemed to scramble to contain this unexpected news; they didn't want anyone else knowing about it. No major news outlet was covering the story, and the State Department wanted to keep it that way.

They asked me questions like, "How do you know Saeed is sharing a cell with Amir? How long has he been in there? What is his health like? Does he know how long he will be held there?"

"My husband…" I said, trying to change the subject back to Saeed.

All of their questions were focused on Amir. This was a typical conversation with the State Department. It seemed like, for them, information was paramount so they could stay on top of the situation for political reasons. They wanted me to give them all the information I had, but they offered very little support or political pressure in return in order to obtain Saeed's release.

It was up to Saeed's family and my family to help him—and, together, we turned into a twenty-four-hour information center with a single goal: to keep Saeed alive.

33

KEEPING SAEED ALIVE

About six weeks after he was incarcerated, Saeed was finally allowed to have visits from his parents. Most of the time, they had to meet with a glass divider between them. However, several times, they were permitted to visit together in a room and hug one another. This closeness sometimes gave Saeed the opportunity to pass along letters for me. During these visits, his parents were able to receive firsthand information about what was happening to him, and it confirmed our fears: he was enduring frequent beatings. One consequence of this was that he had developed a stomach ulcer, and this condition kept getting worse. The following letter I received was a dark reminder of what he was going through every day:

> Hello my dear lovely wife,
>
> When I saw my family for the first time behind the glass walls, I could see my mom four meters away. As she approached me and saw my face, she broke down and could not get closer. She was crying. I understood what she felt because after weeks of being in solitary confinement in Evin Prison, I also got to see my face in the mirror of an elevator that was taking me to the prison hospital. I said hi to the person staring back at me because I did not recognize myself. My hair was shaven, under my eyes were swollen three times what they should have been, my face was swollen, and my beard had grown.

About the time he was allowed visits with his parents, Saeed was transferred out of the cell with Amir and put into a larger cell with prison detainees who were members of al-Qaeda. The Evin officials knew it would be a real threat to a Christian convert from Islam to be in the same cell as al-Qaeda adherents, and they took joy in seeing what would happen. This was another way in which the Iranian government tortured Saeed. These al-Qaeda members threatened him, threw chairs at him, and beat him. The attacks continued from about the end of November until well into January, when Saeed finally had his hearing before the judge.

In addition to enduring constant physical harm, Saeed suffered mental anguish. The prison guards made sure that he could hear the screams of the people who were being executed. Throughout this time, Saeed was continually being interrogated while evidence was being collected against him.

The Iranian government began playing games with us concerning Saeed's case. They said that we could pay for him to be released on bail for 300 million Iranian rials, which is less than ten thousand USD, but when we got the money together to pay the bail, the government increased the price. My father put his business up for collateral to secure Saeed's release, and the authorities gave us hope that they would accept that offer, but then they changed the terms again at the last minute. They loved dangling a carrot in front of us, only to jerk it away just when we thought we could reach it. It was a method they used to show they had power over us.

The government held all the cards, and they knew it. To them, Saeed was not a human being with a family. He was a pawn to be played with on the international game of chess between nations. It was clear that the Iranian officials wanted to get the most mileage out of Saeed that they could. Although Saeed had been born in Iran, the government was hoping he would be valuable to the US government since he was also a US citizen. Iran was willing to hold their own citizen hostage so that they could extract a high ransom price for him.

In November 2012, during one of his phone calls, Saeed said, "They are not going to release me. Go to the media."

We recognized we were not getting anywhere with the Iranian government. Saeed's family and I, as well as the ACLJ, had been afraid that going to the media would make the situation for Saeed's family in Iran dangerous and also make it harder to obtain Saeed's release. We had felt that quietly trying to obtain his freedom using behind-the-scenes requests by countries that were friendly with Iran might be the best option, so that is what we had attempted. We had reserved the media as our last option. Now, after we had unsuccessfully tried the other avenues, we all agreed the media was our only remaining choice. Saeed was still being tortured, and he was being threatened with death every day. If we kept Saeed's imprisonment a secret from the public at large, the Iranian government might still kill him. So, at this point, we felt there was nothing to lose, and we could possibly gain his life.

It was only when we decided to go public that I told our children Saeed was in prison. They had been asking if their father was no longer calling them because he did not care about them anymore, and I knew I had to tell them the truth. Because information about his imprisonment would soon become public, I knew it would not be long before they heard the news from someone else. So, one morning, I called Rebekka and Jacob to me and told them that their dad loved them, and that the reason he was not calling them was that he was in prison. They were both devastated and asked me what the prison looked like. We looked up photos of Evin Prison online, and I was able to show them where Saeed was and what his room might look like. Their father's continued enforced silence and absence caused them great sadness and anxiety.

On December 12, through the help of the ACLJ, we were able to retain a very good lawyer in Iran to help defend Saeed. But, until the time of his trial, the authorities would not allow his lawyer to visit him.

The first media piece appeared on December 19. Lisa Daftari wrote an article on FoxNews.com to spread the word about Saeed's situation, and the article went viral. That same day, because the piece had gotten so much traction on the Fox website, I was invited to appear with Jay Sekulow on Sean Hannity's television show. Being on his program offered an opportunity to get Saeed's story out to the world in a huge way. Because of the short notice, the Hannity team was not able to secure a TV studio in Boise from which I could do the interview, so they sent a camera crew to my parents' home, complete with satellite trucks, utility vans, and suitcases full of equipment.

When the Fox team arrived, they hit the ground running, with crew members rushing back and forth from the house to their vehicles, dragging cables and gear boxes, rearranging furniture, setting up lights, and positioning large, black-boxed cameras.

I had never been on television before, so I called two of my friends and asked them to come be with me and help me prepare. More than anything else, I just needed someone to hold my hand. I felt that I was not a good speaker and did not know exactly what to say.

"Can we get a mic check over here?" one person yelled.

"Going live in thirty minutes everyone!" shouted another.

"Don't worry, Naghmeh, you are going to do just fine," one woman from the team reassured me as she helped me put a microphone in my ear so that I could hear Sean Hannity. "Now, you will not be able to see anyone, but you will hear Sean's voice. Just answer the questions as if you are talking to him, and when you do, look directly at that camera right there," she said, pointing to the camera directly in front of me.

I nodded my head so that she would know I had heard her, but I wasn't so certain I had. There were so many things happening at the same time. I was also thinking about how Sean Hannity had one of the biggest news shows in the United States, and there would be millions of people watching this interview live.

"Lord, give me strength," I prayed. One of my friends swept my bangs as she whisked a touch of hairspray to hold everything in place.

I also prayed to God for wisdom and clarity. I wasn't sure if I was doing the right thing by going on television. I wanted to get the word out about Saeed's wrongful imprisonment, but I also kept thinking that, by doing so, I could be risking his life. There was a strong possibility that Iran would punish Saeed even more because of the international embarrassment the interview would most certainly cause. But if I didn't do anything, he might die in prison.

I had to save my husband's life. I had to get him out of one of the worst prisons on earth and out from under the control of one of the most evil governments in the world—even if it meant risking everything and costing me my life. Speaking out against the Iranian government could make me, as a woman with young children, their target as well.

Yet I felt that my voice was the only one that could campaign for Saeed— he had no one else. He couldn't speak for himself from prison. Saeed's parents and siblings, living in Iran, were understandably afraid of being targeted by the Iranian government if they were to publicly advocate for Saeed. His siblings also had futures that would be seriously jeopardized if they were to get involved. And our diplomatic efforts to free Saeed had been almost fruitless.

Yes, I *had* to do it. Going public was the only way to move forward—and I needed to use the biggest megaphone I could find for Saeed's sake.

When the interview started, I could hear Sean Hannity in my ear asking questions, but there was a slight awkward delay between his questions and my answers due to the satellite transmission. At first, it felt a bit clumsy looking at a camera with lights rather than directly at Sean Hannity while answering his questions, but that feeling passed and was replaced by what felt like a super-natural ease.

Sean started out by asking why I thought this time was different from the other times Saeed had been detained, and my answer reflected what I had come to recognize about the situation: "I believe that this time, the Revolutionary Guard has been handling Saeed's case and previously, the intelligence police was. I believe the recent change from the intelligence police to the Revolutionary Guard has changed the way they have been treating Christians and Christian activities in Iran."[13]

I also explained that Saeed was being physically abused by his interrogators and other prisoners. I shared how Rebekka told me she was forgetting her father's voice but that, early that morning, she had been able to talk with Saeed during a brief, phone-to-phone call through Saeed's parents and hear that he loved her.

Almost as soon as the interview started, it ended. It concluded so abruptly that I felt like I had missed the opportunity to really let people know about Saeed's situation. I had wanted to share so many additional things with the audience. For a moment, a strong feeling of regret flushed over me, and I thought I had ruined the only chance I had been given to get Saeed's story out to the public.

In my mind, I immediately began replaying the answers I had given, wishing I had been more animated or charismatic when responding. I thought of ways I could have made a more emotional appeal. Yet, as soon as I removed the microphone from my ear, there was immediate positive feedback from the Fox News crew in the room—the team actually cheered.

"Great job!" came one comment from across the room from a woman with both of her thumbs in the air.

"That was so good," said a young man helping to remove my microphone. "It is unbelievable that this is your first time. Seriously, that was so good."

"That is everything that we need from you, Naghmeh," said another crew member as she helped pack everything up. "And you look so pretty. I love what you did with your hair. You looked so good on camera."

13. Naghmeh Abedini Panahi, interview by Sean Hannity, "American Pastor Imprisoned While Visiting Family in Iran," *Hannity*, Fox News, December 19, 2012 (revised January 8, 2015), https://www.foxnews.com/transcript/american-pastor-imprisoned-while-visiting-family-in-iran. The quotation has been lightly edited for capitalization.

My heart was overjoyed. This was the first time in years that I didn't feel like a complete loser. For so long, I had been told that I was fat and ugly, and that I couldn't do anything right, but now I was in a room full of people supporting me, praising my ability, and telling me that I was beautiful.

When Saeed was first arrested, I had felt weak and anxious, but through the process of advocating for him, I began to discover that God is my strength. I could rely on Him to guide me and give me the words to speak at interviews and events—and to be bold for the gospel.

I didn't see it at the time, but through Saeed's imprisonment, God was beginning to set me free and help me find my true identity and confidence in Him. Each step I took to free Saeed became a step closer to my own freedom.

34

TORTURED FOR CHRIST

January 10, 2013

When I heard that empty Christmas settings were placed during Christmas as a reminder of my imprisonment and those imprisoned for Christ, tears of joy filled my eyes. I was able to share about this with other prisoners, and they were shocked by the love and support we have for each other in Jesus. I told them how in the Bible we are all considered brothers and sisters (despite race, color, or nationality) and we are to share in each other's pains. This comes from our Lord.

The Word of God says that when we are persecuted for our faith, we are to count it all joy. When I think that all of these trials and persecutions are being recorded in heaven for me, my heart is filled with complete joy. The Bible says that the joy of the Lord is our strength. Without the joy of the Lord we cannot live. It is this joy in our life that gives us strength to continue in this life.

Without strength, we cannot continue the work of the Lord, and without joy, there is no strength. I always wanted God to make me a godly man. I did not realize that in order to become a godly man we need to become like steel under pressure. It is a hard process of warm and cold to make steel. This is the process in my life today: one day I am told I will be freed and allowed to see my family and kids on Christmas (which was a lie), and the next day I am told I will hang for my faith in Jesus. One day there are intense pains after beatings in interrogations; the next day they are nice to you and offer you candy. These hot and cold days only make you a man of steel for moving forward in expanding His kingdom.

When for 120 days you sleep in a room with a giant light that is constantly lit, not allowing you to separate day from night, and when you can only see true sunlight for a few minutes a week, that's when you are becoming His workmanship, and you can be a vessel in bringing His kingdom in a dark place, and you are able to share the gospel of peace and life to the dying world. And this is where you learn you can love your enemies with all of your heart. I am looking forward to the day I can see all of you who are behind me with your prayers and to embrace you in my arms. Thank you for the love you have showed me. What is in us is stronger than what is in the world, and it has conquered the world.

Pastor Saeed Abedini, in chains for our Lord Jesus Christ[14]

I wept as I read this letter from Saeed, which he had hurriedly written on a newspaper and given to his parents during one of their visits. In prison, Saeed was being transformed into the man that God had called him to be. And as I prayed and worked for his release, I was being transformed into the woman that God had called me to be.

As deeply grateful as I was to receive this letter, it also reminded me once again of the gunshots I had heard from the executions at Evin Prison when I was a child, and I was afraid for Saeed's life. Saeed continued to endure countless interrogations, beatings, and torture sessions.

Saeed's case went to trial a little more than two weeks after he wrote this letter. Just before the trial started, the US government began making public calls for his release.

The entire trial was a sham. Judge Pir-Abassi, who presided, was notorious for sentencing people to death—so many so that he had been nicknamed "The Hanging Judge." Saeed never even had a chance to meet with his lawyer until January 20—the day before his trial began. His trial lasted two days, but Saeed and his lawyer were only allowed to be there on the first day—Saeed was not permitted to be present on the concluding day of his own trial!

On January 27, 2013, Saeed was convicted of "threatening the national security of Iran." The Iranian government didn't reveal much beyond this statement, but it was clear that Saeed had been found guilty of the charges because he had met with fellow Christians in private homes and expressed his

---

14. All of the letters from Saeed in this book were translated from Farsi by the author.

religious beliefs. He was sentenced to eight years in prison, although everyone knew he would not survive those eight years. Eight years at Evin Prison was essentially a death sentence for a Christian convert guilty of spreading Christianity in a Muslim country.

A spokesperson for the State Department made a statement saying they were "calling on Iran to respect Saeed Abedini's human rights and release him."[15]

In early February, the ACLJ launched a website, SaveSaeed.org, that allowed people to sign a petition for Saeed's release and share information with others through social media. They also started a #SaveSaeed campaign on Twitter.

After his trial, Saeed was beaten so badly when he was sent back to prison and placed in a regular cell that he experienced internal bleeding. Although he was seen by doctors, he was prevented from receiving treatment.

Saeed wrote that a guard told him, "Deny your faith in Jesus Christ and return to Islam or else you will not be released from prison. We will make sure you are kept here even after your eight-year sentence is finished."

Saeed had been shackled, beaten, electrocuted, kept from medical treatment, forced to watch executions, and threatened with death every day, but he would not bend in his faith. He could have made things so much easier on himself by denying Christ, but he didn't. He refused. During the months he had been incarcerated, we had both grown to be spiritual warriors in ways that we had never thought we could be.

Saeed also gave what I believe was one of the most loving displays of Christianity the modern world has witnessed. He wrote letters from prison that brought me to my knees. Saeed revealed a side of himself that I had never seen before but was everything I had prayed for in a husband.

I pored over his letters again and again. I also shared them with others, and I could see that Saeed's words gave them hope and strength too. The letters he was writing from prison were changing people's hearts and bringing them into a deeper relationship with Jesus Christ. A portion of another letter read this way:

> Maybe you ask, what is the secret of being so happy in such a hard situation?

---

15. "US Pastor Sentenced to Eight Years in Iran," CBS News, January 28, 2013, https://www.cbsnews.com/news/us-pastor-sentenced-to-8-years-in-iran/.

Forgiveness and a change of attitude.

When we forgive, we become free and we become messengers of peace and reconciliation and goodness. And whoever stings us, we can take into our embrace and love them. And in this dark and evil time, we can live full of love and full of peace and full of joy and shine like the stars! Glory be to His name.

I forgave the prison doctor who did not listen to me and did not give me the medication that I needed. I forgave the interrogator who beat me. Every day when I would see the interrogator and for the last time when I saw him, I forgave him. I smiled at him and with respect shook his hand, and I said my goodbye. The minute I forgave them and loved them, that second I was filled with unspeakable joy. I saw in the eyes of the interrogator that he had come to respect me, and as he was leaving, he could not look behind him. Love is as strong as death.

We have to get rid of the poison in our body because if we don't, we will die. We have to get rid of both poisons: first the poison of the snake that bit us and also the poison in us that was created by that bite. We can get rid of the first poison by forgiveness, and we can get rid of the second poison by humility, by dying to ourselves, and allowing the Band-Aid of love and goodness to replace the empty place of the wound. So that we are not a tool of darkness and revenge, but that we can be light and love and a vessel of forgiveness, and we can be transformed in the process.

Surely you have someone in your family, city, work, or environment that has become like a poisonous snake who has bitten you and tried to make you poisonous. So, forgive them and use the antidote of love and be victorious!

One of the chances of forgiveness came when I was blindfolded and a guard was holding my hand guiding me. He asked, "What are you here for? What is your crime?" I said, "I am a Christian pastor." All of the sudden he let go of my hand and said, "So you are unclean! I will tell others not to defile themselves by touching you!" He would tell others not to get close to me. It really broke my heart. The nurse would also come to take care of us and provide us with treatment, but she said in front of others, "In our religion we are not supposed to touch you, you are unclean. Baha'i [religion] and Christians are unclean!" She did not treat me, and that night I could not sleep from the intense pain I had. According to the doctor's instructions, they would not give me the pain medication that they would give other prisoners because I was unclean....

Even though many would call me unclean and filthy and would not even want to pass by me, and they had abandoned me and they were disgusted to touch me because they were afraid that they would also become unclean, I knew that in the eyes of Jesus Christ, and in the eyes of my brothers and sisters, I am like the sewer rat, beautiful and loveable—not disgusting and unclean—and like the rats I can scream with joy within those prison walls and worship my Lord in joy and strength.

The joy of the Lord is my strength. Amen.

"The joy of the Lord is my strength," I said aloud as I read the letter again. "The whole world will read this letter," I told myself. "The entire world will see the testimony of God working in Saeed's life, transforming his life into a story of love, forgiveness, and redemption."

A couple of months after Saeed was sentenced, the authorities allowed additional family members to visit him in prison. During one of his business trips to Iran in March 2013, my father went to see Saeed, and he told me that Saeed had apologized to him for having beaten him. Saeed's life truly seemed to be undergoing a transformation.

After Saeed's sentencing and confinement to a regular prison cell at Evin, he was sometimes able to borrow smuggled phones from his fellow prisoners and call me. However, these calls were rare and quick because Saeed was afraid he would be caught talking on the phone and be punished further.

Saeed was also able to talk with Rebekka and Jacob at times. I knew that he would usually try to call from the prison phone at a certain time on Wednesday nights, which for us in Idaho was Wednesday morning at about ten-thirty. The children attended a Christian school, and that was the time chapel was held, so I arranged with the teachers to allow Rebekka and Jacob to sit with me in our car during chapel in case Saeed was able to call. Several times, he managed to call during that time and reassure the children that he was okay and would be coming home soon. We cherished every moment that we were able to hear Saeed's voice together over the phone because he was given only five minutes to talk—and not a second longer.

I lived from letter to letter and from phone call to phone call. In between, my imagination was not morbid enough to recreate what Saeed was actually going through, but it was vivid enough to keep me awake at night, wet with the sweat of terror for his life.

35

THE CAMPAIGN

Wow! Fox News saw a huge spike in viewers when you were sharing about Saeed," the office manager from ACLJ said over the phone after my appearance on Sean Hannity's program. "The viewers really connected with you, Naghmeh. Your interview is being played everywhere."

The interview with Sean Hannity had gone much better than I ever could have dreamed. And it was doing exactly what we had hoped it would do: getting the information about Saeed's imprisonment out to the entire world.

Interviews with Fox News became a regular occurrence for me. I would speak on one of their programs at least two or three times a week. In addition to Sean Hannity, Judge Jeanine Piro was passionate about helping Saeed and invited me on her program more times than I was capable of accommodating.

Jake Tapper of CNN took a special interest in Saeed's story too. He asked me to be on his program, and I was interviewed on CNN multiple times. The longer Saeed was in prison, the more people's interest in his case grew, and calls for his release began to increase. I started to get additional requests for media interviews.

I felt transformed from a helpless housewife into a fearless freedom fighter.

In December 2012, Congressman Frank Wolf, a US representative from Virginia, reached out to me and invited me to talk with other members of Congress in the spring of 2013. "I have seen you on Fox News," I recall him telling me. "I think Congress needs to hear what you have to say. Would you please consider coming to Washington, DC, and sharing about your husband who is in prison for his faith?"

Congressman Wolf arranged for me to testify on March 15, 2013, before the Tom Lantos Human Rights Commission of the US House of Representatives, which the congressman cochaired. During a layover on my flight to DC for the hearing, my main contact at the State Department, who had heard I was about to testify, called me. She seemed upset and claimed that I had not asked them for help. I assured her that I had indeed asked them for help, but I had been told that there was nothing they could do.

When I landed in DC a few hours later, I met with my ACLJ lawyers to prepare for the hearing. As I read through my written testimony, my emotions overtook me, and tears started streaming down my face. I had to stop reading my testimony and compose myself for the hearing.

Within hours, I was seated in front of Congressman Wolf and a panel of other congressmen and lawmakers, with my ACLJ lawyer, Jordan Sekulow, next to me. While testifying before the commission, I said,

> Saeed holds to what he believes and will not give in under any pressure from the Revolutionary Guards. He is standing up for religious freedom in a country that has no respect for human rights. Are we going to stand with him? Are we going to stand up as a country and protect a citizen whose human right of religious freedom is so clearly violated? Americans are not all Christians; but *every American*—regardless of their beliefs—wants to be reassured and know that our government will take decisive action to protect us if someone uses force to try to make us abandon or change our beliefs.

During a break in the hearing, Congressman Wolf called the new Secretary of State, John Kerry, and demanded to know why the State Department had dropped the ball on Saeed's situation. He wanted to know why Iran had an American citizen in prison for practicing his faith.

Right after the hearing, the ACLJ lawyers told me that we had a meeting with the State Department's Ambassador at Large for International Religious Freedom. At the meeting, in addition to the ambassador, there were some staff members from the State Department, including the woman who had called me earlier that day. This woman was still upset and again proclaimed, "You didn't ask us to do anything!" She seemed to desperately want to pass the blame on to someone else, but Jay Sekulow was having none of it. He pushed back, and the room got heated. One of Jay's colleagues from the ACLJ had been on the phone with me the day they had told me "This isn't Hollywood" and that there was nothing they could do.

Now that reputations and careers were apparently on the line, there was a change of tune from the State Department. After that meeting, the ball started rolling in terms of the US government becoming more directly involved in freeing Saeed. Although the government had started making some statements calling for Saeed's release after I went to the media, the real movement of negotiations on his behalf followed this hearing. Not long afterward, we were also assigned a new contact person at the State Department.

Later in the year, on December 12, 2013, I had an opportunity to testify before members of Congress again, in a joint hearing of two subcommittees of the Committee on Foreign Affairs. I shared about the plight of Saeed and other Christians in Iran. "My husband is suffering because he is a Christian," I said while clutching a black-framed photo of our family. God allowed me to have a platform not just to share about the imprisonment of my husband, but also to highlight the persecution of Christians that happens every day and that we often overlook or even ignore.

The opportunity that made the greatest impact on me came in June of 2013, when I was invited to speak, through the European Centre for Law and Justice, before the United Nations Human Rights Council in Geneva, Switzerland. On June 3, 2013, I did more than just give an update about Saeed's situation—I used this platform to share about the plight of Christians around the world and to introduce people to the gospel message. As I shared, God opened my eyes to the opportunity He had given me: He was using my advocacy of Saeed and other persecuted Christians to help fulfill the deepest desires of my heart to share the gospel with the nations, which I had carried since the day I first read the Bible. I remembered reading Psalm 2:7–8 as a little girl:

> [7]I will proclaim the LORD's decree:
>> He said to me, "You are my son;
>> today I have become your father.
> [8]Ask me,
>> and I will make the nations your inheritance,
>> the ends of the earth your possession.[16]

---

16. NIV.

God was my Father; He had made me His daughter. Since that moment, I had prayed that He would give me the nations as my inheritance, meaning that I would be able to share with people around the world the love of God through Jesus Christ. And here I was, testifying before the nations. Talking about Saeed's plight as a Christian with representatives from countries around the world—having my words being translated into their languages as I spoke them—was a remarkable and powerful time for me. Tears started streaming down my face as I realized that God was indeed using even Saeed's imprisonment to enable me to proclaim the gospel to the world.

As the United Nations became more involved in Saeed's case, over the next couple of years, requests came flooding in from people in the United States, Canada, the United Kingdom, and Europe for me to come and speak about Saeed to various governing bodies, churches, and foundations.

One of the most intriguing moments during these speaking engagements came in Germany in 2015. Arrangements had been made for me to meet with Volker Kauder, the parliamentary group leader of the ruling party in Germany at that time, who was known as the right hand of German Chancellor Angela Merkel.

When I arrived, Volker Kauder's staff appeared cold and matter-of-fact. They told me I would only have two minutes to meet with him, and they made it clear that the lawyers traveling with me would not be allowed to ask him any questions. It was not clear to me why they had even agreed to meet with me. It seemed like I was a burden on their day, and they would have preferred that I stay away.

When I met with Mr. Kauder, he gave the impression of being stoic, cold, and dismissive of my entire campaign for Saeed in Germany. He greeted me in what seemed the most impatient manner, and, after listening to me introduce myself, he grew even more irritable.

As I think back on that memorable day, I remember him sighing, "There is nothing you can do," and adding, "Iran is Iran. You aren't going to change them. I am not going to change them. What do you want from the German government? There is nothing any of us can do."

"I am not giving up," I replied. "I have to knock on every door and talk to every person. I am a wife and a mother of small children. My husband is in prison, and I am not just going to throw my hands up in defeat. I understand your concerns, but I don't share your fatalism. I have faith. I have hope. There is a way to get my husband out of prison, and I will find it."

As I kept speaking, I watched his face soften. His eyes grew kinder, and he seemed more sympathetic to my story.

"This is in God's hands," I said. "Not in mine, not even in yours. But it being in God's hands doesn't mean that mine have to remain idle. It is in His hands, but He has chosen to move His hands through us—through our lives, our mouths, and our hands."

I didn't know if what I was saying made sense to him, but by the look on his face, it seemed that this sentiment had pierced his heart. We kept talking much longer than the two minutes he had originally allotted to me. Whenever a staff member would come by to break up our meeting, he would send them away.

At one point, I recall Mr. Kauder asking, "Would it be okay if I had a photo taken with you, Mrs. Naghmeh?" The way he asked the question seemed so gentle and vulnerable, almost like a small child making a shy inquiry of their teacher. At the beginning of the meeting, he had appeared as hard and cold as a steel rod, but now he appeared as soft as warm butter. When it finally came time to end the meeting, we shared a long embrace, and I was sad to leave. It was definitely one of the most inspiring meetings I had ever had.

Even so, this was not the most interesting meeting I experienced while campaigning for Saeed. Toward the end of 2014, I heard that Donald Trump wanted to meet with me, but I was cautioned that this might not be a good idea.

At the time, I didn't know anything about Donald Trump, so I had to look up his name on the Internet. There I came to understand why I had been cautioned about meeting with him. A movement had started in the United States known as the "Birther Movement," which reportedly promoted the idea that President Obama was not born in the United States, and his birth certificate in Hawaii had been forged. At the time, Donald Trump was one of the leading voices questioning the authenticity of President Obama's birth certificate. For this reason, it seemed Trump had quickly gained the position of being "public enemy number one" to the entire Democratic party. Associating with him might jeopardize my chances of garnering further support from the State Department and White House to free Saeed.

I prayed about the matter before making my decision. After some time in prayer, I felt a strong confirmation that I should meet with Donald Trump. I believed I had to knock on every door possible to help Saeed.

I flew to New York, and, the next morning, I found myself waiting on a couch outside Trump's office in Trump Tower. Two lawyers from the ACLJ were with me. Not long after we sat down, Trump's daughter Ivanka walked into the room. At first, she walked purposefully toward her father's office door, an entourage of four people following closely behind her. Then, suddenly, as if noticing something from the corner of her eye, she came over to me.

With a large, friendly smile, she squatted down, gazing upward at me, and introduced herself. She reached up and pulled my hands toward hers and placed her free hand on top, clasping both of my hands.

"Oh, my gosh, Naghmeh, we have been praying for you and your family," she said with the kind of voice someone uses when they intimately know you. Then she stood up, with one of my hands still in hers, and said, "Come. Let's go to my dad's office."

I smiled because we had been instructed to wait until someone told us when to go in, but Ivanka didn't have to wait to be told when she could go into her father's office. She had the liberty to come and go as she pleased. She walked up to the door and, without knocking or apparently having any fear of disturbing something important, walked right in with me, the ACLJ lawyers accompanying us.

Donald Trump looked up from his desk and seemed a bit confused to see me walking in with his daughter.

"This is Naghmeh," one of the ACLJ lawyers explained as Ivanka swung me around to introduce me.

"Wow, you are beautiful," Trump said right away. Then he kindly invited us to sit down, with my lawyers and me on one side of the table, he on the other, and his assistant toward the corner.

After we sat down, Trump began to open up to us. I knew that he was a busy person, but, in that moment, he acted as if he had no other plans for the day than to be with us. I recall him looking over at me and saying, "You know I am a Christian." He said that he could appreciate the mission work that Saeed and I had been doing. "I had family members who were missionaries," he said fondly. He also mentioned that he had attended Billy Graham's ninety-fifth birthday party the year before. I think he was making kind gestures to demonstrate that we had common ground between us as Christians.

Then, with a burst of passion, he blurted out, "What is wrong with Obama? He should be doing more to get your husband out of there. If I were president, I'd be focusing on this a lot more than he is." His language changed, and he used much different words to describe President Obama than he had his missionary family members.

After we had been in his office for an hour, he asked if I would like to take a short tour. He showed me the different items hanging on his wall, sharing with me their history and what they meant to him. He also showed me the various magazines that had featured him on the front cover.

After our meeting, we took a photograph together. He shook my hand and told me that it had been a pleasure to meet me, adding, "But before you leave, I want to give you something."

He walked back over to his desk, grabbed something from the top of it, and handed it to me. It was a check for $10,000. I gratefully accepted the funds to help with my ongoing travel expenses and continued advocacy for Saeed.

When I flew home to Boise, my bank would not cash the check at first. The bankers didn't believe it was real, unconvinced that Donald Trump had actually written me a check for $10,000. After a few phone calls, they were able to verify that the check was real, and they deposited it into my bank account.

36

A NEW FRIEND

In the hardest moments of fighting for Saeed's freedom, God delivered words of comfort to me through His faithful servants. At the most strategic times, He knew what I needed, when I needed it, and how I would best receive it. When I wrestled the most with my self-worth and ability to do the task that was in front of me, God sent guides to lead me. They provided support and love in a way that I won't ever be able to repay.

Countless people proved invaluable to me during this time. Many of them were close personal friends. I knew them by name, and they reached out to me every day. Some of them were Christians praying for our family from thousands of miles away, individuals that I may never get the chance to meet. Others were business owners and ministry leaders. There were people who used their power and influence on our behalf, even though I could not offer them anything in return, such as the initial thirty-seven members of the US House of Representatives and twelve members of the US Senate who sent letters to Hillary Clinton at the State Department on Saeed's behalf. Secretaries of State Hillary Clinton and John Kerry themselves both demanded Saeed's release. There were also music legends who used their platforms to raise awareness, like Ricky Skaggs, TobyMac, Bart Millard, Kevin Max, Steven Curtis Chapman, Skillet, Rhett Walker Band, Michael W. Smith, Michael Tait, and Josh Turner. And knowing that influential people like President Barack Obama, who mentioned Saeed at the 2013 National Prayer Breakfast, and Donald Trump were praying for Saeed and our family overwhelmed me with gratitude.

In addition to Fox News and CNN, there were several television outlets, newspapers, and magazines who also helped me, including the Christian Broadcasting Network. CBN highlighted Saeed's story and allowed me direct access to their audience to petition millions of Christians around the world to pray.

In March of 2013, while I was at CBN for an interview, I met a representative from the public-relations firm The DeMoss Group. He told me that DeMoss represented Franklin Graham, the son of Billy Graham and the founder and president of the organization Samaritan's Purse, who also now served as the president of the Billy Graham Evangelistic Association. I started thinking about how Franklin Graham might be able to help with Saeed's cause. The idea of connecting with him changed the entire trajectory of my advocacy.

After finding the telephone number for Samaritan's Purse online, I called the organization and introduced myself to the person who answered. Immediately, I was transferred to someone in upper management who told me Franklin Graham was traveling but would get back to me. I really didn't expect to hear back, but, within a few days, Franklin called me and said he had been closely following Saeed's case.

Franklin Graham and I instantly connected. Franklin had the kind of energy and charm that made you feel like you had known him for years, even if you had only just met him. There was also a spiritual element to our conversation that was perfectly timed. From that first phone conversation, it was clear that this was a divine appointment.

Franklin and I worked together to get Saeed's story out to the public in an even bigger way. We didn't just want to inform people—we wanted to involve them. We wanted to bring them in and activate them not only to campaign for Saeed but also to continue to independently fight for oppressed Christians around the world and speak out against religious persecution. As imperative as Saeed's situation was, this wasn't just about him—it was about the oppression that many believers in closed countries like Iran face on a daily basis.

Franklin immediately put his energies into "Operation Rescue Saeed." He put all the resources at his disposal toward getting the word out, including arranging for Billy Graham's *Decision Magazine* to highlight Saeed's plight. Franklin also brought in the weight of both his organizations to issue a worldwide call to prayer at www.SaveSaeed.org. In addition, he encouraged people to join a worldwide prayer vigil being organized for the one-year anniversary of Saeed's imprisonment, which I would later participate in at the Idaho state capitol building. In Washington, DC, the prayer vigil would be attended by

Jane Zimmerman, the Assistant Secretary of State for Democracy, Human Rights, and Labor; Senator Ted Cruz; and other leaders.

I flew to North Carolina and shared Saeed's story at the Samaritan's Purse headquarters in the rural town of Boone, where Franklin and I worked on one of the most ambitious projects that had ever been undertaken to secure a Christian pastor's release from imprisonment for his faith. We would continue to work together as the months went by and Saeed remained in captivity.

Not only did Franklin help to raise the profile of the advocacy for Saeed, but he also used every opportunity to lift up the name of Jesus. During a joint interview that he and I did in 2014 for *On the Record with Greta Van Susteren* at Fox News, he was asked about Saeed's situation.

"Reverend Franklin Graham," Greta Van Susteren said, "he's just a Christian...I mean, that's the whole reason he is sitting in prison for eight years. What do you want to do? What do you hope to accomplish?"

On my right, leaning forward with the eagerness of a child, Franklin responded in such a way as to not let the opportunity pass. He didn't just want to say that Saeed was being persecuted because he was a Christian. He wanted the world to know what it meant to *be* a Christian. He wanted to educate the audience about what the real purpose behind Saeed's persecution was. Saeed was not being persecuted simply because he called himself a Christian. "He's in prison because he believes that Jesus Christ is God's Son, and that Jesus died for our sins upon the cross, was buried for our sins, and that God raised him to life; and, because he believes this, he has been beaten, he has been tortured, imprisoned...."

Franklin also reminded the audience, "He's an American citizen."[17]

---

17. *On the Record with Greta Van Susteren*, September 25, 2014, 1:09, https://video. samaritanspurse.org/franklin-graham-and-naghmeh-abedini-speak-out-in-support-of-imprisoned-pastor-saeed-abedini/.

37

CONFRONTING THE IRANIAN
PRESIDENTIAL DELEGATION

When I wasn't traveling, there were times when I felt helpless at my home in Idaho. Boise can feel far removed from the world when you are trying to run an international campaign to save your husband. The remote mountains of Idaho are a great place to raise a family but an inconvenient spot to stay connected with the pulse of international politics.

In September 2013, shortly before the one-year anniversary of Saeed's imprisonment, I had just started a time of fasting and prayer when I felt a deep conviction to go to New York City. Newly elected Iranian president Hassan Rouhani was coming to America to speak at the United Nations, and a voice inside told me that I needed to be there.

I called the ACLJ and talked with Tiffany Barrans, one of the top lawyers working with me on Saeed's case, and told her I wanted to go to New York.

"You know, we are often allowed into the United Nations," she replied, "but on this occasion we will not be. Security has been increased for this event because of the Iranian president, and only heads of state will be allowed in when he is there."

"What about if we just…." I tried to squeeze out my thought, but I didn't really know what I wanted to do. I just wanted to be in the same city because I felt that was what I should do.

"Just…go there?" Tiffany finished my thought for me.

"Yes! I don't know why, but it just feels like I am supposed to be in the same city as the Iranian president. I can't just sit here in Boise and do nothing."

"Well, to be honest, it is a little late. I think all the hotels around the UN for next week will be fully booked, and if you are not staying in a hotel or don't have a pass, you won't even be allowed in that part of the city. Security is crazy at that time because of all the heads of state."

I nodded in agreement. I knew it sounded like a silly idea, and Tiffany was being logical, but something still told me I was supposed to go.

"Let me see if I can get us a hotel room," Tiffany proposed.

A few minutes later, Tiffany called back and exclaimed, "You won't believe it! I found a hotel room that you and I can share." The hotel was right beside the United Nations building—and there had been only one room left!

I packed my bags and flew to New York, praying that I would somehow get the chance to cross paths with the Iranian president or a member of his senior delegation. Franklin Graham heard that the Iranian president was coming and shared this news with his father. Billy Graham then wrote an open letter to President Rouhani, asking him to release Saeed. To increase the chances that the Iranian president would see the letter, Franklin arranged for it to be printed in the *New York Times* as a paid advertisement.

When I arrived in New York, it was as if the hotel was running the Green Zone in central Baghdad, with metal detectors, body scanners, security guards armed with military assault rifles, bomb squads, sniffer dogs, and muscular security agents in tight-fitting suits with earphones hanging out of their right ears.

I had an interview with *World* magazine, so Tiffany and I met with their journalist in the lobby of the hotel and conducted the interview there.

My back was to the hotel entrance as I faced Tiffany, who was sitting next to the journalist. As I answered questions for the reporter, I could hear a shuffling going on behind me and people speaking Farsi. Before I could turn around, Tiffany called out, "Naghmeh, President Rouhani just walked in!"

Before I could answer her, she quickly passed me a copy of a letter that Saeed had written from prison. Our goal was to hand out as many copies of that letter as possible. I grabbed the letter, turned, and bolted toward the sound of the Farsi speakers.

I could see a security detail surrounding someone, whom I assumed was President Rouhani, although I never found out whether it was actually him or not. The large Iranian delegation was trying to get on an elevator, but they couldn't all fit at the same time. As this was happening, I caught the security detail off-guard and slipped into the middle of their group, but the elevator doors shut just as I ran up to them.

One member of the Iranian delegation who hadn't been able to fit on the elevator was Mohammad Javad Zarif, the foreign minister of Iran. I handed him the letter, and I began to say exactly what I had planned to say if I ever had the opportunity: "I'm the wife of Saeed Abedini, who is in prison for his faith. It is not illegal to be a Christian, and he should not be in prison just because he is a Christian."

Zarif immediately reacted by jerking his body away from me, his eyes wide. He seemed to be trying to figure out how to respond to me. I was a woman, my hair was not covered, and I was not wearing the black chador that women so often are required to wear in Iran. Even more than that, I was talking to him without fear. Nevertheless, he took the letter and said he would give it to President Rouhani.

As he impatiently waited for the elevator, I took each available minute to share with him the agonizing details of what Saeed had been going through. "Read the letter," I said, pointing at what I had just given him. "Read what he has been experiencing in prison. He is not a killer. He is a Christian!"

Finally, the elevator arrived, and Zarif quickly pushed his way onto it. His security detail put out their arms to keep me from getting on with him, and the elevator doors closed.

I stood there in silence, not yet realizing the weight of what had just happened. Without thinking, I had broken through an armed security detail that was trained to eliminate any threat that tried to get close to the president of Iran. They didn't know who I was. I could have been a suicide bomber. I could have had a knife or a gun. They might have killed me, and that would have done Saeed no good at all.

As I made my way back to the interview area, the doors of another elevator opened up. A young woman stepped out and marched to the front desk. She was Mohammad Zarif's spokesperson, and I could hear her issuing a complaint against me.

I wasn't able to make out every word she was saying, but when I heard her state, "She is threatening our safety," I had to respond. I could not allow them to torture my husband in prison, deny him medical care, beat him on a regular basis, and then say that it was I who was the problem.

I thought of all the Christians in Iran who had been tortured and killed. I thought of the children who had been orphaned when their parents were murdered, their bodies left in the trunks of cars. I thought of the night when I had been arrested, blindfolded, and interrogated by men with guns. I thought of my children, who hadn't seen their father for over a year because he was sitting in an Iranian prison, and I wondered who this woman thought she was to say that I made *her* feel threatened.

I grabbed another copy of Saeed's letter, walked over, and handed it to her. "My husband is a Christian," I said to her. "That is his only crime, and for that he has been beaten and tortured, and his life has been threatened every day. He can't see a doctor or go to a hospital for injuries he has suffered from the beatings. If anyone is threatened, it's him. It's our family."

After she walked away, I felt emotionally drained. I retired to my room and collapsed onto my bed. I was not there long before I heard a loud, demanding knock on my door.

When I opened the door, I saw two FBI agents, a man and a woman, standing in the hallway. They showed me their badges and requested to ask me a few questions.

Both of the agents looked Scandinavian but spoke Farsi. One man, with straw-blond hair, spoke Farsi so well that I wouldn't have guessed he wasn't Iranian if I hadn't seen his face. The female agent spoke Farsi well, also, but with a slight accent.

I welcomed them into my room, and the woman pulled out a notebook to take notes.

"Mrs. Abedini," the male agent said, "I have to tell you, the Iranian delegation is not happy."

"The Iranian government is very concerned about your being in the same hotel," the other agent chimed in. "They feel threatened."

"Pfft," I responded at the silliness of the idea that a bloody, murderous regime, responsible for mass executions of thousands of people without trial or thought, would be afraid of a simple mother like me.

"I dunno," the female agent continued, "if my husband was being terrorized by this government, I would do something. Maybe strap a bomb to my chest and jump in front of them," she said, without even trying to pretend to be subtle with her leading suggestion.

"No, no, no. I just had a letter, and I wanted to give it to them. That is all."

"They don't know what you are going to do," said the male agent. "What they do know, however, is that they have your husband in prison, and here you are at their hotel. That has never happened to them before. They are not in Iran and are a bit disoriented.

"Listen, Mrs. Abedini, we don't like the Iranian government any more than you do, but while they are here, it is our duty to protect them. If they feel threatened, or if you do anything more to them, we will be forced to kick you out of this hotel for their safety. If you do anything remotely close to what you have just done, we will have to remove you from the UN secure area. Is that understood?"

"I can reassure you that I will not be a problem for them anymore. I just wanted to give them a letter from my husband." I reached into my pocket and pulled out the schedule for the next couple of days that Tiffany had given me earlier. "You can look here," I said, pointing to the paper. "I have so many interviews lined up with CNN, Fox News, and other outlets the entire time that I am here."

They both leaned in to look at the paper I was holding up. The female agent took it from my hand to have a closer look and then glanced at her partner as if to say that she had seen enough and was satisfied.

"These interviews are going to be all day, every day. I will not even be returning to my room until late in the evenings. So, I do not think you will have any more problems from me while I am here."

Content with my answers, the agents left after telling me they were sorry about my husband.

While staying at the hotel, I never saw the Iranian delegation again. However, I would be lying if I said that, somewhere within me, I hadn't felt giddy for one solitary moment, suspended in time, that the Iranian government had been forced to call hotel security, the police, and even the FBI because they felt threatened by me.

38

HOSPITAL REVELATION

Saeed was suffering from his physical injuries, and his health was deteriorating. He had been taken to the hospital several times in 2013 but was returned to prison before being treated or after having been given only medication. He did not receive the surgery he needed. The US government and the ACLJ put pressure on the Iranian government to allow him to be treated at a hospital. In March 2014, Saeed was finally transported to a private hospital in Tehran to be properly treated.

While Saeed was in the hospital, I was able to talk with him several times through Skype. The first time, he borrowed an iPad from one of the nurses; after that, his family brought him an iPad to use. This was the first time I had been able to see Saeed in a year and a half. When the initial call came in, all I saw was the face of a skinny, gaunt, balding, bearded man with yellow, sleep-deprived eyes looking back at me. Prison had taken such a severe toll on Saeed's body that he looked like he had aged more than ten years. My strong, young husband now appeared frail and gray. Saeed was several years younger than I was, but, suddenly, I felt like the younger one.

He spoke with a weak tone, but I could see him smiling beyond his pain. He looked so helpless lying there in that hospital bed that I desperately wanted to reach out and hold him, caress his face, and nurse him back to health. If I could have pulled him through the screen of my iPad from wishing alone, I would have. I had never wished for anything so strongly in my entire life.

Saeed had been in the hospital about two months when, in May 2014, his situation drastically changed. One day, five angry guards arrived at the hospital to take him back to prison. They had been given strict instructions not to let any medical staff stop or delay their orders, so they ripped Saeed from his bed and dragged him down the hallway, beating him and shocking him with cattle prods as they went.

Saeed didn't know it at the time, but his stay in the hospital ultimately led to the exposure of many of the lies the Iranian officials had been telling the world about his imprisonment—but the revelation of that information came at a price: a return to beatings and even worse prison conditions. In their haste and blind fury that day, the guards clumsily left behind important documentation that confirmed Saeed was in prison because of his faith in Jesus. Most everyone knew that this was the true reason he had been sentenced, but because the court documents had been sealed, no one could prove it. Iran had simply said that Saeed's case was a matter of national security and that he was a threat. Time and again, Iranian dignitaries had denied that his imprisonment had to do with his conversion. Even though the entire international community seemed to recognize this, many in that community appeared more than happy to play the game and repeat Iran's official reason for Saeed's conviction.

Because we lacked any actual proof of the nature of Saeed's sentencing, Iran felt they could deny our claim that Saeed was a prisoner of religious conscience. However, Saeed's mother was with him in the hospital when he was dragged away by the prison guards. She noticed the documents the guards accidentally left behind describing Saeed's crime: undermining national security by gathering with other Christians in homes. She took photos of this evidence and sent them to me.

Now we had the proof we needed to share with the international community that Saeed was indeed being tortured for his faith. The Iranian government learned that I had this proof and attempted to suppress me. Since I was in the United States, they couldn't throw me in prison with Saeed, but they did want me silenced.

I started receiving threatening phone calls late at night. At first, the calls came from Iran, but later they came from local Muslims. "You better shut up!" the anonymous voices would often say on the other end of the phone. "Your husband and his family are going to pay with their lives if you do not shut your mouth!"

One day, when I went to leave the house, I opened the door, and there was a large, broad man blocking the doorway. He hadn't knocked on the door or rung the doorbell. He was just standing there as if he had been waiting for me to leave.

He was Middle Eastern, and he was very muscular; even though he was wearing a heavy jacket, I could see that his arms bulged from the sides, so that it looked like it would be almost impossible for him to straighten his arms at the elbows. He could easily have been a bouncer for a nightclub or a bodyguard for a famous celebrity.

The man looked at me and nodded his head with a greasy smile. "Yes," he said while stroking his beard, "we just wanted to make sure that we knew where you lived."

Family members recognized him from the local Shia community. Family members and friends also reported that they had been pulled aside by a Shia leader and told to relay a special message to me: "Naghmeh better stop doing what she is doing or else...."

Each time I received a direct or indirect threat, I reported it to the State Department.

The police in Boise were amazingly supportive. They kept a special watch over my house and stayed alert regarding my situation. I often saw a squad car cruising through my neighborhood, letting me know that they were never far away. Those police officers will never know how thankful I was for their dedication. Both my children and I were safer because of their presence.

39

A NEW PRISON

When the guards forcibly removed Saeed from the hospital, they threw him into a prisoner transport vehicle, but they did not take him back to Evin Prison. Instead, they took him to Rajai Shahr Prison in Karaj, which was infamous for housing murderers and conducting mass executions.

Political prisoners and prisoners of faith were frequently sent to Evin Prison, but Rajai Shahr Prison was often reserved for Iran's most dangerous prisoners on death row. It was one of Iran's most notorious prisons because there were reportedly many incidents of torture, rape, and murder there. Prisoners taken to Karaj Prison were often not heard from again. This was the main prison where, in 1988, mass executions of thousands of political prisoners were carried out in only about five months.

When I learned that Saeed had been transferred to the prison in Karaj, I really felt that I might never see him again. He had already looked so weak and emaciated when I had Skyped with him at the hospital, and I knew that he might not last long there. The Islamic Revolutionary Guard Corps had their own confinement cells in Karaj that they used to interrogate and torture people for days, without any restrictions or witnesses. If Saeed had been sent to the IRGC cells, it was highly likely that he would never make it out alive.

At Karaj prison, they still carried out "eye-for-an-eye" justice, where prisoners' eyes might be physically plucked out or their hands chopped off. "Eye-for-an-eye" justice is a type of Qisas justice, or a "retaliation in kind," retributive justice system. In traditional Islamic law, Qisas justice provides punishment corresponding to the crime. If Saeed was converting people and leading them to hell, then Qisas justice would either be to kill him in order to send him to hell or to create a living hell for him on earth before his death.

For a short period of time, with all of the support Saeed was receiving from around the world, I had been certain that things would get better. With unified calls from the US Congress, the European Union, and the United Nations, I thought there would be some kind of concession from the Iranian government—but there was not. They were digging in and going even harder against Saeed.

Saeed was first taken to the "murder ward," where they kept the most dangerous convicts. Security between the prisoners was almost non-existent. The sanitation conditions were less than humane: there was not enough hygienic food in the facility to feed all three thousand inmates and staff, raw sewage was always backing up and flooding onto the floor, and disease-carrying rats ran wild.

Like animals in an experimental lab, the prisoners at Karaj were starved of natural light. Only buzzing, florescent lightbulbs, which seemed to snap with waves of uneven electric surges every thirty seconds, provided flickering illumination.

Saeed was banned from using the prison phone, so we were in the dark about what was happening to him or how he was adjusting. I was unable to sleep at night knowing that I might wake up one day to a phone call that Saeed had been killed in prison. I would sit and stare at my phone for hours. I never went anywhere without my phone in my hand or within my sight, hoping for a call from Saeed. When I ate, I placed my phone on the table beside my plate in front of me. If I watched television, I put my phone on the arm of the couch with the screen facing up. When I was in church, I didn't turn the ringer off.

One day, a phone call came through from an Iranian number I didn't recognize, and I dove for the phone. "Hello!" I shouted, almost losing my breath as my heart skipped a beat. My hair was in between the phone and my ear, and I heard a faint voice that sounded like Saeed. "Saeed? Is that you?" I asked aggressively, shoving my hair out of the way.

"Yes," he answered in a somewhat hushed voice. By befriending a guard at the prison, he had been able to get his hands on a phone to call me. After his time in the hospital, he had learned a few things about bribing guards in order to gain access to phones and iPads. Although Karaj Prison was harsher and deadlier than Evin Prison, the guards were also more corrupt and therefore much more apt to take bribes.

Some guards were willing to smuggle a phone for him, but it was going to cost a lot of money. Saeed didn't care what it cost, and he talked a guard into helping him. He knew that I could send money to the prison account to help him pay for the phone, or I could send money to an outside account to get cash to the guard.

Saeed sounded exhausted. He said he wasn't sleeping because he was worried about being killed as he slept.

Sometimes, when we talked, he would turn on the phone's camera so that I could see him. The lighting was even worse than usual because, during the calls, he would try to stay in a place where he would be concealed from the rest of the inmates. But even in that dark, grimy light, I could see that he looked dangerously thin. His beard had grown out, and his body was covered in lice. He said he was constantly miserable.

Because Saeed was too scared to fall asleep, he would ask me to do something to keep him awake. So, I would talk to him for hours about what the family did that day and how the kids were doing in school. When I ran out of things to say, I would read him Bible passages to encourage him. There were certain praise and worship songs that he liked to listen to but was unable to find on the Internet, so I would play them for him directly from my phone. I would also play a Christian radio network called Air 1, with a program by DJ Brant Hansen that Saeed liked listening to. He would close his eyes and dream of being back in America. Sometimes other prisoners gathered with Saeed to listen to the Christian music.

At times, late at night, when he was the most exhausted, Saeed would open up and share some of the most horrible things that he had seen and experienced in the prison.

He felt as if he was being stored in an old warehouse, a damp, mildewy box with moist spores clinging to every particle floating in the air. I could hear the congestion in his lungs as he breathed.

There was almost no public oversight of Iranian prisons. The warden ruled like a king over a fiefdom and answered to no one. The warden was the judge, jury, and executioner.

Saeed was like a play toy for the warden, a ball that he could kick or a bag that he could punch. Saeed wasn't human, with thoughts, ideas, feelings, and pain. He was a Christian—unclean. The guards and prisoners alike felt the same way about it. Saeed didn't need to be asleep for the prisoners to jump him. He was being attacked in the middle of the day. Sometimes the guards would stop it, and sometimes they wouldn't. Why would the guards stop the prisoners from doing the same thing they were doing?

There were no rules in the prison; laws didn't exist there, so how could there be punishment for breaking them? The only law in Karaj was to do what the guards said to do. They *were* the rules, so if they hated you, then the rules hated you, and how was it possible to abide by rules that hate you?

During our calls, I would see marks and bruises on Saeed's face from the beatings he had received. The beatings were a reminder that Karaj Prison was not a place for rehabilitation or even punishment. It was for banishment. It was an isle of exile on which evil men with an insatiable lust for power could play games with men that society had thrown away. It served the purpose of a social garbage disposal, discarding the waste that society would rather forget about while burying the evidence that it ever existed in the first place.

Saeed was one of the very few inmates with a phone, and he passed along information to me that almost no one else knew regarding the prison facility, the staff, and the treatment of prisoners. If the guards had only known what he was sharing with me, he most certainly would have been executed. Saeed knew the danger of speaking about these things, but he did it anyway. Our talks were therapy for his mind. They helped him temporarily escape the hell of Karaj Prison.

When I informed the ACLJ about what Saeed was telling me, they warned me, "You cannot share this information. The government will wonder how you got the information, and they might conclude that Saeed has a secret phone. Make sure you do whatever you can to keep people from knowing that he has a phone!"

No matter how much I wanted to pass along this new information, which was relevant for people to understand how Saeed was doing, I couldn't share it. I didn't want to do anything that would compromise Saeed's safety or make us lose our channel of communication.

However, I would often keep a record of the information that Saeed was giving me, and then, when his family members confirmed the same things through their visits with him, and the time was right, we would incorporate the inside information I had received directly from Saeed with his family's account, and we would release it all together. This helped to mask where some of the information was coming from. I could say I had learned it from his family.

When information about Saeed's condition did eventually come out, the Iranian government would become furious, and the authorities at Saeed's prison would go into a rage. They didn't see that the problem was the cruel things they were doing in secret. They saw the problem as their secrets getting out. They failed to consider why they didn't want their secrets to be revealed in the first place.

The authorities also didn't recognize that there was a simple way to make all the criticism and outrage go away. The easy solution, of course, was to stop imprisoning, beating, and killing people for their faith, and the world would stop seeing them as monsters. Instead, Iran viewed those who revealed what was happening to the people whom they were imprisoning, beating, and killing as the monsters. Their policy was to condemn the whistleblowers—not the actions that the whistleblowers uncovered.

As the second anniversary of Saeed's imprisonment approached, Franklin Graham and I organized another prayer vigil service, with the help of the ACLJ, to be held on September 25, 2014, in Washington, DC.

Prior to the prayer vigil, I had gone on a personal twenty-one-day "Daniel" fast.[18] I spent time in prayer and stayed away from social media, except for the moments when I shared about Saeed.

The Scripture that God gave me during this time of prayer and fasting was Hebrews 12:1–2:

> *Therefore, since we also have such a great cloud of witnesses surrounding us, let's rid ourselves of every obstacle and the sin which so easily entangles us, and let's run with endurance the race that is set before us, looking only at Jesus, the originator and perfecter of the faith, who for the joy set before Him endured the cross, despising the shame, and has sat down at the right hand of the throne of God.*

I saw Saeed and the persecuted church as *"witnesses"* who helped us to examine our personal walk with God so we would rid ourselves of all the sins that so easily ensnare us. As I saw supportive responses to the details about Saeed's imprisonment coming in from around the world, I thought about how persecution causes the church to long for the return of Jesus Christ. Saeed's plight reminded people of the stories they had read in the New Testament about Jesus's disciples being persecuted. The injustice of the world brings us to

---

18. Daniel 10:3: *"I ate no choice food; no meat or wine touched my lips; and I used no lotions at all until the three weeks were over."*

a place where we hunger for the kind of righteous justice, grace, and forgiveness that only God can bring. The Lord showed me that we needed a revival, a renewing, in the United States and around the globe.

The prayer vigil enabled Christians worldwide to stand together in solidarity with Saeed and other prisoners of faith. Many people had participated in the 2013 prayer vigil, and in 2014, those numbers grew: six hundred prayer vigils in thirty-eight countries and territories were organized, while multitudes more who could not be present with us in Washington, DC, watched online. The ACLJ tracked the numbers and reported that an amazing two million people were watching and praying with us that day.

The vigil in DC concluded with a prayer walk. Crowds of people crossed the grassy open area of the Ellipse, in direct view of the White House across the South Lawn, many of them carrying signs in support of Saeed and our family. Our vigil was slowly claiming a slice of the historic Lafayette Square, and many people had their heads bowed in prayer as they silently walked.

When Franklin Graham saw the worldwide outpouring of support, he knew we were on the cusp of something bigger that would not only impact Saeed and our family but would also change the entire conversation about Christian persecution in closed nations. Iran was only the initial focus. Christians had been asleep for too long when it came to remembering their brothers and sisters who suffer every day for their faith. Muslim countries were not the only places that persecuted Christians. Christians were being arrested, beaten, raped, and killed for their faith in Buddhist, Hindu, and Communist nations around the world. Christians in India, Nepal, China, and North Korea were suffering just as badly as, and sometimes worse than, those in Iran.

Saeed's story was highlighting what was happening to Christians worldwide. He was becoming a voice for the persecuted church. Every letter he sent from prison was not just a single message from his cell in Iran—it was like a multitude of letters from Christians languishing in prisons around the world.

40

DOWNWARD SPIRAL

Saeed's time in prison initially brought the two of us closer to God, closer to the calling that God had on our lives, and closer to each other than we had ever been before in our marriage.

Saeed and I would spend hours on the phone in prayer, learning from God and about one another. Saeed had grown into the man that I had always dreamed of. Despite our past, we were ready to fight for our future as a couple. The apostle Paul wrote, *"Those who marry will face many troubles in this life."*[19] I knew that it would not be easy, but I trusted that this trial would only deepen our love for each other, just as hardship deepens our relationship with Christ.

Every marriage takes dedication, commitment, and communication, and somehow we were experiencing all three while Saeed was in prison. We made promises to each other to be better spouses and to make our home one that served the Lord. All of Saeed's anger issues and other problems seemed to be behind us, and I would be a devoted wife serving beside him on the mission field.

The phone was our lifeline of communication, and we recommitted our lives to one another every day. Hearing his voice and sometimes seeing his face brought life to my soul. I had hope that he would one day be released, and together we would raise our family in a loving, peaceful home.

Over time, however, as Saeed's access to a phone grew, things slowly started to change. He noticed how often he was being mentioned on the news and in Christian circles in America, and his interest in his own story increased. He was delighted to hear presidents and world leaders talking about his predicament. Our conversations shifted from working on our marriage to working

---

19. First Corinthians 7:28.

on his image. I couldn't give a specific instance of what he said or when he said it, but I remember hearing elements of the same Saeed that I had sometimes feared might one day return. I had thought that the dark part of him had been crucified in prison and was gone forever, but perhaps it had only been suppressed for a time. The man I had fallen in love with all over again was getting angry at me once more and sending me insulting and degrading text messages.

With the passing months, he was also experiencing more freedom in prison and was getting better treatment, so he was no longer in survival mode. As things got easier for him, his general dissatisfaction with me returned.

His mother and I didn't always agree with one another, and this upset him. Something would happen between the two of us, and she would tell him about it when they spoke on the phone, sending him into a fury.

"How dare you make my mom cry!" he would yell at me the next time we talked. He appeared to be purposefully trying to send me back to the place in my mind where I had to crawl on my hands and knees, kiss his mother's feet, and beg for her forgiveness. "You have disrespected her. You are such a worthless whore!"

He began monitoring my social media. If I shared photos of my side of the family, he would become upset. If I didn't share enough photos of his family, it would throw him into an irrational fit. His angry reactions were always disproportionate to the situation, and I would try to calm him down by apologizing. I didn't have anything to be remorseful over; I just wanted to keep the peace. I didn't want our discussions to be arguments, but, in the final year of his imprisonment, he was easily triggered.

I also tried to avoid disagreements with his family members, but I was reaching a breaking point. There was no escaping them. When his family came to stay in the United States, they lived with me for months at a time, and they had expectations of what I was supposed to do and not do. It appeared that, in their eyes, my job as a daughter-in-law was to care for their every need.

They still did not want to be directly involved in the efforts to raise awareness for Saeed, so they had nothing to do while they were visiting in the US. It seemed to me that the campaign to get Saeed released was almost like a side thought to them. They weren't aware of the endless phone calls I had to make and receive, the emails coming in at all times of the day and night that I had to answer, and the time-consuming preparations I needed to make before interviews and speaking engagements. They didn't have any idea of what it took to set up prayer vigils in cities all over the world and prepare speeches for the United States Congress, the European Parliament, and the United Nations.

At the same time, with my husband in prison, I lived the life of a single working mother, arranging all the transportation for my children to and from their school each day, keeping track of their after-school activities, setting aside time for parent-teacher meetings, and saving money so they could participate in extracurricular programs.

Nevertheless, it was up to me to entertain Saeed's family and find things for them to do. If I didn't, Saeed would feel that his family was being mistreated. Our phone conversations changed from ones that were loving and that deepened our connection with one another to ones where Saeed expressed disappointment in me and called me names. I tried to respond with kindness because of his difficult position in prison.

The stress of the whole situation was weighing heavily on me, but I kept pushing my feelings down, hiding them within me and not talking about them. I wanted to believe that Saeed and I were only going through another downward stage and that things would be up again soon. Yet a small part of me now doubted whether there ever had been an "up" time.

All of our best times together, aside from that last family vacation in Iran, had been when we were talking on the phone during Saeed's most uncertain moments. But had those times been real? Had I ever truly been engaged with the real Saeed, or had I just been talking to the Saeed who existed when he didn't think tomorrow was coming? Had I fallen in love with the scared Saeed? Had I—and perhaps multitudes of other people around the world—fallen in love with the image of Saeed the martyr, instead of Saeed the person?

I was too busy to stop and deal with the reality of what I was experiencing. Every day, I was on a different news station where I had to play the part of the loving wife, even if Saeed had been yelling at me over the phone just before the interview began. Every day, I had to share with new churches or other groups of supportive Christians about Saeed's sacrifice, with echoes of his calling me a whore in the back of my head.

I especially heard the tone of Saeed's voice change when he realized that there was a very real chance he would be getting out of prison soon. President Obama was working on a nuclear agreement with Iran that would allow the Iranian sanctions to be dropped. He was putting maximum pressure on Iran to agree to the deal, and State Department representatives had told us that there were side meetings at the negotiations to try to secure the release of Saeed and other Americans being held.

Saeed was convinced that there would be large amounts of money waiting for him when he got out. He spent hours searching for the kind of house he would like to buy in California when he was released from prison. He sent me photos of massive mansions that he was certain we could afford with all of the support he would receive.

He saw pictures of Franklin Graham's private jet and heard the stories of my flying on it and was intrigued, like a little boy at Christmas. Saeed wanted to buy a jet just like it—or better. He surfed the Internet, window shopping for the best jet that would suit his "ministry needs" after prison.

As he was making all these plans, he sent me specific instructions about things he wanted me to do before his release. One of those errands was to get him a better book deal.

Before Saeed was arrested and imprisoned, Pastor Bob had convinced him to write the story of his conversion and his work with the underground church in Iran. Saeed was able to connect with a respected writer who could coauthor the book. Together, they penned Saeed's story, but the writer did not want to publish the book yet. He felt that God had something else planned for Saeed's life that needed to be included in the manuscript, so he suggested that Saeed wait before seeking publication. Only a few months later, Saeed was arrested. Now, during this time in prison, he saw that there were more publishing options available and that he could make much more money, receive more exposure, and possibly sign a movie deal if he used a different writer. So, from prison, he instructed me to sign a better deal, and I did. We had to be careful how we made this agreement because too many details might leak that Saeed and I were in direct communication on a daily basis, using an illegal phone with Internet capabilities that had allowed him to sign power of attorney over to me.

But Saeed was doing other things with his time besides researching new houses, jets, and book deals. I could see that he had logged on to my video-streaming account and was watching movies with his phone data. What was showing up on my account was more concerning to me than even the pornographic movies he had previously watched. My account history showed a long list of movies that could only be described as homoerotic.

I called and talked to him about it, and his response was the same as the one he used to give me when I had caught him watching pornography: "I don't understand the language."

"Saeed, I looked at the movies you were watching. There was not a lot of talking needed. It is clear what it is in any language."

He responded with silence.

After that conversation, I continued to push aside my troubled thoughts about the downward spiral of our marriage and concentrated on my efforts to free Saeed.

41

PRESIDENT OBAMA

I just saw that Obama is flying to Boise! Is he going to meet with you?" read the message in my email one morning. I was reading my emails while still in bed, but this one woke me up.

"President Obama is flying to Boise?" I said to myself. I leapt inside at the thought of his being in Idaho, because it meant I might have the chance to see him and talk to him about Saeed. Presidents rarely come to Idaho. It is just not a populated area with a lot of influence over the electorate. It has never been a state that would sway an election one way or the other, which made his visit to Boise even more remarkable.

It was about mid-January 2015. I reached out to the State Department and said that I had heard President Obama was coming to Idaho and that I would like to meet with him. They responded that they would connect me with him, but I would not be able to bring anyone along from the ACLJ, and I would not be able to bring other members of Saeed's family with me. Only the children and I would be allowed to see the president. Then they told me to go to Boise State University. "President Obama will be speaking at the university, but before he speaks, we have arranged for you to meet with him." I thought I would just join a group of people standing in a line to shake the president's hand and speak with him briefly.

On the day that President Obama arrived in Boise, I went to the university, as instructed, and I discovered they had arranged for me to have a private meeting with him. The security there was at a level I had never seen before. I went to the building where they told me to go, and the kids and I were whisked into a room where we were met by Secret Service agents.

Saeed had called me on the phone beforehand and said he wanted to know everything as it was happening. However, the Secret Service detail took my phone from me, saying I could not have it while meeting with the president.

We were brought into a room that seemed to be the office of one of the university professors. A senior presidential advisor was waiting for us. She was American but, like me, was originally from Iran. She shared her story of leaving Iran and then proceeded to tell us how to act when the president came into the room, such as standing up in his presence and addressing him as Mr. President.

We waited for a while until Jacob got bored and began to play with one of the office chairs. He was in the middle of making the chair roll across the floor and crash into the other furniture when President Obama walked in.

The president was very kind and immediately made himself warm and engaging. When he talked with me, he leaned in, listened, and kept eye contact. "We are making it a top priority to get your husband out," I remember him saying.

President Obama had been a strong voice for Saeed, calling on the Iranian president to release Saeed and mentioning Saeed at the National Prayer Breakfast the previous year. It had amazed me that the president knew our family by name and had taken special time during the National Prayer Breakfast to pray for Saeed. The month after my meeting with him, he spoke about Saeed and our family again during the 2015 prayer breakfast:

> Last year, we prayed together for Pastor Saeed Abedini, detained in Iran since 2012. And I was recently in Boise, Idaho, and had the opportunity to meet with Pastor Abedini's beautiful wife and wonderful children and to convey to them that our country has not forgotten brother Saeed and that we're doing everything we can to bring him home. (Applause.) And then, I received an extraordinary letter from Pastor Abedini. And in it, he describes his captivity, and expressed his gratitude for my visit with his family, and thanked us all for standing in solidarity with him during his captivity.
>
> And Pastor Abedini wrote, "Nothing is more valuable to the Body of Christ than to see how the Lord is in control, and moves ahead of countries and leadership through united prayer." And he closed his

letter by describing himself as "prisoner for Christ, who is proud to be part of this great nation of the United States of America that cares for religious freedom around the world." (Applause.)

We're going to keep up this work—for Pastor Abedini and all those around the world who are unjustly held or persecuted because of their faith.[20]

During my meeting with President Obama, when I heard him tell me that getting Saeed out of prison was a top priority for the US government, I felt great relief, and a heavy weight was lifted off my shoulders. However, after that meeting, I had no illusions that Saeed's release would be immediate. The president had told me it might be quite some time. In my mind, I thought it might take years. I knew that the US government was meeting on the sidelines of their negotiations for a nuclear deal with Iran to try to get Saeed and other American hostages released. I also remembered learning how, in 1981, the American hostages in Iran had been released only after President Carter's term ended and President Reagan was inaugurated. I thought the same thing might happen, with the Iranian government waiting to see if a conservative president was elected before releasing Saeed.

Nevertheless, I felt that all my advocacy efforts had gotten me where I had wanted to go: I had been granted a meeting with one of the most powerful heads of state in the world, and he had told me that getting Saeed out of prison was a priority of the US government. This was the same administration in which the State Department had told me, when Saeed was first arrested in 2012, that there was nothing they could do.

I had been working so hard advocating for Saeed's release, traveling all over the United States and to other nations to speak, which necessitated a lot of time away from Rebekka and Jacob. I was exhausted and thought that now that I had spoken to the president and received his reassurance, I might be able to slow down a little. The strain of all the travel was taking a toll on me physically, and I had little energy left to give to my children. So, as time went by, I started to cancel various events. However, I couldn't pull back altogether because Saeed wanted me to continue the advocacy, and

20. President Barack Obama, "Remarks by the President at National Prayer Breakfast," Office of the Press Secretary, The White House, February 5, 2015, https://obamawhitehouse.archives.gov/the-press-office/2015/02/05/remarks-president-national-prayer-breakfast.

I wanted to make sure his plight was kept in the public eye. Additionally, I still needed to bring in income to support my children, Saeed's needs in prison, and his family's financial requirements. I had to keep going, even though I felt close to the end of my strength.

42

GOD'S DAUGHTER

On one of our phone calls, Saeed told me that a family member wanted money for a vacation, and that I was to send them three thousand dollars.

"Saeed, I...." I wanted to protest, but I knew it was no use. Saeed thought he and his family should be living a comfortable lifestyle, as they had seen others in American ministry have. Many of the leaders of the ministries that were helping us, especially those that had their own television shows, had extremely enviable lives. They drove nice cars, lived in amazing houses, ate at the best restaurants, and wore the finest clothes. Saeed's family seemed to assume that I was receiving that kind of money through donations, but it was simply not true.

I had been speaking at many venues where I had not received any donations. I took speaking opportunities even if my travel was not paid for. And the majority of the donations didn't come to me. They went to the ACLJ, Samaritan's Purse, and Calvary Chapel Boise to fund efforts to free Saeed and spread the word about his imprisonment. The donations I did receive went toward Saeed's prison expenses and paying for his secret mobile phones. Each phone we had to purchase cost about seven thousand dollars. On top of these costs, I was struggling to pay the bills and the mortgage on our house. I rarely had enough money to fix my secondhand car, which seemed to break down almost every month. And any other money I had left over, I was giving to Saeed's family for their expenses.

One day, his father asked me why I couldn't help to bring two of his other children, who were refugees in Turkey, to the US more quickly. As I explained to him that I was doing everything I could do, I felt like I had reached an emotional breaking point. As a single mother, I was carrying the financial weight not only for my children and myself, but for Saeed's family too. I wanted to help, but I also knew that Saeed's father had other financial means that he could use to help provide for his own family members, yet he was asking me to take care of everything. I felt he should take responsibility as the father of his family. "I am supporting your entire family," I exclaimed. "Ever since Saeed and I were married, I have been the one working. I have been the breadwinner. In fact, for most of my marriage to Saeed, I have been the only person bringing in money. I can't do it any longer for my family and yours." I continued in this way, and I knew that I should be more cautious about the words I chose, but, at that point, I didn't care.

"The money is not yours," Saeed called and told me as soon as he heard what I had said to his father. "You are raising money on my name. You are making money on my suffering in prison. You have no right over the money." Saeed was completely dismissing all the work I had done on his behalf and the reality of how little we actually had coming in compared to the expenses going out. He acted as if I didn't know what the value of money was, disregarding all the years that I had worked hard and carried the entire financial responsibility for our family.

When I protested, Saeed hung up on me.

"Hello?" I said, trying to see if it was just a bad connection. I tried to call him back, but he wouldn't answer. Instead, he responded by sending me texts of vomit emojis, indicating that I made him sick.

I called him again and again until he answered the phone.

"Saeed, I don't want to make you angry. I want to talk about this."

"Listen," he said with a firm voice. "Those crowds at the churches where you are speaking—they aren't there for you. When the politicians applauded you after your speech at Congress, they weren't applauding for you; they were applauding for me. They were applauding what I have done. You were there because of me." His voice was cold and his words were calculated. "When I get out, I am going to divorce you, and you will be nothing, and let's see who applauds you then. Let's see who cares about you then. And when I divorce you, I want you to take my name off your social media accounts, because no one cares about Naghmeh *Panahi*. They only care about you now because you wear the crown of my name: *Abedini*."

With those words, he hung up, and I felt like I was left twisting, naked and alone on the phone line. Saeed was a master at tearing me apart. He knew me in the most intimate ways and understood exactly where to place the dagger. Even though I felt confident about his getting out of prison at some point, I knew that things could change in Iran at any time, and he might not be released. I didn't want to fight with him while he was in prison. But what he had said to me was so ruthless.

I felt low and abandoned. What kind of wife must I be when her husband, who is in prison, doesn't even want her?

I set down my phone and wondered how I was going to speak at an upcoming Baptist women's conference where I was one of the main speakers. I wanted to cancel the speaking engagement, but something inside me would not allow it.

I shook my head, knowing that, yet again, I would have to stand in front of a room full of believers and tell them what an incredible Christian witness Saeed is, and how I was a dedicated Christian wife willing to fight for her husband's life. Once more, I would have to shake off the hurt and pain, pretending I wasn't the most wounded soul in the room.

That night, I spoke on autopilot, not even sure what words were coming out of my mouth. But God's Spirit started working in ways that I still do not fully understand.

After I stepped down from the stage, a woman who was one of the other speakers at the meeting approached me and said, "I feel like I need to pray for you and anoint you." There was something so loving and reassuring about her presence. I had spoken at hundreds of conferences and had been prayed for by thousands of people, but something was happening here that was different.

The woman anointed my head, my hands, and my feet with oil. Then she told me that I was being anointed for a difficult road that I was about to walk down. She didn't know what that difficult road was, but she prayed for me. I was uncertain about what this meant, too, but I thought it might have to do with Saeed's imprisonment.

I had a full day in Boise before my next speaking engagement, so I tried to do as much as I could to assist my mother, who was helping me to take care of the children, including running some errands. One of those errands was to buy some things Rebekka had asked for from a store at the mall. As I walked through the mall, I passed by a jewelry store, and I glanced over at a princess-cut diamond ring in the window. I said a quick prayer to God about how I wished one day Saeed would buy me an expensive ring like that to show

how special I am to him, since he had never bought me expensive jewelry. In fact, I had even needed to pay for my own wedding ring. I thought about my daughter, and I added, "I actually pray that one day I can give a diamond ring to Rebekka so she knows how special she is—so she knows that she does not have to wait to receive an expensive ring on her wedding day to understand that she is special, but that she would know she is special because she belongs to You." This whole conversation with God took about a minute, and I continued with my errands.

The following day, I flew out to speak at another women's conference for a Calvary Chapel church in California. After the conference, a woman came to me with tears in her eyes and handed me a diamond ring. The ring looked exactly like the one I had seen at the mall, although it was much bigger.

"While I was sitting here listening to you," she said, "I felt like God was telling me to give this to you. My husband gave me this ring for our twentieth anniversary. I asked him if it'd be okay to give it to you, and he has agreed. God told me to tell you that you are special."

"No, no, no," I said. "I can't accept this." People sometimes got emotional when they hear accounts of persecution and want to give things away to help. My reflex was to reject the ring.

"It is not for you," she said. "It is for your daughter. Maybe you can give it to her when she gets older."

In that moment, I knew I was to accept the ring. Her comment brought me back to my conversation with the Lord at the jewelry store in Boise. It was a confirmation that God had heard my prayer. I accepted the ring on Rebekka's behalf, and I placed it on one of my fingers. Immediately, I felt many of my emotional and spiritual chains break free. I knew I was God's daughter—I was the daughter of the King.

I was reminded of the time when I had met Ivanka Trump. Almost everyone else in the world, no matter how important they were, had to make an appointment to see Donald Trump, but his daughter Ivanka was special. She had the freedom to walk into her father's office anytime she wished.

The ring that I had wanted from Saeed, God had given to me. I was to pass the ring on to my daughter because she needed to know that she was special to her heavenly Father.

I was holding the ring in my hand and thinking about this when my phone rang. It was Saeed. I told him where I was and that the ladies at the meeting were all praying for him.

"You wouldn't believe it," I added, and I began to tell him about the woman who had given me a beautiful diamond ring. Without mentioning him, I told him how the ring made me feel special in God's eyes.

"Don't think that you are special just because someone gave you a ring. They only gave you the ring because you are connected to me. They were moved by the story that you shared about me."

Again, his words pierced through me and created new inner wounds. But his words felt even more destructive this time. Something quickened in my spirit, and I blurted out, "Saeed, if you can't be nice to me, then I don't want to talk with you anymore."

He paused for a moment as if I were joking with him. The statement hadn't come out the way I had wanted it to, but it expressed my sentiments.

"I mean it, Saeed. If you can't be nice to me, then I don't want you calling me."

I don't know what I expected, but I didn't expect him to hang up.

Instantly, I was overcome with regret and wanted to take the words back, but it was too late. If I could have rewound my life to only five minutes earlier, I wouldn't have said those words. But I am glad I didn't have that chance. My words were long overdue.

I sat and looked at the phone for a moment, waiting for a text, but a text never came. I waited for a call, but a call never came. I didn't want to cut things off with Saeed; I only wanted him to treat me better, but that seemed too much to ask from him.

He didn't call me again after that day.

43

CONFESSION

It was the beginning of November 2015. Hours had dragged into days as I waited for Saeed to call. I was living in a silent bubble, unable to tell anyone what I was going through. I was used to pouring out my heart to Saeed for hours about my every thought as we talked on the phone, but now I was cut off from him. I kept calling him, but he didn't answer.

How could I possibly share with anyone else what was happening to me in my marriage? I was wrestling with things that I hadn't fully thought through myself. I didn't know if there was anyone I could trust enough to help me process all of my conflicting thoughts and feelings about Saeed and the way I was living my life.

I was still being asked to speak at churches and special gatherings, but I was losing heart. I was expected to share Saeed's story of being a hero of the persecuted church, but I was running out of reasons why I should. I knew who Saeed was and who he was not. I, also, was not who people thought I was. I was living a secret that no one else knew. I was playing a part.

I wasn't sure how long I could hide the tempest that raged within me. If I spoke openly about what I was going through, Christians might condemn me for bringing up the abuse. Most important, support for Saeed could drop, leaving him stranded in prison. But if I didn't share what was happening between Saeed and me, he might get out of prison, start a ministry, and fool thousands of people about what he was really like. Everything I had said during my advocacy campaign about his unjust imprisonment and life-threatening situation was true, and no matter what Saeed had done to me, I desperately wanted to see him released from prison. He had been arrested and incarcerated for sharing the gospel; there was no doubt about that. He was being tortured for refusing to deny Jesus Christ, and that too was not debatable. I needed to keep advocating to get him out of prison, but, unless he changed, I could no longer plan for a life of ministry with him afterward.

I tried to work through the most immediate problems first. "I can't do the book anymore," I thought aloud. "How can I get out of writing a book with Saeed?" I knew that a book could lead to a movie deal and a worldwide ministry reach that I could not participate in.

I emailed my book agent. "What happens if I don't want to write a book with Saeed?" I asked. I didn't give him any details—I only presented the idea as a hypothetical dilemma. He was confused and didn't know exactly how to respond, but he said, "You don't have to write about Saeed or with Saeed. Your contract just says that you have to write 'a' book. The book can be about anything that you like."

I thought about it and felt that he had just given me a means to be released from doing a book jointly with Saeed—I could write a different book myself. I had just spoken at a church in California after having given a talk to a group back on the East Coast. Now, I boarded a plane to fly back to North Carolina to speak at another large church. During a layover at an airport, I posted on my social media that I was going to write a book.

That evening, in response to my post, Pastor David Chadwick, my host in North Carolina, asked me about the book. He and his wife had taken me out to dinner, and I had shared with them what I had told a thousand people. I went on and on about how Iran was persecuting Christians and how Saeed was not bending under pressure but standing true for Christ. As I spoke, I was halfway between automation and reality.

"You two are such precious believers," Pastor David said. "I can't wait to read your book. When is it coming out?"

When he said that, I couldn't look him in the eye. It had been a week since I had last talked with Saeed, a week of painful silence. I was exhausted from all my travels, and my emotions were swirling within me. For such a long time, my mind had been on an endless loop, trying to figure out why Saeed had continually attacked me when I loved him so deeply and had tried so hard to free him from prison. I was struggling, shaking with heartbreak and confusion. Yet, not imagining what was really wrong, Pastor David didn't at first recognize my desperation. He and his church, together with a multitude of supporters across the nation, still considered my husband a Christian hero. In many ways, Saeed was a hero—but I knew him in the ways that he wasn't.

Suddenly, like the raging waters of a flood that force along everything in their path, my inner being insisted on pushing out the fearful truth. The overwhelming emotion started in my chest and permeated throughout my body.

Time seemed suspended as I looked down into my lap. My practiced social autopilot turned off, and tears started flowing down my cheeks. I knew that my mascara was going to run down my face like two broad streaks of black tar down the side of a new barrel. I was used to paying close attention to how I appeared in public, but now I didn't care.

"What's wrong, Naghmeh?" Pastor David asked. I sensed in his voice that he assumed I was crying over Saeed's prison sentence. People expected me to cry over Saeed's imprisonment. And I was, but not in the way he thought.

In that moment, as the truth rushed out, I could feel all the strings that had been holding down the darkness snap loose. All the murky issues were coming to the surface, and I couldn't force them back into the depths of my soul.

"I can't write a book," I blurted out. Pastor David looked over at his wife as if to ask her what I was talking about. "I am sorry," I continued. "Look at me. I am sitting here crying and ruining your dinner with my problems."

"It's okay, Naghmeh. You are in a safe place. Let it all out."

I started sharing small details about my marriage, nibbling at the edges by confessing to domestic troubles that were more socially acceptable—ones that were only a little gray rather than the black abyss I was experiencing. I talked about the conflicts that every wholesome marriage has—the kind described in the self-help books you buy on the shelves of Christian bookstores. But confessing the smaller, more common problems in my marriage made room for me to reveal the bigger issues.

I still wanted to stop the flow of my words, but it felt impossible. Years of confusion, dissatisfaction, and shame poured out. Many people hailed me as the courageous Christian wife that any husband would only dream of having. They said things like, "Look at all of the advocacy you have done to get Saeed out of prison. He must be so proud of you." No, he wasn't proud of me—he disdained me.

I opened up to the Chadwicks about Saeed's extramarital affairs and how he had forced himself on me and beaten me. I talked about the pornography he had frequently viewed, how he had constantly put me down, and everything else I could remember.

For years, these hidden realities had haunted me, robbed me of my sleep, and picked apart at every relationship in my life. I had come to that dinner glutted with accumulated secrets, but now I was heaving confessions like vomit; it was as if I were expelling them onto the ground in front of Pastor David's feet. I didn't know why this was happening, but once I started, the process felt cleansing, and I wanted to continue sharing until I was dry heaving even the most modest sins from my past.

When I finally stopped speaking and looked up at the expression on Pastor David's face, my heart plummeted. He had thought he was going to dinner with an unshakable hero of the faith, but instead he was looking into the eyes of a broken woman. A woman who had just unveiled the dark side of one of the most beloved persecuted Christian heroes in recent times. I couldn't imagine the betrayal he must have felt, especially because I had just spoken at his church.

In a desperate attempt to demonstrate what I was saying—even though I knew it was a risk to share Saeed's communications from prison—I pulled my phone out of my purse and began to show him the most recent text messages Saeed had sent me.

"Wait, wait, wait, Naghmeh," Pastor David said. "You realize that I am not just a pastor, right? I have a doctorate in psychology."

Why was he telling me this right now?

"From what you have shared with me, I can tell you that you are an abused wife."

His words stunned me. I had known things were very wrong in my marriage, but, despite everything I had gone through, somehow, I had not thought of myself as an abused wife.

That phrase, that night, changed everything—because I was finally diagnosed. The fog of confusion began to lift, slowly replaced by the dawn of clarity. Of all the people that I could have confessed my troubles to, God allowed me to confess to Pastor David. I had no idea that he had spent years dealing with abuse. It was clear that God had arranged this dinner long before I knew why.

"Naghmeh," Pastor David continued, "after listening to you, I also need to tell you that you must stop all advocacy. You need to stop everything right now. The book, the tours, the speaking engagements. It all needs to stop. You are not in a place to do this. You are being abused and manipulated, and it can only stop after you clear your calendar of all these events."

"But…" I began, trying to think of all the commitments I had lined up. There were so many groups that had already booked venues, paid deposits, arranged travel, promoted dinners…. I couldn't just let them down.

"No, Naghmeh. Look at me," Pastor David said in a firm but loving way. "You can't do this anymore. You need to cancel all of it now."

That evening, my emotions still in turmoil, I went back to my hotel room. I was now alone, trying to process on my own the enormity of what had just occurred. I started canceling some of my speaking engagements. Afterward, I couldn't sleep, so I pulled out my laptop and did a search of "abused wife" on the Internet, and, as I read, everything in my marriage began to make sense. The silent treatments, verbal assaults, putdowns, projections, deflections, and double-standards in my marriage were not isolated events—they were all symptoms of a larger, more ominous reality. I was not dealing with "normal" marriage issues. This was not like a common cold that could be soothed by an over-the-counter pain reliever. What had entangled me from the beginning when I had first met my husband was like a cancerous tumor that had taken over my body and was now strangling me.

I had known that my body was falling apart and that I seemed to be slowly dying inside, but I hadn't known why. Now I knew. Drastic, intensive treatment was the only path to survival. The common Christian marriage advice of submission to one's husband—no matter what—which I had earnestly tried to follow, was only feeding into the disease and enabling it to spread. Although it would be a long road, putting a name to the dark fog I was in set me on the path to freedom. These words of Jesus came to me: *You will know the truth, and the truth will set you free.*[21]

---

21. John 8:32 (NASB, NIV).

44

THE EMAILS

My flight left North Carolina at six o'clock the next morning, November 2. Having slept little, I cried all the way to my layover in Texas, feeling completely exhausted, emotionally spent, and alone. I was still struggling with the intense inner conflict over what I knew to be true about Saeed and what others believed about him. While waiting for my next flight, I resolved that the only way to relieve this turmoil was to stop delaying and finally come clean with all of the people who had been supporting me and standing with me to help get Saeed out of prison. I could no longer hide what was going on. I owed them the truth.

I looked at the blank screen of a new email message and watched the blinking cursor. What would I write? How would I start off? How much did I really want to share?

The people I was emailing were not just random individuals from an accrued email list. They were a dedicated group of over a hundred friends and supporters who were leading grassroots efforts to free Saeed. They believed in me, and they believed in Saeed. I knew that the content of this email would crush them, but I myself was living under a relentless crushing weight, and I finally needed to tell the truth. I had shared deep and personal information with this email group in the past, and they had always been faithful to keep it private. I trusted them completely.

As I sat in the airport writing the letter, tears fell with every keystroke. I felt the power of the Holy Spirit come down upon me. It didn't feel good—but it felt right. For the first time in years, I was finally allowing the sunshine to disinfect the disease.

I intended to write only a couple of lines, but the longer I sat there, the more I wrote. I opened up about the scope of my troubles, saying that they included "physical, emotional, psychological, and sexual abuse (through Saeed's addiction to pornography)."

I let them know that the abuse had been going on since we were first married. I explained that Saeed had access to a phone and that we had been calling and Skyping one another. "His abuse has continued over the last 3 years and it has gotten worse as his name has grown. It is very serious stuff and I cannot live a lie anymore. So, I have decided to take a break from everything and seek the Lord on how to move forward." I asked for people's prayers that the Lord would free Saeed not only of his physical chains but also of the spiritual chains that had held him for such a long time.

After writing the email, I hit send, closed my laptop, and got on the plane.

I didn't realize it, but during the few hours of that flight, my whole world was being transformed. When I landed and checked my phone, I had countless voicemails. Franklin Graham, Jay Sekulow, and many others had left messages saying I needed to contact them right away.

There were even messages from members of the press asking me to call them back. Unfortunately, the content of my email had been leaked to the news media. To this day, I don't know who leaked it. Various recipients of the email had forwarded it to family members and friends, so it was impossible to trace.

Pastor Bob's wife from Calvary Chapel was at the airport to pick me up. As I met her, my phone rang. I saw that it was Franklin, but I didn't want to answer the call. I felt that I first needed to talk with the pastor of my home church and tell him everything I had told Pastor David. I needed to confess everything to him. It was part of the cleansing process that Pastor David had started me on. So, his wife drove me directly to their home, where I met with Pastor Bob and explained everything that had happened and what I had been struggling with, including Saeed's verbal and emotional abuse from prison. Pastor Bob agreed that I should stop all advocacy. He also advised that I not talk to anyone about Saeed and the abuse because he was concerned that the Christian community would turn against me.

When I returned home, I systematically went through the rest of my commitments and contracts, and, one by one, I made phone calls and sent emails canceling them.

The next day, in response to the email leak, I wrote a second email to my supporters, saying, "I have trusted you with a great burden because I have believed that you love Saeed and that you can see the warrior of Jesus that he is and that he has refused to deny his faith and has shared with many about his faith.... But that does not mean he has not been battling with his own demons, which I am believing that he can be freed of." I also said, "I wanted to be real and ask you to pray for real things (I have opened myself up to you), but without judgment and without losing your love for your brother Saeed who is fighting for his life in the dark prison.... This is going to be a different season of endurance and perseverance for me. It will be on my knees. I ask you to join me and to keep EVERYTHING confidential."

Some people encouraged me to backtrack on my emails, saying that I had been under a lot of stress, had been on strong medication, and was mentally unwell and didn't realize what I was saying. However, I didn't listen to those voices. I wasn't mentally unwell or on strong medication, and I was done with the cover-up, done with pretending that all was well in my marriage.

The ACLJ issued a statement that my family was going through a lot, and we would appreciate our space. I asked them to help me be released from certain obligations that I had committed to. Some obligations were easier to cancel than others. I knew that there were a few financial obligations that I would have to pay to get out of, and I was okay with that. Completely canceling the book contract, for instance, would require me to sell property to raise funds, because I didn't have enough money to repay the advance. I didn't know how I would get out of every contractual obligation, but I was determined to sell everything I owned if I had to in order to free myself of all agreements that involved my campaigning for Saeed.

It was not an easy process, but there was freedom in the midst of the pain. With every event I canceled, I felt another emotional shackle fall off. The links in the chain that bound me grew shorter and shorter. Many people pulled away from me because of my revelation of abuse, so I found myself losing my reputation but gaining my freedom. For the first time in years, I was coming clean before God and others.

I started to read a book called *What to Do When You Are Abused by Your Husband* by Pastor Robert Needham and Debi Pryde. I connected with Pastor Robert, and he personally walked me through the entire counseling process to recover from the years of abuse I had been going through.

I needed a completely fresh start, so I got off social media and didn't post anymore. I shed the skin of public advocacy and retreated into a shell of privacy.

After cleansing my conscience, I began to cleanse my environment. I had a sudden urge to transform those parts of my life that reminded me of the abuse I had suffered from Saeed. It might not make sense to some people, but this process made a huge impact on my mental ability to adapt to my new life: I changed the color of our bedroom, discarded the old furniture, and purchased new furniture. I redecorated other areas of the house, including simply moving the couch and dining room table to new locations.

I also took off my wedding ring and silently prayed, "God, I give this over to You." In my mind, giving my marriage over to God was my "Isaac moment."[22] I was taking my marriage, the most sacred part of my life, and laying it on the altar. I wasn't holding anything back. I gave everything over to Him. I was willing to take off my ring and sacrifice my marriage with the prayer that it would be given back to me.

Each step gave me more resolve. Each step made me stronger.

22. See Genesis 22:1–18.

45

RELEASED FROM PRISON

What is going on?" Franklin Graham asked when we finally talked, clearly confused by the email I had sent out, and miffed at the situation.

He deserved to know. He had been one of the loudest advocates of Saeed and one of the strongest supporters of our family. He and his ministry had invested a lot in us—spiritually, emotionally, and financially.

I poured out my heart to him, telling him everything.

What I told him was all new to him. He had been with us through almost the entire process of Saeed's imprisonment, but he had not been privy to any of the intimate details of our marriage. Like the rest of the world, he had been left in the dark about it.

"Naghmeh, can I ask you a question?" Franklin said.

Tearfully, I answered yes.

"Are you cheating on Saeed?" he asked bluntly.

"What?"

I knew that I must have shocked him with what I had shared, but I am not certain it was as shocking as what he had just asked me. I was not even certain where the question had come from. "Definitely not!" I blurted out. I had never cheated on Saeed. He was the only man I had ever been intimate with in any way. I had not expected Franklin to be as open as Pastor David had been toward me, but I was not ready to be accused of having an affair.

Soon after that call, I talked with Dr. George O. Wood, General Superintendent of the Assemblies of God in the United States, the denomination of which Saeed was a member. He asked, in effect, "Naghmeh, what's going on? Why are you coming out with this now? Why have you gone all this time and not told anyone? We are all confused."

"I am so glad you are doing this," he said finally, after hearing me explain everything. "We knew something like this might be going on, but we couldn't confirm it until you came out." He informed me that, shortly after Saeed was arrested, he had heard from several people that there were reports about Saeed's abusive behavior and desire for fame and money, but as long as Saeed was in prison, it was difficult to address the situation. Dr. Wood reassured me that I would have his support, although it was clear that they were watching to see which direction I was going to take before they acted. Because of Franklin Graham's response to me, I asked Dr. Wood to send Franklin a letter explaining that he was aware of reports of the abuse, and he did.

Responses from other supporters were mostly painful. At best, people were silent about the matter. But there were people I had been very close to who called me and said they thought I had intentionally leaked the email to the press. Like Franklin, they imagined that I was cheating on Saeed and was using accusations of abuse to undermine him to get out of my marriage. Other people felt that by speaking up about the abuse, I was damaging the cause of Christ, giving the church a bad reputation with the world. They wanted me to be quiet about it—and, for a season, I did go silent again as I experienced this backlash.

Weeks passed, but Saeed still did not call me from prison. He was no longer contacting me but communicating only with his family members. What I had written in my emails had already been circulated around the world and, although I was unaware of it, Saeed had heard the news and was very angry about it.

I followed Saeed's sisters on social media, and, one day in January 2016, I noticed they had posted a very cryptic message, saying, "Please Pray for Pastor Saeed as the Situation Develops."

"As the situation develops?" I asked myself.

The next morning, January 16, I woke up early and saw that a friend from England had sent me a link to a news story reporting that Americans had just been released from prison in Iran. I immediately called the State Department to confirm it, and they said, "Please, for the safety of the Americans, don't talk about this." They told me that Saeed and the other Americans were at the Swiss Embassy but were not yet out of Iran, and they didn't know if radicals in the country might still try to detain them. Once the Americans were safely out of Iran, they would make the announcement that they had been freed.

Later, I wondered if, since I was no longer in contact with Saeed or actively talking to media about his situation, this might have caused the Iranian government to realize they could no longer take advantage of my involvement to increase the price of releasing the hostages, so they finally decided to free them. In fact, the State Department told me that my not advocating for Saeed any longer, not being so public, was a good decision for our family. Only weeks later, Saeed was released.

News crews from NPR, Reuters, CNN, Fox News, and local TV stations rushed to my house so they could be there when I received the special phone call from Saeed telling me that he was free.

Franklin Graham called and asked how I was doing and if I was going to Germany to see Saeed. "I am glad you are doing good," he said in an elated voice. The day that we had both been praying for had finally arrived. It just hadn't arrived in the way that we had thought it would. "I can fly you to Germany on my plane to see Saeed," he volunteered. "Naghmeh, it would be good for you to be there. I will have Greta Van Susteren with me, and she can cover the entire story."

I agreed. I wanted to go and see Saeed even if he didn't want to see me. And even though Saeed and I were not on speaking terms, the children needed to see their father. I ended the conversation quickly, telling Franklin that I needed to keep the line clear in case Saeed tried to call.

Then I began to pack for Germany. However, as I was getting everything together, I realized that my passport was missing. I searched the entire house before thinking that I must have left it in our safe-deposit box at the bank. Because of a local bank holiday, the bank would not be open until Tuesday of the next week. I panicked and talked to my congressman, who knew the president of the bank. The president said that there was no way of getting into the bank because the facility was on a timed lock.

I called Franklin and told him that I would not be able to leave until after 9:00 a.m. on Tuesday morning because my passport wasn't available.

When the news came that the plane carrying the four freed Americans had arrived in Germany, I continually called my contact at the State Department for updates, asking her, "Where is Saeed? Is he okay?" She told me he looked healthy and seemed fine and that he was joking around with her. They were going to take him to a hospital where he could rest for a while. She was sure he would call me. I wanted to speak to him, but I still didn't know how angry he was because of the leaked email about his abuse.

Messages flooded in from around the world announcing that Saeed had called his parents, his sisters, Jay Sekulow, and even Franklin Graham—but he didn't call me.

The news crews standing idly by in my house in anticipation of that special moment were following social media on their phones. They could see that Saeed had been released. They were reading the posts about Saeed's phone calls to his family members and friends. They were still waiting for him to call me.

It was so embarrassing to have all of those news crews waiting for a call that never came. One by one, the media representatives left, and it was more silent in my home than I ever remember it being. In the silence, a message popped up on my phone from Saeed's sister. Saeed wanted to talk to the children, but he didn't want to talk to me. She sent me a number to call to have the kids speak to him.

As soon as I received the number, I called it, and Saeed answered.

"Hello?" both of us asked simultaneously.

As soon as he heard my voice, he replied, "I don't want to talk to you. I want to talk to the kids."

"But I want to talk to you." I waited. I had gone through a lot of changes in the last few weeks. "I just want to ask you: Have you ever cheated on me?" It wasn't a real question. I knew the answer, but I wanted to hear him say it. I needed to hear him say it.

He scoffed. "Huh, I am not going to answer that question. You'll just use it against me. Have you cheated on me?"

"No, Saeed. I didn't have sex before marriage because I wanted to honor God. Why would I have sex with someone else while I am married to you?"

"I just don't want to talk to you. You have ruined everything. You have destroyed my reputation. I am done with you. My sister will be in charge of my publicity from now on. My only goal right now is to divorce you, leave you in the gutter where you belong, and move on with my life." He said he would take the children and return to Iran with them, which alarmed me.

Saeed also told me that in the Old Testament, God had given the Israelites a "certificate of divorce" because of their spiritual adultery.[23] He equated my not being fully obedient and submissive to him with my having committed spiritual adultery, which he said was far worse than any "physical" adultery he might have committed. And my "spiritual adultery" apparently justified his entering into other relationships.

After that, he hung up.

I went and got the kids. They were not to blame for any of this, and I knew they would love to hear from their father. I called Saeed back and, this time, let the kids talk to their daddy. Tears rolled down my face as I watched our new norm take shape.

The following day, I took my next step of cleansing when I stopped paying the bills for Saeed's family members. I removed all their phones from my account. I stopped sending them money and ceased paying for their rent, laptops, vacation and travel expenses, and food allowances. I would no longer be carrying their financial load. Although my relationship with them came to a messy end, I felt lighter with each step I took.

While I was waiting for my passport to be available, I contacted a lawyer for advice. I talked with her about the trip to Germany and how I wanted the children to see their father, but I was concerned about going because Saeed had told me he was going to take the kids back to Iran with him. When she heard about my plans and what Saeed had said, she immediately told me, "Don't leave the country with your kids! Once you leave the US, you will not have the same rights as you do here. If Saeed decides to take the children, you might not have any power to stop him. It is a risk that I am advising you against taking."

I called Franklin with the bad news. "We are not able to go to Germany, I am sorry," I said. "With the relationship between Saeed and me in shambles, I've been told by my lawyer that I should not leave the country." I told him about my conversation with Saeed and that I couldn't risk losing my children to him in Germany.

Not one to easily give up, Franklin called back with another offer: to fly Saeed from Germany to North Carolina and to fly the kids and me from Idaho to North Carolina so we could be there to greet him when he landed.

---

23. See Jeremiah 3:8.

He proposed arranging a time for us to be together as a family at his ministry retreat center, where we could work on our marriage.

I agreed to do this, but on the day we were supposed to leave, a rare snowstorm hit North Carolina, and we were not able to travel there. Saeed had traveled before the storm hit, so when he arrived, he was greeted by Franklin and by his parents and sister, who had flown in from southeastern Virginia, where they were living. Fox News' Greta Van Susteren conducted the interview with Saeed from North Carolina.

The new plan was for me to wait until the storm cleared up, but when I told Pastor Robert Needham about this during a counseling session, he immediately advised against it. He firmly believed that Saeed first needed to go through counseling alone before I was placed in the same room with him. "You cannot go through counseling with an abuser before the abuser goes through counseling for abuse. That counseling needs to happen separately," he said.

My lawyer agreed with Pastor Needham. She also felt that the state laws of North Carolina would not be favorable to me if Saeed filed for divorce and custody there.

I felt obligated to go to North Carolina, even against the advice of my lawyer, because I thought I had already let Franklin down by not going to Germany. There were also media reports that Saeed and I were going be reunited. Franklin was really pushing me to come. He had sent me some forceful emails saying I needed to be there, indicating that if I didn't come and spend time with my husband, this meant that I was the one who didn't want the marriage to work. I still wanted to make my marriage work, and I also had a desire to concede to Franklin's wishes because I had looked up to him. He had been putting in so much effort to make things happen, but I still felt he did not comprehend the abuse I had gone through, and I didn't know if he would have the mindset to even listen.

I prayed to God, asking for confirmation about whether I should go, and the Lord answered my prayer through Franklin's sister, Anne Graham Lotz. I emailed her asking for her counsel on the situation, saying that I didn't feel safe leaving Boise. I trusted her judgment and felt that I needed to write to her. She immediately responded to my email, saying, "Your email, beloved Naghmeh, is an answer to my prayers. I prayed for you throughout the night last night. When I awoke early this morning, I found myself praying for you deep down in my spirit...then I prayed for you during my devotional time.

What you shared below is the right thing to do! I totally confirm that you are to stay in Boise, where you have your network of support. You are right, Franklin does not understand. And I can also tell you, Franklin is not a good listener. Just never mind him, if that's possible."

Anne followed up the email with a phone call, confirming that I should not go to North Carolina.

Again, I found myself regretfully making a phone call to Franklin to break the bad news to him. I thought about how much Franklin had done to help our family. At my request, he even had been willing to arrange for bodyguards to protect me and the children so we would be safe. I was fearful for my life around Saeed. I knew that he could be violent. He had just come from prison, and I didn't know what state of mind he might be in. Franklin had also been willing to arrange for marriage counselors to help us through this hard time, but both my lawyer and my counselor were telling me not to go.

My lawyer had informed me of the risk my children might be in with Saeed now in the United States. He was a legal parent, so it would be completely legal for him to come and pick up the children from school without my knowing about it and fly away with them to a location where he would have more leverage. To keep that scenario from happening, she recommended that I file for divorce, but I was adamant that I didn't want a divorce.

She then recommended that, if Saeed were to come to Boise, I should file for legal separation so the kids could not be legally moved to another district, and that I should also file for a protection order. I agreed to this advice, but with Saeed in North Carolina for what seemed to be the foreseeable future, I didn't sense that the need was imminent.

A little more than a week after Saeed arrived in America, at about ten o'clock in the morning, I received a phone call from a reporter from Reuters news agency. He basically said, "How do you feel about your husband coming to Boise?"

"What?" I said. "He's not coming to Boise."

"Oh, he's coming," the reporter replied. "I just got confirmation that he is on the plane. How do you feel about that?"

I told him I had no idea, and I ended the conversation. I started shaking with fear. I had traveled from North Carolina to Idaho many times, so I thought I had perhaps four hours to prepare before Saeed arrived. Pastor Bob's daughter came and drove me to the courthouse so I could file for separation and obtain a protection order, with the understanding that Saeed would be served at a later date, whenever I might see him.

Afterward, as we pulled into my driveway, I was on the phone with Pastor Bob, explaining everything that was happening. He was on a missions trip to India, and he said he wished he could be there to help me through this difficult time.

Suddenly, when the car came to a stop in my driveway, another car pulled up right beside us, with Saeed inside! Franklin had flown Saeed, Saeed's family, a bodyguard named Tim, and the marriage counselors to Boise without my knowledge.

I screamed over the phone to Pastor Bob.

"What? What is happening?" he asked, disoriented by my screaming.

"It's Saeed! He is here!"

"What? How?"

"I don't know, but I am freaking out right now."

"Give the phone to him, Naghmeh. I can talk to him. I will explain to him that you have a protection order against him, so he can't go into the house."

Saeed had gotten out of the car. I tossed the phone to him, saying, "Saeed, here's Pastor Bob. Talk to him!" Then I pivoted and ran into the house.

I am not certain what Franklin was thinking when he sent Saeed, his family, and the counselors to my home without letting me know ahead of time. Perhaps he thought that things would work themselves out if people just spontaneously showed up at our house, but I was scared. Maybe it is not possible for those who haven't gone through abuse to understand the level of anxiety someone can feel when coming face-to-face with their abuser without warning.

While I was running into the house, the kids were running outside to see their father and give him a hug. At the same time, Pastor Bob was attempting to explain the court order to Saeed over the phone. When I returned outside, Saeed's mother was in a rage, having learned about the protection order.

As Saeed and his other family members tried to calm down his mother, I approached Tim on the side and handed him a copy of the protection order. From working with Franklin, I knew Tim pretty well and felt safe around him. "Here is this," I told him, pointing to the order. "He is going to get served. I don't want him to be embarrassed in front of the media. Where are you staying so we can arrange for him to be quietly served? No one else has to know."

"Well, our plan was to leave tomorrow."

"What? You planned to come here and pick up the kids and me without telling us and take us back to North Carolina the next day?"

Tim shrugged.

Later that night, he gave me the name of a hotel, and Saeed was served.

46

AN UNWANTED DIVORCE

Would it be possible for us to meet, Naghmeh?" Saeed's voice was the kind, gentle, loving voice I had fallen in love with during all those long nights in Iran. "Franklin is doing a nationwide tour with a stop in Boise, and he asked me to come with him to Boise so we can meet with you. I really want to meet with you and work this out."

Franklin had helped Saeed get back on his feet in America and was encouraging him to keep working on our marriage. There were pictures on social media of Saeed cutting grass and chopping wood. When I saw those photos, I knew Franklin had to be some kind of miracle worker, because I hadn't seen Saeed do manual labor before. Even with our own yard, it had been either my father, my mother, or me who mowed the lawn. Saeed hadn't done outdoor work.

"I have confessed everything to Franklin, and I want us to find a way back to each other," Saeed said.

Listening to him gave me hope once again that we could really have our family back together. I agreed to the meeting.

"If you meet with Saeed, you will need two witnesses there with you, Naghmeh," my abuse counselor told me. He suggested that I bring my pastor and a lawyer. Pastor Bob and my lawyer agreed to be present that day.

Franklin Graham was scheduled to speak in Boise on August 10, 2016, as part of his Decision America Tour. He and Saeed came to Boise the day before, and we met with them at six o'clock in the evening in a conference room of the hotel where they were staying. After making some opening comments and saying a prayer for our family, Franklin seemed to set the parameters for the meeting:

"Saeed has had hour upon hour upon hour of counseling. He's had a lot of people talk to him. I have not found Saeed to lie to me. I have asked him questions that he did not answer, and that's his business not to answer. But I found everything that he has said to me has been true, when I have asked him a question, and he has answered some." Then he turned to me and said, "And I think, Naghmeh, for both of you, that this can be fixed, Naghmeh. And it can be fixed easy. If you want it fixed..... I'm not a marriage counselor, Naghmeh, okay, that's not what I do. I wouldn't do that for all the tea in China, I promise you. I don't have a gift at this. But I'd like to see this marriage, if it's God will, to survive."

As the conversation went along, I felt that Franklin was firmly pushing me to seek marriage counseling with Saeed, but I had to stay with the advice of those around me, such as my abuse counselor, who warned me against seeking counseling with Saeed before he received abuse counseling himself. I had also seen this advice in other sources that discussed abusive situations. Although Franklin said that Saeed had received much counseling, it seemed that this counseling had been more geared toward addressing Saeed's experiences in prison than addressing the abuse in our marriage, and the discussion that followed confirmed this in my mind.

It appeared that Franklin was trying to say Saeed was not really an abusive person. "You're talking about a relationship where the wife comes home every night and she's being beaten. And she's being stomped on. These are the types of situations, and that's not what you've been facing. Your husband has been in prison."

"I was beaten," I pointed out, not wanting Franklin to get away with the idea that Saeed hadn't beaten me.

"Your husband has been in prison for three and a half years. And he's not the same person that went into prison."

"He's gonna be the more dangerous; he might have PTSD." I started to explain that I had talked with military wives who had experienced the trauma of their husbands coming home with PTSD; these wives wished there had been a transition time during which their husbands could have received counseling before coming home, because they were experiencing abuse.

"PTSD?"

"Yeah."

"Post-traumatic syndrome. So you think he's got that?"

"He's been in a prison. He was abusive before prison. He was verbally and emotionally abusive in prison. And he was three and a half years in a prison. Should he not...?" I then explained about what I had heard from the military wives, although Franklin claimed he had often successfully counseled military couples who had gone through conflict in their marriages, including when the husband had been severely injured in combat. Even if that was the case, one of his examples was not at all convincing. And, as we continued to talk, I felt Franklin still didn't understand the ramifications of domestic abuse.

With the conversation clearly not going the way that he wanted it to go, Franklin said, "Listen, it takes two people to make it work. If you wanna make this work, you're going to have to move a little bit, okay?..."

"Not in abuse," I said.

"...Saeed's going to have to move a little bit," Franklin finished.

"I'm sorry, but in abuse...."

"Don't tell me you're sorry, because it doesn't matter to me, Naghmeh...."

I addressed Saeed directly. "Yeah, I'm sorry, Saeed, but the abuse has to be dealt with."

I felt like this was the same way that many churches had been dealing with abuse for centuries. I was the one who had been abused, but I was expected to make things better for the abuser. I was the one who had to compromise. I was not going to compromise the safety of my children and myself any longer.

I told Saeed, "You know more than anyone how much I loved you." I reminded him of all the efforts I had made on his behalf while he was in prison, how I had spent the majority of my time and resources to help him and his family, only to receive terrible insults and rejection in return.

Looking back, that reaction from Saeed is what had finally woken me up to the reality of my situation. I had prayed, in bewilderment, "God, what am I doing wrong? You were supposed to protect me; You said that if I loved him enough, then he could change." But as I continued to pray and read the Bible, I realized that what I had been taught years earlier about what it meant to submit as a wife had been erroneous teaching. God had not been telling me to submit to corruption or abuse—that had been a man-made idea. It was biblical for me to create boundaries in my marriage until the abusive situation was addressed, if it ever was.

In the meeting with Franklin, I talked about Saeed's pattern of behavior, where I saw no repentance on his part, and what I had learned scripturally about how I should respond. I also reminded Franklin of how he had asked me if I was having an affair.

In apparent frustration, Franklin seemed to shift the blame back to me and my pastor, asking why we hadn't said anything about the abuse earlier. He felt as if he had been left in the dark about Saeed.

At one point, Pastor Bob interjected, "Be careful, okay? Because you don't know what you don't know." The atmosphere was getting even more tense, and Franklin and Pastor Bob began talking over one another.

"No, all I'm saying is—" Franklin tried to explain, still maintaining control of the conversation. He had been talking more than anyone else in the room, and Pastor Bob knew that there needed to be clarification, because my voice was not being heard.

"No, wait, don't interrupt me," Pastor Bob said.

"No, I'm saying what she told me."

"I know you're a big shot—don't interrupt me."

"No, what she told me, she said you knew everything," Franklin said, again seeming to grasp at the chance to maintain control of the conversation.

"Do I have a right to talk?" Pastor Bob asked.

"You go right ahead," Franklin said.

"I'd appreciate it, because you said something about me, and I'd like to explain.

"Okay."

Pastor Bob said that he knew Saeed and me well from our interactions with him over the years, including our weaknesses, but that he hadn't known Saeed was abusing me and viewing pornography while he was in prison. Pastor Bob then steered the conversation back to what I had hoped would be settled in this meeting: all I wanted was for Saeed to receive abuse counseling before we could move on with the restoration of our marriage.

"We're all equal in this room right now, okay?" Pastor Bob said. "We are all facing a crisis. You want it fixed. She wants it fixed. I want it fixed. He says he wants it fixed." Pastor Bob then pointed to me. "I've watched them fight. I've watched the interaction. I've watched the verbiage; and the things that have happened, that she said in November, were similar to the things, to conflicts, that they had before, okay?... She does not want a divorce, and she has a simple request: 'I want to feel safe psychologically.'" Then he turned back to

Franklin and said, "Mate, you've never been around, obviously, psychological abuse, because if you have, it is worse by far, sometimes, than any physical abuse."

"Listen, we deal with this; I understand it," Franklin replied.

"Well, I'm serious."

"No, I know you're serious. I understand it."

"Then let's respect it, because...."

"I'm not disrespecting it," Franklin insisted.

"But you were saying that her weakness in this situation is she's not getting beat up, so, therefore, it's not real abuse. It's kind of mental abuse that can be dealt with by talking it over."

As we continued, it was clear that we weren't getting anywhere, but before the night ended, Franklin was able to get Saeed, who had said very little, to agree to participate in abuse counseling before I would commit to couples counseling. Sadly, I heard that he did not follow through with the counseling.

It appeared that once Saeed realized I had drawn a firm line and was not budging, he filed for divorce. He sent me this message: "You have been good to me and you have been a good wife." That message had a kind of finality to it, and I knew it was the end of our marriage. I didn't want the divorce, and I would have done anything to save our marriage, but I needed him to deal with his abuse and adultery. It didn't happen.

Saeed stayed in an expensive penthouse apartment in downtown Boise while we went through the divorce proceedings. As the months went on, his behavior continued to deteriorate. Even though I had a restraining order against Saeed that excluded all communications except for matters pertaining to the children, he would often send me text messages letting me know that he could see exactly what I was doing. I was frightened because he seemed to be stalking me. I sent the text messages to the police, and they kept an eye on him, but Saeed didn't appear to care. He continued to break the restraining order by sending insulting or ominous messages.

For the rest of 2016 and the early part of 2017, we went through all the legal proceedings. In April 2017, our divorce was finalized. The court awarded me both full legal and full physical custody of the children.

I had not wanted my marriage to end. I had drawn healthy boundaries regarding the abuse and then trusted God with the results. When Saeed filed for divorce, I was devastated. I felt that meant I was not worth fighting for.

But, over time, I came to believe this outcome was part of God's rescue of me. Although I could not see it at the time, He was using this means to release me from an abusive, harmful marriage because I could not bring myself to divorce Saeed. Over time, God would continue to rescue me from the effects of years of accumulated hurt and pain.

Unfortunately, in March 2018, Saeed broke the restraining order again and was arrested. He was soon released on bail but immediately left Idaho before the legal charges were settled. More than two years earlier, when my emails about Saeed were leaked, I had been the recipient of angry comments and mistrust from the media and fellow Christians who didn't believe—or want to believe—my account of the abuse. But the world was eventually able to see the real Saeed: the judge in our divorce hearing concluded that he was "a habitual perpetuator of domestic violence," and he spent five years with a pending warrant for his arrest in the state of Idaho. He didn't see the children throughout this period.

In 2023, he finally returned to Boise, took care of his outstanding warrant, and went through a reunification process so that he could visit with Rebekka and Jacob again.

When God helped me to see that it was biblical to create boundaries with Saeed because of the abuse and adultery, I discovered that He cares more about the person within an institution such as marriage than about trying to keep the institution intact. This was a revelation to me. Jesus came to save people, not institutions. God reminded me that, when Jesus was on earth, many of the religious leaders had been so concerned about keeping the Sabbath day that they actually objected when Jesus healed people on the Sabbath. Their man-made rules for the Sabbath became more important to them than the well-being of suffering people, and they failed to understand these words of God spoken by the prophet Hosea: "I desire mercy, not sacrifice."[24]

Similarly, we can be so concerned that a marriage be preserved that we do not step in to help the one who is being abused in that relationship. As Christians, we are held to a high standard in how we treat other people, especially our spouses. We are called to treat our spouses with love and care— the kind of love and care we ourselves have received from God. In this way, having regard for marriage sometimes means that a union will end in divorce because the person within that union needs to be respected and protected, not bound forever to mistreatment. God values the lives of His children above

---

24. Hosea 6:6 (NIV); see also Matthew 9:9–13.

the institution of marriage. Therefore, if an institution that God has set up—whether it is the institution of marriage or the church itself—to shield, provide for, and serve people is harming them instead, then that institution is no longer submitted to God, and He calls us to rescue the individuals who are being harmed.

For generations, wives have been told that their marriage is sacred, and they need to do everything they can to save it. God loves marriage, but marriage was made for the husband and wife, not the other way around. God hates divorce, but it is an insult to believe that He doesn't hate violence against His children more.

47

IN THE WILDERNESS

The stress of the long divorce proceedings was finally over, but I was still living in the middle of the confusing new world that had begun the day I wrote the first email about the abuse. The unknowns of being a single mother were frightening. But my confusion went beyond even navigating that complicated territory. Ever since November 2015, I had felt as if I were wandering in a completely new land, bewildered about where I was and what I was to do. This time of wandering would last well into 2018. My original plan had been to step back from all the advocacy to pray and fast, focus on my children, and believe for the reconciliation of my marriage. But I was unprepared for the force of the spiritual and emotional upheaval that crumbled to dust the foundation of my identity.

Ever since I was a girl, I had wanted to share God's love through Jesus Christ to the nations. And when I was the wife of a pastor, God had used me to minister to the underground church in Iran and to proclaim the gospel to millions of people around the world through the platform of advocating for Saeed. When the news of the abuse first came out, I was advised by several prominent Christian leaders to backtrack on my statements and cover up the abuse, or I would no longer be useful for ministry. Covering it up meant moving forward with a book deal and a movie deal, continuing to receive invitations to speak, and receiving the praise of the Christian community. Not covering it up meant losing everything.

I could not cover up the abuse anymore, and so I lost everything. I felt as if my sense of self had been completely torn away. I was no longer a pastor's wife, a ministry partner, an advocate for the persecuted, or a hero. My Middle Eastern culture rejected me because I was a rebellious woman and a divorcée. The majority of the Christian community that had supported me during Saeed's imprisonment turned against me. I was judged to be a liar, an adulteress, and a "jezebel" who was trying to take the lead in her family by drawing boundaries with regard to the abuse. Many people were also upset because they hadn't gotten the happy ending they had been hoping for: seeing our family reunited after Saeed came out of prison. Becoming an outcast in the church was devastating. As each former title was stripped from me and stones of accusation were thrown at me, I was left bare and bleeding by the side of the road, "untouchable" by religious leaders.

Almost no churches or Christian events were interested in contacting me anymore because I was tainted, a disgraceful Christian wife—all for having dared to talk about domestic abuse. I had already canceled most of my speaking engagements, and that was the way I still wanted it. But, at the same time, it was sobering to recognize that I wasn't welcome or "marketable" in the world I had been living in for the past few years. Associating with me could cost someone their ministry. I was no longer profitable to be around.

Saeed had told me that when he divorced me, I would become worthless in the Christian community, and in some ways he was correct—but not in the way he thought. It was not because I was now *disconnected* from his name— it was because I was still connected to it because of the abuse, and people couldn't face that fact about me. They didn't want to be reminded of it.

In the midst of this rejection and isolation, I didn't lose my faith, but I no longer understood who I was, and I no longer knew how God viewed me. God had just rescued me from the slavery of abuse, but now I found myself alone in a wilderness, and only He could reach me and guide me through this new land:

> *But then I will win her back once again.*
> *I will lead her into the desert*
> *and speak tenderly to her there.*
> *I will return her vineyards to her*
> *and transform the Valley of Trouble into a gateway of hope.*
> *She will give herself to me there,*
> *as she did long ago when she was young,*
> *when I freed her from her captivity in Egypt.*
> *When that day comes," says the* Lord,
> *"you will call me 'my husband'*
> *instead of 'my master.'"*[25]

---

25. Hosea 2:14–16 (nlt).

Just as God led the Israelites in the desert for forty years, cleansing them of their idolatry toward Egypt and its gods, He led me through this wilderness time, during which He was setting me free from idols that I didn't know had bound me: first, the idols of ministry and marriage. He also showed me I had succumbed once again to the idol of comfort, as well the idol of people-pleasing. I had allowed all these things to define me and shape my personality. But each step I took with God brought me closer to freedom.

The Bible says that *"perfect love casts out all fear"* (1 John 4:18). Through the passage in Hosea and other Scriptures, God also helped me to untangle all the lies I had been told through spiritual abuse about His disapproval of me. The more I came to know who God is and the perfect love He has for me, the more He alone became the One whom I sought to please. He wasn't angry at me or seeking to punish me—He was kind, gentle, and tender. He was patient and full of grace, and my mistakes did not define me in His eyes. When I understood all this, my fears left me, and I was released to become what God had created and called me to be.

This included letting go of other false ideas that had been built in my mind through manipulation and control in my marriage. For years, I had been told that my dark skin and dark hair were ugly, and that I was fat. I had tried to cover up my face and body to the best of my ability. In the years when I was married, I would pile on the makeup. During this wilderness period, one night, as I stepped out of the shower, I flinched when I looked in the mirror and saw the imperfections and stretch marks on my body. It was difficult for me to look at my crooked eyebrow and the dark circles under my eyes. I wanted to cover myself up as fast as possible. But, almost immediately, Song of Songs 1:15 came to mind:

> How beautiful you are, my darling,
> How beautiful you are!
> Your eyes are like doves.

I started to pray, and I became overwhelmed by God's great love for me. I understood that I was beautiful in His eyes, and that was enough! God Himself had created me as I was. I was *"awesomely and wonderfully made"*[26] by Him. I was accepted just the way I was. Recognizing the fingerprints of my Maker for the first time, I now didn't recoil when I looked at myself. My imperfections became beautiful to me. I was able to embrace myself with all of

---

26. Psalm 139:14.

my flaws and even to see loveliness in them. After that night, I was set free to leave the house without wearing makeup. No more covering up.

In the wilderness, God released me to be myself. This freedom went beyond how I felt about my appearance. I began to experience a freedom to express my opinions and show my emotions without being afraid that people would judge me for them or that there would be repercussions for them. Once I had found my identity in Christ, I knew that, despite all my other losses, no one could take that away from me.

I came to accept that I had lost everything, from an earthly perspective. I did not need to engage in ministry or receive the praises of people in order to be whole. Knowing that I was a child of God—that I belonged to the King of Kings and Lord of Lords—was more than enough for me.

48

A NEW KIND OF MINISTRY

Just when I thought ministry was over for me, God started to do something new in my life—leading me into a new kind of ministry with a different focus. This ministry was like a *"roadway in the wilderness,"* guiding me into God's unexpected plans for me:

> *Do not call to mind the former things,*
> *Or consider things of the past.*
> *Behold, I am going to do something new,*
> *Now it will spring up;*
> *Will you not be aware of it?*
> *I will even make a roadway in the wilderness,*
> *Rivers in the desert.*[27]

This time, ministry did not come in the form of a platform within a church or with a famous ministry that is led more by people than by God—it came in the form of helping other women who had been left broken and bleeding outside the church walls.

The seeds of this new ministry, which sprang up as new life at the end of my wilderness journey, had been planted four years earlier. In September 2014, I had been invited to be one of the speakers at a fundraising event sponsored by the Family Research Council. As I was sitting at one of the nicely decorated round tables, waiting to speak, I could hear whispers about a woman named Mariam Ibraheem entering the room. I had remembered seeing her compelling story on social media. She had gained the attention of the Christian community when she had been on death row in Sudan, suffering deeply for her Christian faith, and she had recently been released from prison.

27. Isaiah 43:18–19.

I was told that Mariam might seem standoffish at first, that it took time for her to warm up to people. But as soon as we saw each other, our hearts connected, and we hugged. From that moment, our friendship was immediate and deep. When Mariam got up to speak, she had a translator, but she spoke these words in English: "God is good, all the time!" I was amazed by her faith, and I knew she was someone I wanted to know better.

At the time, we were both very busy with travel, so we stayed in touch by texting and calling a few times a month. When Saeed was released from prison, some people reached out to Mariam to see if she could help get Saeed and me back together. She messaged me about it, but I was in a very exhausted state and weary of having to explain everything about Saeed's abuse to others. So, I pulled back from our friendship, and we weren't in touch for a couple of years.

Then, in mid-December 2018, I woke up at about five o'clock in the morning and saw a Facebook message from Mariam. She said that she really needed to talk to me, and she gave me her current cell number. This time, something seemed different about her message, and, after praying, I felt God was leading me to call her.

When I phoned Mariam, she was riding on a bus full of people, heading to work—and she was in tears. She kept saying that her marriage was bad and she needed help to get a lawyer. I immediately set up a call for the two of us with my abuse counselor. On that call, as Mariam described her marriage, it became evident that she was being emotionally and physically abused—she was struggling with isolation, verbal putdowns and threats, control, intimidation, and physical mistreatment.

It was clear that she and her two children were not safe in that environment. And, as Mariam talked, she herself began to understand the extent of the abuse—and her need to get to safety. I remember her stark statement: "What I am experiencing in my marriage is worse than being on death row in Sudan, In Sudan, I knew who the enemy was. In domestic abuse, the enemy is from within, and it is very confusing. No one wants to help me. No one wants to touch this."

Mariam later told me that she had reached out to many organizations for assistance, but no one was willing to help. When she prayed to God, He put it on her heart to contact me. As I did what I could, I watched the spontaneous formation of a network of women who worked together to help set one woman free.

Mariam had no money and nowhere to go. She didn't have a lawyer, and she didn't know what steps she should take to become free from the abuse. Mariam lived in another state, so I could not physically be there to help her, but I called one of my good friends, Anne Basham, a human rights advocate who lived in the Washington, DC, area, to tell her about Mariam's situation. Anne was only four hours from Mariam by car. Christmas was approaching, and we both agreed we wanted to see Mariam and her children safely settled in a new home before then. Anne quickly moved into action. She drove to where Mariam lived, enabled her to obtain a protection order, and helped her to find a new apartment and get other assistance she needed. I had another friend who lived near Mariam, and after I contacted her about Mariam's predicament, she donated furniture to furnish Mariam's new apartment, filled her house with groceries, and showered her with gift cards.

I knew that, now that Mariam and her children were in a safe place, they needed more substantial financial support. Mariam also needed to retain a lawyer right away. I created a private GoFundMe account for Mariam and started sending the link to some well-known Christian friends, musicians, and pastors, asking them to help. I appealed to people who had cared about her imprisonment in Sudan for her religious beliefs. After a few days, it seemed that no one was going to contribute. The Christian community is often unified in helping oppressed believers escape persecution. But Christians are often hesitant to help an abused woman leave her marriage. Again, they are afraid to touch the institution of marriage even at the cost of the person who is wasting away in it.

As I waited for donations to come in, I prayed and sought God, and the Lord spoke to me through Matthew 14:15–16:

> Now when it was evening, the disciples came to Him and said, "This place is secluded and the hour is already past to eat; send the crowds away, so that they may go into the villages and buy food for themselves." But Jesus said to them, "They do not need to go; you give them something to eat!"

I was doing everything I could to get others to help Mariam, knowing full well that I had tens of thousands of dollars sitting in my savings account as security for the future of my children. That money had been designated for their upcoming school fees, to purchase computers and a car when needed, and as the beginnings of a college fund. Everything within me wanted to hold on to that financial security—I was depending on it. I was a full-time mother who did not have much money coming in. I was also still weary from having gone through my own struggle with abuse, fighting for my own safety and the safety of my children. I wanted to close my eyes to the need. I wanted to say, "Send them away, Jesus. They're not my problem. Use some well-known, wealthy Christians to help. Can't you see I am struggling?"

But, through those verses in the book of Matthew, I could hear Jesus speaking to me: "I want you to give Me your all. Give me all the fish and bread that you have and trust me for your daily provision." Understanding His clear message, I wept deeply, crushing the idol of financial security at the feet of Jesus. I used a good portion of my savings to help Mariam pay a retainer for a lawyer.

I think that God often tests us to see if we are willing to give our all for the sake of others. As we trust Him for provision not only to feed the multitudes but to have much left over for ourselves, as well, He will take care of us. He wants us to be free to show others His love, expressed not only spiritually but also materially. It has been a challenge and a process to trust God for all my needs, but, over the years, I have seen Him provide in miraculous ways.

It was through helping Mariam that I realized how many women are often stuck in an abusive situation because they don't have the money for housing, legal fees, education, and job training—especially women like Mariam who also do not have family or close friends nearby to help relieve some of the financial pressure.

About the time I was involved with helping Mariam, I was also contacted by three women in the underground church in Iran, each of whom had suffered from domestic abuse and been abandoned by their husbands. These women had been part of the house church that Saeed and I led in the early 2000s, but they had become churchless after the many church splits that had occurred. They wanted me to teach them the Bible via Skype. I agreed to meet with them online to pray and study the Bible together. Within six months, our group had grown to several hundred believers, all of whom were converts from Islam.

Yet, as the numbers of converts grew, so did the persecution. In March 2019, one of the young women was arrested by the Iranian Revolutionary Guard Corps. That young woman was Maral, from the city of Shiraz, whom I had first met when she was an inquisitive ten-year-old, asking me question after question about her new Savior, Jesus, and teaching other children about

Him. Maral was put into solitary confinement and tortured as she awaited trial for her Christian faith.

Thankfully, we were able to get her out on bail by retaining a lawyer for her in Iran. It was moving to see the video of her being released, after months of being in jail, and being reunited with her mother and sisters. At that point in my life, I knew I did not want to become involved with public advocacy. However, I had a group text with Mariam and Anne, and I sent them the video of Maral being released. I asked Mariam what could be done to help her. Mariam later told me that when she received this text, her eyes welled up with tears. She remembered how she had felt when she was released from prison, and she wanted to do everything she could to make sure Maral would not have to go back there. Mariam called me, still in tears, and told me that she had been invited to speak at an event in Washington, DC, in June 2019. She suggested I go to DC at the same time so we could talk with religious-freedom supporters there and see what could be done for Maral and her family. After Maral's release, her mothers and sisters had needed to flee to Turkey from Iran because they were also being threatened with arrest. I agreed to go to DC, and Anne also cleared her schedule to join us.

Soon, the three of us were in Washington, DC, and doors were opening for us to meet with the Ambassador-at-Large for International Religious Freedom at the State Department, senators, congressmen, and other religious-freedom advocates. At each and every meeting, we were advised to start a nonprofit organization in order to be more effective in advocating for women who were being persecuted because of their religion.

A few months later, Mariam, Anne, and I founded the nonprofit Tahrir Alnisa Foundation (TAF). Tahrir Alnisa is an Arabic term meaning "Setting Women Free." Mariam and I knew that with our experience with domestic abuse, we had to include helping abused women get to safety as part of what TAF did, in addition to addressing religious persecution. We were struck by the commonality between the two needs: in both religious persecution and domestic abuse, the one in power—whether the government or the spouse—was abusing their power by controlling, abusing, and oppressing. TAF was formed to help women and children caught in domestic abuse and religious persecution in the United States and around the world through both relief efforts and advocacy.

Funding a new nonprofit is a challenge; therefore, as I continued to obey God's call to help others, I used the rest of my savings toward starting TAF so that we could rescue persecuted women—first as refugees in a third country and finally to a safe country—and enable abused women to escape their environment and get back on their feet emotionally and financially. We were very grateful to be able to assist Maral in leaving Iran, and she is now safe with her family in Canada.

Over the years, I have seen abused and persecuted women whom God has used TAF to help set free find their voices. I have watched them move from being in survival mode to having a thriving life and becoming world-changers. Today, Mariam travels all over the globe advocating for religious freedom. Another woman God helped through me was given a high position at the Department of Justice and has been used to affect policy regarding domestic abuse. Others have started podcasts and founded their own nonprofits for abused women. Women are helping women who are helping women who are helping women....

Seeing women who were once bound in the chain of abuse and struggling to survive now flourishing and using their voices for change has brought me great joy. My suffering has been worth it as I see others set free.

49

PROCESSING THE PAST

My newfound identity in Christ had brought me much spiritual and emotional healing. I had come through the wilderness period with an unexpected new ministry in which God was using me to help rescue the persecuted and the abused—those who, because of my own experiences, were especially close to my heart. Over time, it became clear to me how dear they were to the heart of Christ as well. I seemed to be at the beginning of a path that, if not yet fully clear, was leading me in my next steps in life.

Then, in August 2020, my life was upended once again: my beloved father became ill with Covid-19 and passed away. Until Baba was taken from me, I had not realized how much I had relied on him. For my entire life, he had been a rock that had given me protection and stability. When I was a child, he had been a strong and calming presence in the chaos of revolution and war in Iran, cradling my brother and me in his arms as he took us to safety in the basement of our apartment building. When we moved to America, he encouraged me through all the uncertainties of starting a new life in a foreign country. He believed in me, and he gave me confidence in my abilities as a businesswoman. And throughout my abusive marriage, he had been an ever-present shelter and source of hope, while also providing for me physically and materially when I needed it most.

Following the initial shock of Baba's passing, I spiraled into a deep depression. I had no appetite, and I could not keep my mind focused, even to listen to worship music. I was in a dark world of despair, and I saw no light in the future. I began to withdraw from many of my daily activities—including eating and walking. When the depression was at its worst, I found it difficult to take care of my children, and my mother and good friends came alongside me to help.

No amount of telling myself I should simply pull myself out of this dark condition helped. Before I became crippled by depression, whenever I faced difficult times, my theology was to simply shake it off and move on, just as the apostle Paul shook off the poisonous snake that bit him and continued on with his business as if nothing had happened.[28] Yet, no matter how hard I tried, in my battle with depression, I could not just shake it off.

I had to find a way for this darkness to be lifted from me. I imagined myself as the woman in the Bible who had suffered from bleeding for twelve years and who, in desperation, had reached out and touched Jesus's cloak so she could be healed.[29] Spiritually, I clung to Jesus's cloak, begging Him to heal me. As anguish and anxiety surged within me, I could only cry out, "Help me, Jesus!" Time crept by, and I found no rest. I stayed on the couch all day, waiting for the day to end. I would go to bed at six or seven in the evening, but my anguish continued into the night. I felt a restlessness and a darkness that I could not overcome. I seemed to be trapped inside my body in a place no one could access. No one else could help me—no one except the One who had formed me and called me. With no other alternative, I continued to cry out to Jesus, refusing to let go of Him.

I started to listen to a book by Joni Eareckson Tada called *Joni: An Unforgettable Story*, in which she shares how, when she was a vibrant seventeen-year-old, her life suddenly changed when she had a diving accident and became a quadriplegic. In her book, she talks about coming out of her despair and finding faith and hope in Jesus. Although I was not physically disabled, this book seemed to describe my own experience because my depression had paralyzed me spiritually and emotionally. Sometimes I even seemed to be affected physically; my legs were still functioning, but I could not seem to make myself move. I would lie on the couch and gaze out the window, which overlooked the walkway to a park near my house. I watched people walking their dogs, running, and pushing their children in strollers, and I would plead with God to give me the strength to be able to walk that path again. Life had lost its meaning for me, and I had no inner hope to motivate me. But Joni's story encouraged me and helped me to stand up and start taking little steps again.

This period of intense pain became a doorway to spiritual and emotional growth for me. Over time, I learned that the depression I was going through

---

28. See Acts 28:1–5.
29. See Mark 5:24–34.

was for a season—that dawn would come after the night; the warmth of spring would arrive after the cold, harsh winter. God knew all about the unresolved pain that had been hidden inside me. I believe He permitted this dark season in my life to bring me to a place of desperation and surrender before Him, where I would finally fully submit to Him. I learned not only in theory but also in reality that I can do nothing without Him—that every breath I have comes from Him, that *"in Him we live and move and exist."*[30] In that place of surrender, I learned to depend on God in an even deeper way; I began to pray continually about every matter in my life, and to thank Him in each situation.

During my struggle with depression, I looked back on all the rubble of my life and everything that had been lost or that "might have been"—such as a good marriage and family life. And I looked to the future with anxiety, desperately desiring to be married again and even to have another child. I thought I might be able to rewrite my story with a "do-over" or "happy ending." But in learning to trust God, I came to understand that in whatever situation I found myself, my life could be full—and I could have peace and joy—because *He* was with me. As Philippians 4:11 says, *"I have learned to be content in whatever circumstances I am."*

Processing my past enabled me to make peace with much of the trauma I had experienced in life. But, in other ways, reviewing the past pushed some disturbing questions, which I had pondered over the years, to the forefront of my thoughts. I especially had questions about the spiritual and physical abuse I had seen—and the ways in which the church was enabling it and, in many ways, causing it. As I assessed my experiences with the underground church in Iran, the abuse epidemic in America, and the "Christian celebrity" culture and self-absorbed church world I had encountered during my travels and speaking engagements across the globe, I gained a new perspective on these questions and began to see a path to renewal.

In my wilderness period, I had discovered the freedom of knowing who I was in Christ; and, in my battle with depression, I learned what it meant to be content in life no matter what. Both of these seasons brought me to a place of intimacy with Christ and desperation to love Him for Himself and to serve Him more—and it was beautiful. Through all the storms of life, especially the loss of my marriage and the loss of loved ones, I discovered that Christ Himself was more than enough for me. He was my source of comfort, peace, joy, and identity. I learned what it means to walk daily in dependence

---

30. Acts 17:28.

on Christ and to submit to the leading of the Holy Spirit. As I did, God began to show me through His Word how spiritual revival is closely related to our brokenness before Him—discovering and acknowledging that we have nothing in ourselves apart from Him—and our spiritual desperation for more of Christ. He showed me that the persecuted church and those who are being abused have such brokenness and desperation in common, and we are called to defend them and lead them to the healing and hope found in Christ alone.

50

A RENEWED VISION

I did not set out in life to face the "Goliath" of abuse in the church. But, looking back, I see how God was preparing me for this challenge. In the Bible, David didn't go up against Goliath until he had already won battles against wild animals in the wilderness that threatened his flock, and until he had found his identity and confidence in God alone. Only then was he able to face the fierceness of his Philistine enemy.

Most significantly, David said to Goliath, *"I come to you in the name of the Lord of armies, the God of the armies of Israel, whom you have defied."* [31] The epidemic of abuse is God's battle, and He has equipped me to join this fight by training me through various experiences in my past. He allowed me to be bullied by the radical Islamic government in Iran as they attempted to force me to deny my faith. While I was under persecution there, I lived with an ongoing fear that I would be arrested, raped, or killed. It was not until I was actually arrested and threatened with rape and death that I knew I could stand firm in my faith, through God's grace, and proclaim that I was a Christian. Seeing our Islamic interrogator become emotional upon hearing the gospel and ask for a Bible caused me to realize that I should not fear people. My time is in God's hands. He could and would save me from the lion's den if it was not yet my time to go. Later on, while I was advocating for Saeed, the Iranian government—or those acting on its behalf—was breathing down my neck, threatening me in an attempt to convince me to stay quiet about calling for his release. I could have backed off to protect myself, but God gave me courage to continue to fight for justice and to trust in Him to defend and protect me.

---

31. See 1 Samuel 17:32–51.

These experiences, as well as other situations that have stretched and strengthened my faith, have prepared me to confront a different type of bully—those within the church who are determined to hold on to their power and prestige at the expense of the weak. Women who report abuse often come up against authorities that try to silence them. I had to stand firm in the face of backlash from Christians when my claim of abuse was disbelieved, dismissed, and turned against me. Now, I hope to challenge the attitudes in the church that create an environment for neglecting or harming those who are most vulnerable, and this task will take courage as well.

Seeking the Lord for His solutions to the epidemic of abuse and the neglect of the poor, needy, and defenseless among us has led me to see that the solution does not lie in new programs or a new curriculum—a common way in which the church likes to approach problems. The solution is to return to the truths and principles of the Bible and to Christ Himself. God began to reveal this solution to me through my involvement with a single mother who was on the verge of becoming homeless. When she went to her church for help, she was given just a few hundred dollars and told not to expect any more assistance. She belonged to a large church that had yearly tithes in the millions of dollars. While the church had certain upkeep and expenses to meet, I wondered why it couldn't find any more money to give to this mother who was in desperate need, for whom a few hundred dollars would not stretch very far. I saw similar scenarios occurring in many churches across the nation.

In America, many "building" churches (churches that meet in buildings rather than in believers' homes) have essentially become organizations that spend 70 to 80 percent of their income through tithes and offerings on constructing or maintaining their buildings and on overhead for running the activities of the church. The church as a whole has not prioritized helping those whom Jesus says we should be paying the most attention to—the widows, the orphans, the outcasts, the oppressed, the poor, and the hungry. We allocate few resources in our church budgets to helping the struggling and destitute who are part of our own church families and local communities. God showed me in His Word that, in order to serve Jesus directly, we must help the *"least of these"* among us. Jesus said, *"Truly I say to you, to the extent that you did it for one of the least of these brothers or sisters of Mine, you did it for Me."*[32]

A substantial obstacle to serving "the least of these" is the top-down leadership structure that is so prevalent in the church, and in which many

---

32. Matthew 25:40.

well-intentioned pastors and elders have become trapped. This structure supports a style of leadership in which the head pastor (or team of pastors) carries the majority of the load as they preach and minister to the flock and simultaneously try to manage the "business" of the church. Under this top-down structure, at best, these pastors and leaders frequently become burned out, so the flock that Christ has called them to feed, defend, and protect is often neglected. At worst, those in high leadership positions become so "elevated" and separate from the rest of the church that, having little to no accountability for their lives and actions, they either fall into personal sin or use and abuse their flocks for their personal gain.[33]

As a result, the "least" important members of the body of Christ—whom the Scriptures say are supposed to be elevated, protected, and given *"special care"*[34]—are often forgotten, while the "celebrity" pastors are given the most attention and treated as special. The abused flock is often scattered and isolated without a shepherd to gather them and bind up their wounds. Many people cannot bring themselves to step into a church building any longer because of disappointments, hurts, and traumas they experienced at church; and many of those who do step into a church are so afraid of experiencing additional hurts that they resist becoming more involved in the church.

Our church structures, Sunday-morning routines, and programs are often based on tradition and man-made ideas, so that we no longer rely on the Holy Spirit to lead us. This is the source of our weakness. Having been involved in leading one of the largest underground churches in Iran, and having seen the powerful move of the Holy Spirit in my birth country, I have often longed for revival and the move of the Holy Spirit in America, the country I now call home. In the same way I cried out to the Lord to give me the nations as my inheritance and to see Muslims come to know Jesus, I have prayed and cried out to God for revival in our churches in America and across the world. The more I have sought God and studied His Word, the more He has taken me back to the book of Acts, which describes how the believers met in homes, gathered money for the poor and needy, and were continually guided by the Holy Spirit. Some pastors might call the book of Acts merely *descriptive* of the church's origins rather than *prescriptive* for church life today. But perhaps we are overlooking or dismissing the wisdom of God in giving us this pattern

---

33. See Ezekiel 34:2–6.
34. See 1 Corinthians 12:22–26 (NLT).

for the church, which enabled the early believers to reach the world with the gospel even under intense persecution.

The house church movement and revival in Iran that God allowed me to be a part of closely followed the same pattern. Until the early 2000s, Iran had largely followed the model of the Western church by meeting in church buildings. But as the persecution by the government increased, and pastors were being martyred, the believers went underground. An underground Bible school was created, and over thirty students were handpicked to be trained to start house churches. After the church went underground, a revival began. The Iranian authorities saw these underground churches—small, weak, and poor fellowships that met in believers' homes—as the number one threat to their national security! In response, they tried to shut down the churches that still met in physical buildings—but it was too late to stop the exponential growth of Christian converts. The underground fellowships were already established, and, even with increased persecution, the church continued its remarkable growth.

Why do we see such powerful moves of the Holy Spirit in areas of the world where the church has been forced to go underground? It is because the believers in those regions have no other option but to depend on God. They are desperate for Him—they continually pray and listen to the Holy Spirit so they can receive His provision, protection, and direction.

Generally speaking, for the first several hundred years of the church's existence, believers met in homes, and they had a significant impact on the world for the gospel. But soon after the church became "established" and built buildings for people to gather in, it lost its vitality and spiritual influence. Other religions began to be dominant in regions that were once chiefly Christian. The institutional church grew to be powerful in worldly terms—it oppressed and committed violence against people in order to protect the institution. But, spiritually, it became weak. I see the same pattern today in the Western church, with the church becoming more focused on worldly platforms and power while becoming increasingly weak spiritually, so that it has slowly fallen into a deep sleep.

It is not people with worldly status who impact the world for the gospel. It is often the weak and the unknown whom God uses to do this. In the house churches, people are rarely given titles; instead, everyone calls each other "brother" and "sister." If you were to walk into a house church in Iran, it would probably be difficult for you at first to identify the pastor. That is because the pastor is often the one serving the meal and cleaning up afterward. For these pastors, leading a church is not about seeking to have a "platform" for ministry—it is about seeking to serve others. When people pursue a ministry platform for personal gain, it enslaves them to their own self-interests, while their flock suffers from a lack of protection. Because being a leader in the underground church is personally costly, it deters self-interested "wolves" from seeking a leadership role there.

Leadership in the Western church has become about titles, status, and financial gain. In the underground church, leadership means servanthood and laying down one's life for the sheep—including being imprisoned and even killed in order to protect the flock. There, the position of leader in the church is not one that many people are fighting over, nor are they having deep theological discussions about what leadership entails.

In his first letter to the Corinthians, Paul calls the apostles *"weak," "without honor," "hungry," "thirsty," "poorly clothed," "roughly treated,"* and *"homeless."*[35] In his second letter to the Corinthians, he reminds the believers that it is the parents who save up for their children, and not the other way around. Then he expresses that he *"will most gladly spend and be expended for* [their] *souls."*[36] Can we say the same thing about many of the leaders in the Western church?

Another obstacle to our ministering to the "least of these" among us is the Western church's failure to treat women with honor. Women are generally considered inferior to men, and they are frequently hindered from using their God-given gifts and talents. In the house church in Iran, women are accepted as equal partners in the gospel. The believers there don't have endless theological debates about the role of women in the church.

I know many brave women in Iran who are leading house churches; they have suffered greatly for Christ and have laid down their life for their sheep. Why is God using women, who have historically been treated as second-class citizens in Iran, to lead house churches? Could it be that honoring the women in our churches is how we exhibit the radical love and respect that Christ Himself showed toward women? This has been the case in Iran, where many Muslim women have been drawn to the church because they want to know who this Jesus is who gives such honor and equality to women.

---

35. See 1 Corinthians 4:10–11.
36. Second Corinthians 12:14–15.

God's ways are not our ways. His ways require living the sacrificial life-style of the cross that Jesus demonstrated for us; they require traveling the narrow road.[37] In certain ways, the church in America has grown big—but its impact and influence on society have become small. What if, to grow big in the best sense—being strong and influential spiritually so we can change the world through the message of the gospel—we have to become small, moving into the model of the home church? Likewise, what if addressing the epidemic of abuse in the church and properly shepherding God's people requires becoming small? What if humility, brokenness, and desperation before God are required for Him to lead us? What if impacting the world means that we tend to the least of these and gather the scattered? What if the woman at the well, rejected and alone, is actually the key to the city?[38]

Changing the nature of the church in the West will require courage and a commitment to obedience to God's Word that only He can supply for the benefit of His people. We must be led by the Holy Spirit instead of by religious traditions, religious structures, and human wisdom that have distorted the true meaning of the gospel and lulled the church to sleep. Planning a new activity or financing a large building to house a country-club type of Christianity is not the answer to the many needs of the church and the world today. The answer is to return to our *"first love."*[39]

Repenting and seeking God's plan for His church is the only way we can address both the epidemic of abuse[40] and the widespread neglect of the needy. The Holy Spirit withdraws when we embrace self-reliance and have unrepentant hearts. God resists the proud.[41] But when we humble ourselves, He becomes involved in our lives in remarkable and miraculous ways. I believe we will see a great movement of God's Spirit in the Western church if we turn from the ways in which we have become self-reliant and have allowed tradition to replace obedience to the Word of God. Experiencing revival in our midst will require repentance, complete reliance on God, and submission to the leading of the Holy Spirit.

---

37. See, for example, Matthew 7:13–14; 16:24–26.
38. See John 4:7–41.
39. Revelation 2:4.
40. For more information about domestic abuse and how to address it, please refer to Call to Peace Ministries at https://www.calledtopeace.org/ and Psalm 82 Initiative at https://www.psalm82initiative.org/.
41. James 4:6 (NKJV).

I call upon the shepherds who long to obey Christ and to follow Him: Become small. Take the form of a bondservant, with Jesus as your example: *"He...did not consider equality with God something to be grasped, but emptied Himself by taking the form of a bond-servant."*[42] Reject the ways of the world and the poison of seeking platforms and positions. Carry your cross and follow Him. He will use you to bring positive change and revival to your land.

I also want to speak to the abused, broken, and rejected: You are useful in the Master's hand. Even though people have rejected you, He has not rejected or abandoned you. Jesus, too, knows what it is like to be rejected.[43] He will comfort you and strengthen you to build His church.

Let us all submit to God to give us a renewed vision for His church:

For I am about to do something new.
  See, I have already begun! Do you not see it?[44]

---

42. Philippians 2:6–7.
43. See, for example, Psalm 118:22.
44. Isaiah 43:19 (NLT).

EPILOGUE

Those of us who have endured abuse often cling to what is familiar, no matter how bad it is. I am grateful that, with all that I went through, *I Didn't Survive*. My old self had to die so I could be set free to become someone new—someone God intended for me to be:

> But now, this is what the LORD says, He who is your Creator, Jacob,
> And He who formed you, Israel:
> "Do not fear, for I have redeemed you;
> I have called you by name; you are Mine!"[45]

When I first learned that Saeed had been imprisoned in Iran, I felt that God was being cruel to add more turmoil to my life. I didn't realize that in my struggle to free Saeed from that prison, I, too, was being freed—in the way a butterfly struggles out of its cocoon. The struggle had to occur so that I would be able to fly. God made me stronger through that struggle in order to release me from all that had bound me.

Through each battle, I discovered that my past does not define me. My successes, my failures, my marriage, my divorce, my culture, my citizenship, my language, my ministry, or what other people think of me—none of these things defines me. Even what I think of myself cannot define me. Only God defines me.

Understanding this truth and experiencing a fundamental change in my thinking was a process as I released my past and gave up my false mindsets and values. The process encompassed a long period of recovery from the damage

---

45. Isaiah 43:1.

of abuse and being stripped of a counterfeit identity so I could find my true identity in God.

My fears *didn't survive*—but faith and hope took their place.

My poor self-esteem *didn't survive*—but new self-respect rooted in Christ emerged.

My old, earthly dreams *didn't survive*—but they were exchanged for God's eternal dreams.

The lies *didn't survive*—but God's truth remained.

My story is not over yet. God continues to write my story as I let go of what holds me back and trust Him, no matter what happens. He is my anchor. God has used all the twists and turns and suffering in my life to enable me to grow, both spiritually and personally—for the benefit of His church and for His glory. And I am thankful for that!

This is my story, but the same truths can bring you freedom: *"You will know the truth, and the truth will set you free."*[46]

---

46. John 8:32.

ABOUT THE AUTHOR

Naghmeh Abedini Panahi is a speaker, a Bible teacher, and the cofounder and executive director of Tahrir Alnisa ("Setting Women Free") Foundation, which serves women and children around the world impacted by domestic abuse and religious-motivated violence. Naghmeh made national news when she publicly advocated for the release of her then husband, Saeed Abedini, who was imprisoned in Iran for his Christian faith, and ultimately freed. Through Saeed's imprisonment, not only was Naghmeh able to bring worldwide attention to the plight of persecuted Christians, but she was also able to proclaim the gospel to millions of people across the globe by speaking to human rights groups, major news outlets, the United Nations in Geneva, the European Parliament, and the US Congress, and to have personal meetings with President Barack Obama and Donald Trump. Naghmeh's story is the remarkable account of how God saved an ordinary immigrant Muslim girl from Iran and used her to proclaim His gospel before kings. It is a story of persecution, abuse, unwanted divorce, and God's amazing grace through it all.